John B Harris

CAMBRIDGE
DEC. 1949

THE CLASSICAL MOMENT

THE
CLASSICAL
MOMENT

STUDIES OF
CORNEILLE, MOLIÈRE
AND RACINE

BY

MARTIN TURNELL

───────

"I recommend theatrical representations to you, which are excellent at Paris. The tragedies of Corneille and Racine, and the comedies of Molière, well attended to, are admirable lessons, both for the heart and the head. There is not, nor ever was, any theatre comparable to the French"

—Letter from Lord Chesterfield to his Son

HAMISH HAMILTON
LONDON

First published 1947

PRINTED IN GREAT BRITAIN
BY WESTERN PRINTING SERVICES LTD., BRISTOL

FOR HELEN

PREFACE

"ENGLISHMEN," said Lytton Strachey, "have always loved Molière. It is hardly an exaggeration to say that they have always detested Racine."

It is due very largely to Strachey's two brief studies that Racine now has a certain following among admirers of French literature in this country. The production of *Phèdre* by members of the Comédie Française in London last year was a great step in the right direction, but there is still much to be done before his work is recognized for what it is—one of the summits of European poetry. It would, perhaps, be an exaggeration to say that Englishmen to-day "detest" Racine, but we are still far from the happy state of affairs described by a Belgian observer. In an article written shortly after the liberation of his country, he declared that the English are the most civilized people in the world because English bankers spend their leisure pruning their rose trees and reading Racine. For Racine remains a difficult writer for many English readers, and the author of an article on "Un-English Tastes," which appeared in *The Times Literary Supplement* a year before the war, remarked:

"There are, no doubt, genuine English 'fans' of Racine, though surely not many. But with all the good will in the world and complete faith in the standards of French classicism the rest of us sigh heavily over the resounding syllables of *Andromaque* and *Bérénice* and prefer to think of *Antony and Cleopatra*. Racine, we agree, loses nothing of his stature because we cannot greatly enjoy him; our trouble, perhaps, is that we have not yet so habituated ourselves to values of literature other than our own as to experience the delight he offers."

These difficulties seem to me to be real ones and the attitude of respectful incomprehension much more promising than the arrogant dislike of former generations. It has long been recognized by the French themselves that Racine presents a serious obstacle to foreigners and it is curious to observe that a remark of M. François Mauriac's confirms in its own way the findings of *The Times* critic:

"Of all our authors," he writes, "Racine is one of the least accessible to the peoples of other countries. His realm is that borderland between the head and the heart where no one can penetrate who does not belong to the French family. When a foreigner tells us that he is fond of Racine and recites a few lines in a certain tone of voice, we know that he has nothing left to learn about France."[1]

The writer in *The Times* seems to put his finger on one of the main difficulties when he points out with M. Mauriac that it is precisely because he is so French that Racine is so difficult for foreigners. Now an understanding of Racine means primarily an appreciation of his greatness as a poet. It is, unfortunately, a problem that our French friends can do little to help us solve. They realize like M. Mauriac that Racine is peculiarly "inaccessible," but they cannot help us to overcome difficulties which for them simply do not exist. Popular works on Racine from Jules Lemaître to the admirable M. Pierre Brisson are in the main penetrating psychological studies of Racine's *characters*. They have comparatively little to say about his poetry beyond holding up for our admiration a few lines here and there which to many English readers are no more than "resounding syllables."

There are lines in Racine which are "poetical" by any standards. When he says

Dans l'Orient désert quel devint mon ennui!

huge vistas of desolation unfold before us and the one word, *désert*, welds the desolation of man and the desolation of nature.

He has only to say

C'était pendant l'horreur d'une profonde nuit.

for a bottomless abyss of terror to open before our eyes.

In spite of the "formal" language, a single line conjures up the peace of night and the silence of sleeping armies:

Mais tout dort, et l'armée, et les vents, et Neptune.

or the decadence of an Eastern potentate:

La molle oisiveté des enfants des sultans.

Racine is a master of the single line certainly, but it would be shirking the main difficulty to pretend that the bulk of his poetry is as easy to appreciate as these lines. Although Racine seems to

[1] *Journal*, III, Paris, 1940, p. 203.

present special difficulties, they are only part of a larger difficulty
which is well brought out by *The Times* critic in the same article.

"There is no foreign literature," he writes, "to which English taste is
so sympathetic as the literature of France; but only a relatively small
part of French poetry 'appeals' to the French-speaking Englishman, and
even in a great deal of French fiction he discovers a less than sympathetic
and sometimes faintly inimical quality."

The movement and style of French poetry and the mind behind
it may sometimes appear very different from English, but French
poetry is not a special kind of poetry. It can be enjoyed by anyone
with a good sensibility and a reasonable knowledge of the language;
but in order to enjoy Racine to the full, to attain that "delight"
which so tantalizingly eludes *The Times* critic, we are called upon
to make a definite mental adjustment. It is a question not of choosing
between Shakespeare and Racine, between English and French
poetry, but of extending our experience by accustoming ourselves
to fresh ways of thinking and feeling, to a new vision. It is not
enough to rid ourselves of a number of critical preconceptions;
we must realize that poetry which lacks many of the qualities that
we have come to think inseparable from all poetry may yet be among
the greatest poetry that there is.

The only way to enjoy Racine is to soak oneself in his poetry,
to surrender oneself completely to his sensibility. There is no short
cut, no convenient text-and-translation. Shakespeare has been trans-
lated into French, Molière and much more recent poets into English,
and a good deal of these writers has survived in translation; but
Racine remains one of the few great masters who is absolutely
untranslatable. When you know him, almost every line he wrote,
however simple, however commonplace the vocabulary, has a
charm and music of its own; but if you try to translate him everything goes. Racine in English dress is practically indistinguishable
from the authors of the minor tragedies of the Restoration
period.

It has seemed natural in writing of Racine to include in the same
book studies of the two other great French dramatists of the seventeenth century—Corneille and Molière. Corneille is in some ways
a more difficult poet for Englishmen than Racine because on the
surface he appears still less "poetical" and his syllables are, as they

are certainly meant to be, "resounding." Moreover, an appreciation
of his genius was scarcely helped by the sort of production of his
plays that we witnessed in England between the wars until, like
Racine, he, too, was tactfully dropped from the repertoire of our distinguished visitors. For those who know and love his work Racine
is incomparable and irreplaceable; but it must be admitted that of
the three poets discussed here, Molière is far and away the most
"accessible." Yet though "Englishmen have always loved Molière,"
it will hardly be maintained that we are overburdened with good
criticism of his work in English or that he is as widely read and
enjoyed as he should be. The very fact that he is so "accessible"
also helps us to appreciate the contrast with Corneille and Racine
and, I hope, to make them more intelligible.

There is another reason for studying the seventeenth century in
general and its three greatest dramatists in particular at the present
time. After being cut off from France for over four years, Englishmen admire French literature more passionately and await the latest
books and periodicals from Paris more eagerly than ever before.
While this is an attitude that we must all applaud, there is a reserva-
tion to be made. The French tradition is far more homogeneous
than our own and the connection between writers belonging to
different centuries is far closer than in England. It is difficult to
obtain a real insight into French literature or, as M. Mauriac puts
it, to become a member of "the French family," if we limit our
reading, as we are tempted to do, to the great nineteenth-century
writers, who have had a decisive influence on contemporary English
literature, and to living authors.

The English critic takes a knowledge of the classics of his own
literature for granted; it is an essential part of his critical equipment.
Unless he knows Donne he cannot speak with any confidence of
Eliot, and the profound linguistic originality of Hopkins can only
be grasped by someone who knows Shakespeare. The same thing
is true of French literature. We cannot hope to appreciate French
poetry to the full, or to the fullest extent of our capacity, if we
approach French writers as isolated individuals. We have to soak
ourselves in the French tradition until we are almost a part of it.
For we can only judge French writers when we find ourselves automatically comparing them with the great French classics. We cannot understand Baudelaire unless we know Racine and are capable

of perceiving the force of Gourmont's remark that his poetry is a
return to traditional French versification. Unless we know the
seventeenth century as well as the eighteenth, we cannot understand what Laclos was attacking in the *Liaisons dangereuses* or why
the attack was made, so that without its proper background the
book may appear to be no more than a pornographic novel written
with uncommon psychological insight and an uncommon sense of
style instead of the masterpiece that it undoubtedly is. Unless we
know the seventeenth and eighteenth centuries, we shall undoubtedly
miss much that Constant and Stendhal have to offer. Flaubert is
naturally one of the key-figures in the development of the modern
novel; we cannot appreciate Henry James and Conrad in England
or Proust in France without understanding his peculiar technical
accomplishment. We must go further than this and say that it is
difficult to appreciate either the undeniable originality of Flaubert
himself or his painful weaknesses without a sound knowledge of
the classic French novelists and of the atmosphere of Flaubert's
formative years. It is only when we realize this that we can begin
to form a true picture of the development of European literature and
to understand the significance of the great French writers for us as
Englishmen.

It is evident that the more we read, the greater will be our
enjoyment and the surer our judgment of French literature. I do
not pretend that a knowledge of the three writers discussed here or
even of the whole of seventeenth-century literature is sufficient; but
it does seem to me to be the essential foundation.

It remains to add that none of these studies makes any claim to
completeness. I have tried first to give a general account of the
three poets in relation to the social and literary background of their
age, then to illustrate what seem to me to be the essential qualities
of their poetry by a closer examination of the texts of some of their
greatest works. If I have done something to encourage English
readers to study them more carefully and with greater pleasure and,
above all, to help them to enjoy stage productions of their work
when the opportunity occurs, my labour will have been well repaid.

I have to thank my friends Professor P. Mansell Jones and Miss
Sonia Brownell for their kindness in reading the proofs and for
making a number of valuable suggestions.

Parts of this book have appeared in somewhat different form in *Horizon* and *Scrutiny* and I am indebted to the Editors of those journals for permission to reproduce them here. Acknowledgments are also due to Messrs. G. Bell & Sons, Ltd. for allowing me to quote from Mr. John Palmer's *Molière: His Life and Works*, and to Mr. W. Somerset Maugham and Messrs. William Heinemann, Ltd. for *The Summing Up*.

August, 1946   M.T.

CONTENTS

LIST OF ILLUSTRATIONS

THE
SEVENTEENTH CENTURY

1

THE seventeenth century in England and France was one of the greatest ages in European civilization. We are inclined in England to take the *grand siècle* too much for granted, to treat it as a textbook phrase without appreciating the reality for which it stands or the splendour of its achievement. The literature of the country which produced Corneille, Molière, Racine, La Fontaine, Bossuet, Pascal, Fénelon, Descartes, La Bruyère, La Rochefoucauld, Saint-Simon, Saint-Évremond, Madame de La Fayette and Madame de Sévigné was certainly not inferior to that of any other European country. France had no Shakespeare, but between 1600 and 1700 she probably produced more great writers than England, and their range and variety were in some respects wider. The greatest of the English writers were nearly all poets. England had no religious writers of the stature of Bossuet and the depth of Pascal, no moralists and memoir-writers who were the equals of La Rochefoucauld, La Bruyère or Saint-Simon, no novelist who wrote anything which is so obviously a "classic" as the *Princesse de Clèves*. Saint-Évremond's literary criticism makes Dryden's sound like the essays of a respectable member of the sixth form; and compared with Descartes Hobbes appears crude and shallow.

In both countries it was an age of violent contrasts, of great successes and resounding failures, of great splendour and appalling squalor; but though the same spirit seems to dominate the whole Continent, French literature makes a very different impression on the mind from English. We shall only understand the reasons for this and learn to appreciate the masterpieces produced in both countries to the full when we know something of the historical background.

The Englishman who approaches the poetry of the *grand siècle* for the first time misses the colour and fantasy, the racy colloquialism and the love of homely detail which are native to the English genius. It was not always so. In the Middle Ages English and French poetry was often very close. Chaucer and Villon possessed the same firm grasp of the world of external reality and the same power of placing things vividly before our eyes. It was because they had their roots deep in the common life of their time and spoke for the community as an undivided whole that we are more conscious of their resemblances than their differences, that they are far closer to one another than Racine is to Shakespeare.

The close of the Middle Ages, the disruption of Christendom and the rise of the nation-state split Europe in two. They mark a parting of the ways for the cultures of the Northern and the Mediterranean peoples in general, and of England and France in particular. The Mediterranean peoples retired behind the Pyrenees and the Alps, the English to their island, only emerging to do battle with one another in an attempt to impose their own systems on their rivals. Germany was in a state of chaos and, in spite of her geographical position, France suffered from the same disadvantages as her neighbours.

The effect of this cleavage on European art was immense. English poetry retained its native vigour, and the primitive folk-element which was present in all medieval art, until the latter part of the century; but in France poetry became more and more the expression of a civilized *élite*. The emphasis falls on decorum, on the virtues of clarity and order, and there is a growing horror among French writers of "Gothic barbarism":

> Cette grande roideur des vertus des vieux âges
> Heurte trop notre siècle et les communs usages.

It is not difficult to see why this was so. In England, the country where the Reformation triumphed, the people were united in their opposition to Spain. The merchant-adventurers, who were also the men who defeated the Armada, contributed to the unity and Shakespeare's "rabble" were the "other ranks" who manned their vessels in the same struggle. In France, the country where the Reformation was signally defeated, the unity was much less broadly based and far more precarious; it was the unity of throne and nobility; and while English culture remained in many ways a popular one, French came to depend more and more on the aristocratic idea. Neither country was directly affected by the Counter-Reformation and there was practically no Baroque art. (Eighteenth-century Rococo was a different matter.) England, however, was less isolated culturally as she was less isolated politically. The influence of the Italian and Spanish schools of poetry was introduced by scholars and travellers like Donne and a Catholic convert like Crashaw; but the innovations were assimilated by the English genius which for the next two hundred years set its face steadfastly against the Latin virtues.[1] France was preoccupied with the problems of internal and external security and concentrated on the development of her natural virtues to the virtual exclusion of foreign elements. The tendency to rhetoric, which is inherent in French verse, becomes more pronounced during the seventeenth century and is a sign that the poet is already conscious of the instability of the society in which he is living.[2]

This fundamental cleavage has persisted down to our own times. In the nineteenth century English readers found the French romantic poets and, much later, Verlaine, more to their taste than the seventeenth-century masters; but it is only during the present century that there has been a genuine *rapprochement*. In many ways the poetry of the School of Baudelaire is closer to the Metaphysical Poets than to other kinds of English or French poetry written in the nineteenth century. It is the bridge between the Metaphysical Poets and contemporary English and French poetry and, indeed, between English and French poetry as a whole. The intellectual as well as the territorial frontiers, one feels, have been abolished. There is a common *malaise* and a common use of imagery drawn from industrial civilization and from experimental psychology.

It is, however, with the seventeenth century that I am mainly concerned here, and the differences between English and French poetry will be more readily apparent if we compare a few lines from Donne's *Calme* with the description of the calm in Racine's *Iphigénie*:

> As steady' as I can wish, that my thoughts were,
> Smooth as thy mistresse glasse or what shines there,
> The sea is now. And, as the Iles which wee
> Seeke, when wee can move, our ships rooted bee.
> As water did in stormes, now pitch runs out:
> As lead, when a fir'd Church becomes one spout.

[1] V. Praz, *Secentismo e Marinismo in Inghilterra*, Florence, 1925.
[2] There were Spanish and Italian influences in Corneille and Molière, but they were not of the kind or extent which invalidates the general thesis maintained here.

And all our beauty, and our trimme, decayes,
Like courts removing, or like ended playes.
The fighting place now seamens ragges supply;
And all the tackling is a frippery.

.   .   .

Tu te souviens du jour qu'en Aulide assemblés,
Nos vaisseaux par les vents semblaient être appelés.
Nous partions; et déjà, par mille cris de joie,
Nous menacions de loin les rivages de Troie.
Un prodige étonnant fit taire ce transport:
Le vent, qui nous flattait, nous laissa dans le port.
Il fallut s'arrêter, et la rame inutile
Fatigua vainement une mer immobile.

The first thing which strikes us is that Donne builds up his picture by accumulating a great number of significant details which place the *physical* scene compellingly before our eyes. The ships are "rooted" like the islands for which they are making, and later in the poem they become our "bed-ridde ships." The molten pitch pours out in the sweltering heat whose fiery blast strikes at us from the printed page. The next thing we notice is that the lines are at once popular and colloquial and extremely erudite. In the terse reference to the lead streaming out of a "fir'd Church" which has become a single "spout" of flame, the poet is a spectator, is "one of the people," mingling with the sweaty London crowd which gazes idly, helplessly with open mouth at the fire. The ship's tackle, once so elegant, "decayes" and becomes a "frippery," reminding him—for he is an aristocrat as well as a man of the people—of the tawdry stage properties left behind when the court removes or the play comes to an end.

There is nothing comparable to this, you may feel, in Racine's lines; but his aim is very different from Donne's. It is no part of his intention to paint a vivid picture of the physical appearance of the scene or to amuse his audience with the quaint and erudite reflections that pass through the mind of a cultivated man who is stranded on the high seas as Donne does in

Onely the Calenture together drawes
Deare friends, which meet dead in great fishes jawes:
And on the hatches as on Altars lyes
Each one, his owne Priest, and owne Sacrifice.

Racine's interest is concentrated on the drama that is going on inside the character's mind, on the contrast between the excited warriors anxious to "get at" the Trojans—

> . . . par mille cris de joie,
> Nous menacions de loin les rivages de Troie.

—and the sense of hopeless frustration caused by the calm. The commonplace, colourless little words do somehow contrive to suggest the great fleet eager like the crews to join battle:

> Nos vaisseaux par les vents semblaient être appelés.

Then the calm descends in all its suddenness:

> Le vent, qui nous flattait, nous laissa dans le port.

The *flattait* is a characteristic example of Racine's elegance. In the final couplet the tension reaches its last extreme. The skilful mingling of the r's and m's and the liquid l's makes us feel the oars beating helplessly against the heavy, motionless waters; but the emphasis falls on *fatigua*, on the sense of complete and hopeless frustration.

I think that we can go on to describe the principal difference between the literatures of the two countries by saying that English literature was a literature of *expansion* and French a literature of concentration and *consolidation*. This statement, however, needs some qualification. In the sixteenth century the literature of both countries was a literature of expansion, but at the end of the century we notice a change in France. It was in the poetry of Malherbe that French literature formally turned its back on the Gothic past and began the process of consolidation which will distinguish it all through the seventeenth century. There was no such change in English literature which was dominated for most of the seventeenth century by a spirit of adventure and discovery, by a determined attempt to extend the whole field of human experience. In his essay on "The Metaphysical Poets," Mr. T. S. Eliot has spoken of "a mechanism of sensibility which could devour any kind of experience." The words describe with felicity the way in which the frontiers of poetry were extended and we see the process at work in a line of Donne's where he addresses his mistress as

> . . . my America! my new-found-land.

The great geographical discoveries of the age are reflected in its poetry and are paralleled by the discoveries which the poets make about the human mind. Their borrowings from the language of philosophy, astronomy, mathematics and the other sciences reveal the effort to map the inner world with the same care and thoroughness with which the great navigators were mapping the outer world, to establish relations between realms of experience which seem at first to have little in common.

This, however, is by no means the whole of the story. We must go on to point out that English poetry in the seventeenth century reflects a state of great emotional turmoil, a sense of unending and, at times, well-nigh intolerable spiritual tension. Its principal figures are almost all *tourmentés*, fighting a relentless and solitary battle against death and doubt. Donne, fretting silently in his room over the ravages of the "new philosophy," is the classic example of what has been well called "the Baroque doubt"; but scarcely one of them escaped from the gentle Herbert, wondering whether he really belonged to Canterbury or Rome, to Milton who wrote a "Christian epic" which betrays in every line his utter disbelief in the fundamental tenets of the Christian system.

The short journey across the Channel introduces us to a world which appears to be as different from ours as it could well be. There are modern French writers who speak to me more urgently, more intimately than any of the seventeenth-century masters, who seem more necessary to me; but I always return to the seventeenth century with a sense of undisguised relief. For here, one feels, is something solid and firm on which the mind can rest; a circumscribed world no doubt, but a world with clearly defined boundaries; a world which speaks with many voices, but on all the major problems of human life each voice proclaims the same message, delivered without the slightest hesitation. French society was highly centralized and very compact, and there is a passage in the *Critique de l'École des femmes* which throws some light on its structure. The speaker, who represents Molière's own views, declares that

"la grande épreuve de toutes vos comédies, c'est le jugement de la Cour; que c'est son goût qu'il faut étudier pour trouver l'art de réussir; qu'il n'y a point de lieu où les décisions soient si justes; et, sans mettre en ligne de compte tous les gens savants qui y sont, que, du simple bon sens naturel et du commerce de tout le beau monde, on s'y fait une manière d'esprit qui, sans comparaison, juge plus finement des choses que tout le savoir enrouillé des pédants."

The keynote of the century is authority and the word which occurs perhaps more frequently than any other is *les règles*. There are rules in religion, in conduct, in art. "There is an immense effort," writes M. Daniel Mornet, "to establish everywhere an order which is as reasonable as the order of mathematics, to organize a sort of social and æsthetic geometry."[1] France was not without her rebels, but it must be emphasized that the authority of "the rules" was not in the main a tyrannical one. The history of authority in the seventeenth century is the history of an authority which was freely accepted because it was felt to be *reasonable*. In art, in particular, the application of the rules was tempered by what Molière calls in the passage I have just quoted the "simple bon sens naturel" and the "commerce de tout le beau monde."[2]

I have already suggested that the movement towards consolidation began in France in the second half of the sixteenth century, and it is worth while examining this point a little more closely. When we turn to French literary criticism in the seventeenth century, we discover that there were two main trends. There were the liberalism of Saint-Évremond and the conservatism of Boileau, and their interaction did much to give the literature of the seventeenth century its geniality and its poise. I do not think that Boileau was a great writer, but, as so often happens, the cross-currents of an age are more apparent and easier to follow in the work of secondary writers than in the work of the masters. In an impressive defence of Sainte-Beuve, Remy de Gourmont said that a critic must be a "creator of values"; and he went on to show that in the seventeenth century Boileau had determined or "created" the values of the French poets of the Middle Ages and that his "placing" of them had lasted for two hundred years.[3] There is no doubt that Boileau's influence was immense and his career is very instructive

---

[1] *Histoire de la littérature et de la pensée françaises*, Paris, 1927, p. 75.

[2] The foundation of the French Academy in 1635 was at bottom an expression of a felt need for a central authority, but once founded the Academy tended to foster repressive tendencies.

[3] "Sainte-Beuve Créateur de Valeurs" in *Promenades philosophiques*, I, Paris, 1913.

for anyone who wishes to understand the seventeenth century. He was not, perhaps, a particularly original thinker, but he was undoubtedly the spokesman of his age or more precisely of its conservative tendencies which he proceeded to express in remarkably lucid and logical form. The influence which Gourmont rightly attributed to him was exercised not by a large work in many volumes, but by a few lines of his *Art poétique*. When he wrote:

> Durant les premiers ans du Parnasse Français,
> Le caprice tout seul faisait toutes les lois.
> La Rime, au bout des mots assemblés sans mesure,
> Tenait lieu d'ornements, de nombre et de césure.
> Villon sut le premier, dans ces siècles grossiers,
> Débrouiller l'art confus de nos vieux Romanciers.

he succeeded in branding almost all French poetry down to the end of the sixteenth century as clumsy and incomprehensible, and in reducing Villon to a talented barbarian who might have done quite creditably in a more propitious age. His propaganda was so effective that living French critics are still busily engaged in removing the stigma and rediscovering the sixteenth century.[1]

The shortcomings of Boileau's approach are fully apparent when, a few lines later in the same passage, he remarks:

> Ronsard qui le suivit, par une autre méthode
> Réglant tout, brouilla tout, fit un art à sa mode:
> Et toutefois longtemps eut un heureux destin.
> Mais sa Muse en Français parlant Grec et Latin,
> Vit dans l'âge suivant par un retour grotesque,
> Tomber de ses grands mots le faste pédantesque.

The crux of this passage is not the slighting reference to Ronsard's achievement, but the line

> Mais sa Muse en Français parlant Grec et Latin . . .

For it was precisely the linguistic experiments of the sixteenth-century poets and their power of assimilating words from other languages which were the signs of their immense vitality, of their tendency towards expansion which Boileau and Malherbe before him were so eager to curb.

The *Art poétique* also contains a vigorous statement of Boileau's

[1] V. Thierry Maulnier. *Introduction à la poésie française*, Paris, 1939.

positive values, is indeed a veritable breviary of the *mots d'ordre* of the seventeenth century:

> Quelque sujet qu'on traite, ou plaisant, ou sublime,
> Que toujours le Bon sens s'accorde avec la Rime.
>
> Aimez donc la Raison. Que toujours vos écrits
> Empruntent d'elle seule et leur lustre et leur prix.
>
> Tout doit tendre au Bon sens: mais pour y parvenir
> Le chemin est glissant et pénible à tenir.
> Pour peu qu'on s'en écarte, aussitôt l'on se noie.
> La Raison, pour marcher, n'a souvent qu'une voie.

It was, however, in the famous eulogy of Malherbe that Boileau's talent proved most effective and, in view of the subsequent history of French literary taste, I think we must add most dangerous:

> Enfin Malherbe vint, et le premier en France,
> Fit sentir dans les vers une juste cadence:
> D'un mot mis en sa place enseigna le pouvoir,
> Et réduisit la Muse aux règles du devoir.
> Par ce sage Écrivain la Langue réparée
> N'offrit plus rien de rude à l'oreille épurée.
> Les Stances avec grâce apprirent à tomber,
> Et le vers sur le vers n'osa plus enjamber.
> Tout reconnut ses lois, et ce guide fidèle
> Aux auteurs de ce temps sert encor de modèle.

In a sense the whole of the seventeenth century is there with its air of authority and its finality, its *Bon sens, juste cadence, règles du devoir*, its *grâce*, its *pureté* and its *clarté*. The whole of the seventeenth century, we may add, except its inspiration and its incomparable sensibility.

It is time now to pursue our investigation in a somewhat different field.

> Le bon sens est la chose du monde la mieux partagée . . .

The opening words of the *Discours de la méthode*, with their confidence and their obvious reasonableness, emphasize one of the basic values of the *grand siècle*, and the way in which they reinforce the tenets of the *Art poétique* demonstrates the remarkable unity of thought in that age. It is no doubt true that the work

B*

of Descartes spelt the ruin of traditional philosophy, marking the change from a philosophy of *being* to a philosophy of *knowing;* but on the fundamental values of civilization Descartes himself was completely intransigent, and so far from undermining them, his aim was to justify and strengthen them and to provide them with a philosophical basis. He was at pains to prove at every step that his "method" was a reasonable one, and when he overthrew the authority of Aristotle, he did so in the name of *bon sens* and at once proceeded to set up in its place a new authority which was not less solid.

It is the existence of authority that gives the literature its external order and its internal tension. Descartes and Boileau speak naturally of *bon sens*, *raison* and *nature*, but these were only some of the terms which express the "basic verities" of seventeenth-century civilization and which recur in all its writings. Others are *ordre*, *mesure*, *équité*, *bon goût*, *justesse*, *bornes*, and *esprit*. A critic like Boileau was constantly trying to determine their place in poetry, while a moralist like La Bruyère tried to determine their correct relations to one another or, to put it in another way, to consolidate the essential human values. When he writes

"Talent, goût, esprit, bon sens, choses différentes, non incompatibles.
"Entre le bon sens et le bon goût il y a la différence de la cause à un effet.
"Entre esprit et talent il y a la proportion du tout à sa partie"

—we know that this is the voice of a man living in a world in which it is natural to speak of measure and proportion. The whole tendency of the century was to express itself in brief, pithy maxims.

We find the same tendency at work in definitions like the *honnête homme*, the *belle âme* and the *grand cœur*. We shall never appreciate the literature of the age to the full until we realize that these terms are in no sense abstractions, but stand for something as vivid and real as the life which pulsates in the words *amour*, *passion*, *gloire* and *honneur* which enshrine values of a different kind. Descartes' preoccupation with *idées claires et distinctes* is symptomatic. The only things, he said, of which we can be sure are those of which we have clear and distinct ideas, and that describes the whole policy of the century. The policy can be defined as the conquest of experience. There was an unceasing effort to translate more and more of human experience into formulas, to reclaim it from the vast hinterland which lay just beyond "reason" and "good sense." For as soon as this was achieved, the field of human experience was automatically extended; fresh territories had been brought under the dominion of "reason," more pointers were available to help people to live a "reasonable" life, and the danger of going off the rails and plunging into anarchy was correspondingly diminished.

This process was certainly very different from the one that was going on in England. The English poets were extremely conscious that they were living in a dangerous and perplexing situation, that they were constantly up against the Unknown and that at any moment someone might make a fresh discovery which would shatter their conception of the world. There was, as we shall see, plenty of tension in some of the French writers; but it was in the main tension within a stable world or a world which appeared to be stable, and they were free from the radical uncertainty of the Englishmen. Their work was not a voyage of discovery into the Unknown; it was a minute exploration of a known reality which can best be described as an *approfondissement* of everyday experience. The literary forms chosen by poets and prose-writers—the alexandrine, the maxim and the character—were used both as an intellectual discipline and to present complex material in the most lucid and orderly manner possible; and it is largely the skill with which they handled their medium that gives much of their work an air of disarming simplicity and sometimes made their discoveries appear superficial.

The price that they paid for their achievement was a substantial, but not an exorbitant, one. Their conception of life was limited but it is easy to exaggerate its limitations, as I suspect that M. Daniel Mornet does in the excellent manual to which I have already referred. He tells us that discussion of political, religious and social problems was to all intents and purposes banned and that in social life fantasy and independence were excluded. It is true that "self-expression," as we understand it, was not exactly encouraged, and it may be true that when La Bruyère came to write the *Caractères* he found no rebels in the grand manner and had to confine himself to the *tics* and *manies* of a few eccentrics. It must be remembered, however, that he was not composing a psychological treatise in the manner of Descartes' *Traité des passions de l'âme*, but a work of art. His book is less valuable for its psychological *aperçus* than for a particular kind of wisdom which informs it and transcends the simple phrases. His habit of looking at everything, however trivial it may appear, from the standpoint of unchanging principles produces flashes of insight which illuminate the human scene in a way that is peculiar to the age. When he writes

C'est une grande difformité dans la nature qu'un vieillard amoureux,

we see the amorous old man for the first time and realize why he is shocking and ridiculous.

When M. Mornet goes on to say that the seventeenth century "had no sense of history, no sense of the instability and transitory nature of human societies and of a great number of human rules," he seems to me to give a misleading impression.[1] It is characteristic of the people of the classical ages that they believed very firmly in their own time, believed that they had achieved such a high degree of civilization that the future could only lead to decline. Now there seems to me to have been far more change and development in seventeenth-century France than is commonly allowed, and it is almost certainly the perfection of its literary forms and the regularity with which human experience was "reclaimed" that have obscured the process and produced the impression of a static civilization. Some of the writers were conscious of the uncertainty of the future, and the sense that civilization was disintegrating beneath the polished surface is reflected in individual writers like Racine and Saint-Simon; but it was of the essence of their achievement that this did not undermine their belief in the fundamental sanity of the *universe*. One cannot help being aware in *Athalie* of the doom which is hanging over civilization; but there is also the impression that if the whole Kingdom collapsed and disappeared overnight, Reason, Order and Nature would survive untouched. This is the basic difference between the English and French writers of the seventeenth century. It was not for themselves or their society that the English writers feared; they were the victims of an *angoisse métaphysique* which led them to doubt the ultimate sanity and reasonableness of the universe and which made the French confidence unthinkable for them.

[1] *op. cit.*, p. 76.

2

It is worth glancing next at the subject-matter of seventeenth-century literature:

"About the year 1548," writes M. Georges Duhamel, "France decided to embark on a great work and to spend centuries on it. All Frenchmen who have been associated with it, have been conscious of their part in the great undertaking and have accepted the high degree of discipline which was necessary for so majestic a task.

"What was this work that was undertaken by a whole people? What is this monument which French literature set out to build? The reply can be given at once. It is a portrait of Man.

"French literature has worked untiringly at its task which is nothing less than a full-length portrait of man: the Individual man and the Social man, the Inner and the Outer man, the Visible and the Invisible man, the Subjective and the Objective man."[1]

These words have much to tell us about French literature and the French language. They explain the continuity of French literature from the middle of the sixteenth century down to our own time and the French love of tradition. The great undertaking was undoubtedly helped by the nature of the French language, but here the influence of subject and instrument is a reciprocal one. The French language is singularly well adapted to psychological analysis; but it is also true that the preoccupation with man and his nature has helped to mould language, to make it more the language of the intelligence than the emotions.

It is clear that the great work must, as M. Duhamel points out, last for centuries, must indeed last as long as there are writers. For though man's nature is finite, there is room for change and development; and it thus happens that in each age the accent falls in a different place. Some ages have stressed the Social, others the Individual man; some the Objective, others the Subjective man; but it is because they have all accepted certain fundamental assumptions about human nature that the work of writers as different as Montaigne, Saint-Simon and Proust is clearly part of the task described by M. Duhamel.

[1] *Défense des lettres*, Paris, 1936, pp. 280–1.

"La passion," wrote Pascal in what must have been an unguarded moment,

"La passion ne peut être belle sans excès. Quand on n'aime pas trop, on n'aime pas assez."[1]

In these sentences Pascal puts his finger on the great problem of the seventeenth century. The side of human nature on which they chose to concentrate was precisely the conflict between reason and passion or what Pascal himself, in a more solemn mood, called the "guerre intestine de l'homme entre la raison et les passions."

"This internal war of reason against the passions," he goes on, "has divided those who desire peace into two sects. The first would like to renounce their passions, and become gods; the others would like to renounce reason, and become brute beasts (Des Barreaux). But neither can do as they wish, and reason still remains to condemn the vileness and injustice of the passions and to trouble the repose of those who abandon themselves to them; and the passions always remain alive in those who try to get rid of them."

The dilemma is plain. Whether one liked it or not—many of the seventeenth-century writers emphatically did not—man is endowed with "reason" and "passion" which are in a state of perpetual conflict. "Reason" is constantly trying to bring more and more of human nature under its dominion; "passion" is continually trying to upset the balance and to drive man to the edge of the abyss, to the *espaces infinis* whose silence was a source of fear to Pascal and his contemporaries. Perfect equilibrium was impossible and would indeed be contrary to nature. "For," wrote Pascal in another chapter of the *Pensées*,

"Nothing is so insufferable to man as to be completely at rest, without passions, without business, without distraction, without study. He then becomes aware of his utter nothingness, his forlorness, his insufficiency, his dependence, his weakness, his emptiness. There arise immediately from the depths of his heart feelings of weariness, gloom, sadness, fretfulness, vexation, despair."

The message of these passages is clear. Neither "reason" nor "passion" alone is sufficient to produce "the good life." A man who

---

[1] In the *Discours des passions de l'amour*. It should be observed that in the quotations from the *Pensées* which follow, Pascal does not limit the word "passion" to love; he uses it in the general sense of emotion.

is at the mercy of his passions falls into anarchy, but the man who
eliminates or tries to eliminate them altogether is condemned to
sterility. A perfect balance between the two is equally unacceptable
as a solution because it produces the *plein repos* which opens the
door to "weariness, gloom, sadness, fretfulness, vexation" and
finally to "despair," which bring him by a different but not less
certain route to the abyss.

The only healthy condition is a regulated tug-of-war. The
peculiar vitality of French literature in the seventeenth century
lies in a very delicate poise between "reason" and "passion," in a
sense of tension-and-repose which is quite different from the tension
of the English writers and which is the result of an ambivalent
attitude towards authority. Authority is not accepted passively.
It is accepted-and-resisted, and it is this that gives the literature its
life, its high degree of emotional vitality combined with a high
degree of order.

The regulated tug-of-war is the real theme of the great imaginative writers of the age, of Corneille, Molière, Racine and Madame
de La Fayette. It is in no sense an artificial conflict. For, said Jacques
Rivière, in the French analysis of human nature "morality itself
becomes a psychological element."[1] It is not, save in the case of
Pascal, an *angoisse métaphysique*. The writers are haunted by fear of a
concrete threat to society, by the fear that it may suddenly be swept
away by the excesses of passion; and it was because Racine seemed
to his contemporaries, as indeed he was, a reckless champion of
the primacy of passion that his work caused such a scandal. There
are two short passages at the beginning of the *Princesse de Clèves*
which provide a particularly instructive example of the seventeenth-
century approach to the subject:

"La magnificence et la galanterie n'ont jamais paru en France avec
tant d'éclat que dans les dernières années du règne de Henri second . . .
Jamais Cour n'a eu tant de belles personnes et d'hommes admirablement
bien faits; et il semblait que la nature eût pris plaisir à placer ce qu'elle
donne de plus beau dans les plus grandes princesses et dans les plus grands
princes."

"L'ambition et la galanterie étaient l'âme de cette Cour et occupaient
également les hommes et les femmes. Il y avait tant d'intérêts et tant de

[1] *Le Français*, Paris, 1928, p. 27.

cabales différentes, et les dames y avaient tant de part, que l'amour était toujours mêlé aux affaires, et les affaires à l'amour. Personne n'était tranquille ni indifférent: on songeait à s'élever, à plaire, à servir, ou à nuire; on ne connaissait ni l'ennui ni l'oisiveté, et on était toujours occupé des plaisirs ou des intrigues."

The contrast between the calm, measured movement of the first passage and the breathless, feverish movement of the second shows that the issue was essentially a living one and how deeply the danger was felt.

There is another passage in the same novel which is worth looking at:

"Je lui dis que tant que son affliction avait eu des bornes, je l'avais approuvée et que j'y étais entré; mais que je ne le plaindrais plus s'il s'abandonnait au désespoir et s'il perdait la raison."

This passage is a dramatic statement or, more precisely, an enactment of the seventeenth-century doctrine. Passion cannot be excluded, but it is only permissible so long as it is kept within decent limits, is kept in subjection. Whatever the provocation, the "limits" are absolute; once they are exceeded everything goes.

In a brilliant study of the *Princesse de Clèves*, M. Albert Camus has called the style of the classic writer *une sorte de monotonie passionnée.*[1] It would be difficult to discover words which better describe the effort of the seventeenth-century writers to impose a proper discipline on the emotions that they express, to regulate them by style. This emerges very clearly at the end of *Bajazet* when Osmin announces the death of her lover to Atalide:

> Bajazet est sans vie:
> L'ignoriez-vous?

The studied casualness of the tone in which the momentous announcement is made provokes a violent shock and, at the same time, controls it.

In that very remarkable letter in the *Liaisons dangereuses* in which Madame de Merteuil gives some account of her moral education, she remarks:

---

[1] In *Problèmes du roman*, Brussels, 1945, p. 193.

"J'étudiai nos mœurs dans les Romans; nos opinions dans les Philosophes; je cherchai même dans les Moralistes les plus sévères ce qu'ils exigeaient de nous, et je m'assurai ainsi de ce qu'on pouvait faire, de ce qu'on devait penser, et de ce qu'il fallait paraître."

This passage brings home very clearly to us the sense in which the great French writers are a living force, are an *école de vie* as well as an *école d'art*. Thought and emotion do not stand still. We have learnt a great deal about human nature since the seventeenth century; considerable progress has been made with the "great work" described by M. Duhamel; but the literature of the seventeenth century as a whole remains a contribution of singular veracity and power to the collective undertaking of all French writers which Stendhal once declared was "the study of the human heart."

"There exists outside Rousseau," wrote Jacques Rivière in a passage which only yields its full savour when it is read in French,

"Il existe quelque chose, en dehors de Rousseau, de fort, de puissant, de juste, d'imperturbable, d'impitoyable, une manière directe, stricte et réservée de voir les sentiments, un instinct positif, une lucidité sans phrases, une aptitude à se passer d'appuis et de consolations en face du chaos de l'âme humaine, une délimitation immédiate de ce qui s'y offre de connaissable, qui sont des vertus proprement françaises, et qui ont amené des résultats, aussi bien au point de vue psychologique qu' esthétique, dont on ne soulignera jamais assez l'irremplaçable importance."[1]

These are the virtues which we shall discover in the three great writers whose work is studied in the pages that follow.

[1] *Moralisme et littérature*, Paris, 1932, p. 66.

"THE GREAT
AND GOOD CORNEILLE"

1

IT is Corneille's misfortune that no English writer has done for him what Lytton Strachey did for Racine. Whatever the short-comings of Strachey's criticism, it did much to dispose of academic prejudice and to present Racine as a *poet*. It is true that Corneille has never aroused the same antipathy as Racine once did and that he has his place among the immortals on the Albert Memorial; but it is also true that he has never enjoyed the relative popularity which came to Racine with the publication of Strachey's essays. The insistence of living critics that Racine is not merely a great poet, but a great *contemporary* poet, has brought him closer to us, while the figure of Corneille has receded farther and farther into the past. For many of us he has become a sort of historical monu-ment, the lonely representative of a vanished civilization. His poetry suggests Versailles with its vast porticoes and the rigid stone figures hiding coyly among the *bosquets* of its trim gardens or, more formidable still, a scratch troupe from the Comédie Française dressed in those strange, those impossible accoutrements which seem inseparable from the performance of high tragedy, declaiming the *Cid* to an audience of schoolgirls armed with the Hachette plain text. It is ironical to think that the veteran Rodrigue, a little hoarse of voice, a little "gone in the knees," who rants and stamps through five acts for the edification of the School Certificate class, should have become the symbol of the great writer who was all his life the champion of youth in revolt against the corruption and pretence of an older generation.[1]

It is perhaps reassuring to find that this impression is not due entirely to insular prejudice and that Corneille's own country-men have experienced similar difficulties. The most striking thing about the distinguished French critics of the last century is their profound dislike for the great masters of their own literature. Of

[1] It must be added in fairness that these criticisms only apply to the sort of productions we used to see before the "reform" of the Comédie Française towards the end of the 'thirties.

PIERRE CORNEILLE
From an engraving after a portrait by J. Gigoux

Racine they could scarcely bring themselves to speak with patience. "*Bérénice*," wrote Sainte-Beuve in a characteristic sally, "peut être dite une charmante et mélodieuse faiblesse dans l'œuvre de Racine, comme la Champmeslé le fut dans sa vie." In spite of Stendhal's timely championship of "the great and good Corneille," Corneille himself fared no better. "I admire his characters," said Taine, "but from a distance: I should not care to live with any of them." "C'est beau, admirable, sublime, ce n'est ni humain, ni vivant, ni réel," said Brunetière.

That was the verdict of the nineteenth century. Corneille was widely recognized as "the Father of French Tragedy," but he had become the professor's poet, a "classic" whose proper place was not the playbill, but the examination syllabus. Racine has long since come into his own in France, but it has been left to the younger French critics of our own day to discover in this staid classic, whose *Horace* delights or was supposed to delight the populace at the free matinée on Armistice Day, a much more exciting figure. According to one of the latest of his critics, Corneille's world is not a world of flourishes and lofty feelings. It is a world of corruption and intrigue inhabited by doddering, time-serving fathers and criminal stepmothers plotting the ruin of their children who are drawn with a ferocity that is worthy of Racine.[1]

There is, perhaps, a danger of exaggerating the sensational element in Corneille and the reason is not hard to discover. Contemporary admirers are a little too anxious to profit by the popularity of Racine and to discover similarities between the two writers, though it is clearly the differences which ought to detain us. One of the most important of these differences is brought out in the first chapter of M. Jean Schlumberger's valuable study when he speaks of the contrast between

"an heroic art and an art which aims at entertainment or pure knowledge, an art which builds up an exemplary picture of man and an art which destroys this picture by analysis and excessive refinement."[2]

It is a curious fact that few French critics manage to be fair to both poets and that their "rivalry," which is merely of historical interest, still influences critical opinion. Stendhal spoilt his defence

[1] Robert Brasillach, *Pierre Corneille*, Paris, 1938.
[2] *Plaisir à Corneille: Promenade anthologique*, Paris, 1936, p. 9.

of Corneille by declaring roundly that he was "immensely above Racine"; and it is one of the drawbacks of M. Schlumberger's study that he is inclined to diminish Racine's greatness in order to make his defence of Corneille more convincing. This is surely a mistake. No one seriously believes that he is as great a poet as Racine, but they are not "rivals" and they are not interchangeable. Without Corneille there would be a gap in French literature which Racine could never have filled.

Racine belongs to an age of transition from the old order to the new, from the old social solidarity to the new individualism. His impact on French poetry produced what was virtually a change of direction—a movement away from all that Corneille had stood for —and for this reason he seems to me to be much more the predecessor of Baudelaire than the successor of Corneille.[1] Corneille is not in himself a difficult poet, but an appreciation of his poetry has been made difficult by changing circumstances. He is more than most other great poets the test of a catholic taste in poetry, because to enjoy him it is necessary to realize that poetry may be "sublime" *and* "human, living and real." He wrote heroic plays and it is as an heroic poet that he stands or falls. A criticism of his work is primarily an elucidation of this uncomfortable term. M. Schlumberger's suggestion that an appreciation of Corneille involves an appreciation of Hugo and Claudel seems to me a strategic error, and Croce's invitation to us to discard Corneille's four most famous tragedies and to discover the true Corneille—Corneille the Poet—in the final plays simply shirks all the difficulties.

2

Corneille's achievement becomes more comprehensible when we consider it in relation to his own age. The reign of Louis XIII opened appropriately with an assassination. France was governed by a despotism, but an uneasy despotism. The first part of the century is dominated by Richelieu. The spectacle of Richelieu entering La Rochelle at the head of the King's troops to celebrate the Mass of thanksgiving for the fall of the town is a symbol of the

[1] There is perhaps a parallel here between Racine and Donne which seems more striking when one considers the recent history of their reputations in their own countries.

contradictions of the age and of its strange mixture of piety and
opportunism. It was an age of rival factions and incredible intrigues,
an age that delighted in great exploits and violent actions. France
had been shaken to the core by the religious wars of the previous
century; and though the worst of them were over, the country was
still split in two by the conflict between Catholic and Protestant.
It was also a period of intense religious revival in which the chief
figures were St. François de Sales and St. Vincent de Paul. Although
it has seemed to later generations that theology and philosophy
parted company in the seventeenth century, Corneille's contemporaries saw no conflict between the old religion and the "new
philosophy." Descartes and the theologians were at one in their
interest in psychology and their preoccupation with moral problems; and Pascal and Bossuet were both admirers of the Cartesian
philosophy.

In Corneille's poetry all these different and sometimes contradictory elements found a place. The interest that he shows in
family feuds in the *Cid*, in political intrigue in *Cinna* and religious
dissensions in *Polyeucte*, is clearly a reflection of events that were
going on around him. The relation of a great poet to his time,
however, is primarily a matter of temper, and it was left to Sainte-
Beuve to define it in a sympathetic moment in his description of the
famous *journée du guichet* in *Port-Royal*:

"It is the same struggle, the same triumph; if *Polyeucte* moves us and
carries us away it is because something of the kind is and remains possible to human nature when assisted by grace. I will go further than
this. If the genius of Corneille was capable of producing *Polyeucte* at
this time, it was because there was still something in his surroundings
(whether Corneille himself was aware of it or not) which matched its
spirit and achieved the same miracles."[1]

The fact that internally France was in a state of turmoil undoubtedly produced a considerable effort towards consolidation.[2]

---

[1] *Port-Royal*, II, Paris, 1848, p. 115. The *journée du guichet* was the day
when Arnauld was refused admission to the Abbey by his daughter, the abbess,
to prevent interference with his children's religious vocation. Sainte-Beuve's
words are still more significant when one recalls what a large part of Corneille's
work was occupied with conflicts between parents and children.

[2] The propaganda for absolute monarchy, which is prominent in all Corneille's
plays, seems to be a sign of the political uneasiness of the times and of the
"effort towards consolidation."

In spite of its contradictions, Corneille's age was in many ways an age of reconstruction. A sense of effort, a striving towards a moral end, seems to me to be the deepest thing in his poetry. It is well expressed in a characteristic couplet from one of Auguste's last speeches in *Cinna*:

> Je suis maître de moi comme de l'univers;
> Je le suis, je veux l'être.

In the first line we notice that the personal problem is related to the social one, and in the second that the statement is significantly followed by the aspiration.

A direct preoccupation with morality and the constant recurrence of words denoting moral qualities like *honneur*, *gloire*, *grand cœur* and *mâle assurance* are usually a sign of literary decadence—a sign that society is becoming self-conscious about qualities that it is in the process of losing. With Corneille this is not so. Much of his work—particularly the heroic element—is sixteenth-century in feeling, but it also marks the transition from the wild and extravagant sixteenth century to the reasonable seventeenth century. In his poetry, as surely as in Pope's, the words represent "robust moral certitudes" which were the product of centuries of civilization and the common heritage of the people. France was engaged in setting her house in order, in trying to work out a fresh code after the upheavals of the previous century, and this produces a literature of great vitality. Corneille's heroes are not, as they are sometimes said to be, mere abstractions or metaphysical entities, but the embodiment of all that was best in the middle class from which the poet came. They are human beings realizing their aspirations in *action*. It is the integrity of this middle class—*la solide vertu*, as Horace calls it—which gives his poetry its personal idiom and its peculiar strength. For this reason Corneille's poetry, in spite of a certain narrowness, possesses a maturity of outlook which makes the lesser Elizabethans in England seem crude and immature by comparison.

The political triumphs of the latter part of Louis XIII's reign made possible the *external* stability of the reign of Louis XIV. They also account for some of the main differences in the poetry of the two periods. M. Schlumberger suggests that Corneille's work is the product of an age in which civilization was threatened and

Racine's the product of an age of security, an age which encouraged disinterested speculation without the necessity of translating thought into action. Racine's elegance, as we shall see, belonged to a civilization which had reached its zenith, but a civilization which had within it the seeds of its own dissolution. Corneille's verse sometimes appears clumsy in comparison; but it is a clumsiness which comes from living in a difficult age and not the clumsiness of a man who is not the master of his medium. Racine's age did not possess the same internal stability and its moral fibre was less fine. I think that one might defend the view that Racine made greater poetry out of a poorer philosophy.

When we compare

> Il est doux de revoir les murs de la patrie
> > (*Sertorius*)

with

> Dans le fond des forêts votre image me suit
> > (*Phèdre*)

or

> Tous les monstres d'Égypte ont leurs temples dans Rome
> > (*Polyeucte*)

with

> Dans l'Orient désert quel devint mon ennui!
> > (*Bérénice*)

or

> . . . sur mes passions ma raison souveraine
> Eût blâmé mes soupirs et dissipé ma haine
> > (*Polyeucte*)

with

> Il n'est plus temps. Il sait mes ardeurs insensées.
> De l'austère pudeur les bornes sont passées
> > (*Phèdre*),

we may think that though Racine's lines are finer, they are not obviously more "poetical." It is clear, however, that the lines are the product of two very different sensibilities. Corneille limits and defines and finally sets a particular feeling against its background. Racine's method is a process of infinite suggestion; the lines seem to expand·in the mind, to set up waves of feeling which become more and more subtle and elusive. In the first line *patrie* has a precise geographical connotation and limits the emotion to a definite area.

In the second there is no barrier; *fond* suggests an infinite extension which has no limit and no term. In the third line—a description of the perverse Eastern cults which are tolerated in Rome while Christianity is persecuted—Corneille deliberately strips the East of the glamour with which Racine's *Orient désert* invests it. The squalor and degeneracy of the East are set against the moral integrity which Rome so often suggests in Corneille's poetry. In the last example, the "barrier" is purely a moral one; but the *raison souveraine* (which is deliberately placed after *passions*) is so vividly apprehended by the poet that it gives us a sense of physical repression. In Racine's couplet, on the contrary, the "limit" is only mentioned in order to tell us that it has long since been exceeded.

The differences become still more pronounced when we compare longer passages:

> Quoique pour ce vainqueur mon amour s'intéresse,
> Quoiqu'un peuple l'adore et qu'un roi le caresse,
> Qu'il soit environné des plus vaillants guerriers,
> J'irai sous mes cyprès accabler ses lauriers.
>
> (*Le Cid.*)

> Je le vis, je rougis, je pâlis à sa vue;
> Un trouble s'éleva dans mon âme éperdue;
> Mes yeux ne voyaient plus, je ne pouvais parler,
> Je sentis tout mon corps et transir et brûler.
>
> (*Phèdre.*)

The speakers in these passages are both victims of a conflict between what might provisionally be called "duty" and "inclination." In Racine, Phèdre's personality crumbles and disintegrates at once; the emotion of the passage is split up into its component parts, but though there is analysis there is no synthesis. Chimène's character is different. She is not passive, but active. The two conflicting impulses are balanced against one another and the conflict is resolved by the will acting in obedience to a principle. There is nothing specious about it; the solution springs necessarily from the *données*.

The great passage from which Racine's lines are taken will be discussed in more detail in another place. I must now record that the four lines from the *Cid* seem to me to be one of the glories of Corneille's poetry. The first three lines have an extraordinary lyrical élan which is intensified by the obvious sexual connotation of *intéresse*, *adore*, *caresse*, and the suggestion of "action" and "vitality" contained in *vainqueur* and *guerriers*. This feeling of expansion, this sense of personal liberation which comes from the momentary identification of Chimène with Rodrigue and his exploits, is suddenly checked by something altogether impersonal in the last line. The spreading foliage of the cypresses, with their sinister hint of darkness and death, comes down like a pall and stifles the "life" which is now concentrated in *lauriers*. The final effect of the passage, however, is not negative. The emotion of the first three lines is skilfully transformed so that the last line has behind it the force of the whole passage. It will be seen that there is no casuistry and no argument here: Corneille's method is a purely poetic one and depends on the opposition of *cyprès* and *lauriers* and the triumphant use of the word *accabler*. The image in the last line is fully adequate to the emotion; it stands out against the sober background of Corneille's verse and glows with a sombre splendour.

I hope that these comparisons have given some indication of the structure of Corneille's world. It is a finite world whose geographical boundaries are marked with such clarity that we sometimes have a feeling of almost physical oppression in reading him. His conception of the nature of man is defined with the mathematical precision of Descartes' *Traité des passions de l'âme* which gives his poetry its certainty and forthrightness. He is only interested in a few aspects of human nature and therefore only master of a limited range of emotion.[1] Within these limits he is a great writer, but when he ventures outside them the results are disastrous. He is, it need hardly be said, a more pedestrian writer than Racine, and the hard, metallic clang of his verse is in strong contrast to Racine's sensuous, flexible rhythms. There are no surprises in his poetry, none of those sudden glimpses into a subconscious world of primitive instinct that we get in Racine. For Corneille's aim was to bring that world of primitive instinct under the dominion of reason before reason was overthrown by it and society reduced to a state of chaos. Corneille's vocabulary was no smaller than Racine's, but it is

[1] It is this tendency to select, to isolate emotion, which is responsible for the sense of remoteness from common experience that we sometimes have in reading Corneille, and it may have inspired the criticisms of Taine and Brunetière given above.

probable that his language has less power of suggestion than that of any other great French poet. Words are scientific terms which mean exactly what they say. He did not possess Racine's gift of revealing mysterious depths with the most commonplace words as, for example, when Hippolyte says:

> Je me suis engagé trop avant.
> Je vois que la raison cède à la violence.

Corneille's four most famous plays are really variations on the same theme. They show the Cornelian hero in relation to the code of chivalry, to patriotism, to politics and finally to religion. In the later plays there is no doubt that Corneille was sometimes inclined to play the showman and to write without any inner compulsion and it is this, perhaps, which has led critics to say that his characters are artful mechanical contrivances without contact with living experience. The simplicity of his psychology and the ease with which he could define his position have undoubtedly lent currency to this view. In a remarkable passage in the Epistle Dedicatory to *la Place Royale* he wrote:

"It is from you that I learnt that the love of an *honnête homme* must always be voluntary; that we must never allow our love to reach the point at which we cannot stop loving; that if we do, love becomes a tyranny whose yoke must be shaken off; and, finally, that the person whom we love is under a much greater obligation to us when our love is the result of our own choice and of her merit than when it is the result of a blind impulse and is forced on us by some influence of birth which we are unable to resist."

This is a statement of principle which underlies the whole of Corneille's work, and our opinion of him as a poet depends on whether it is a living principle which produced vital poetry or an assumed position which led to a frigid formalism. It is plain that we have here a conception of love which is completely opposed to the one that dominates the poetry of Racine and of almost every great French poet who has since written. Hostile critics have always maintained that Corneille's was an artificial system deliberately imposed on living experience. Its authenticity can only be fully tested by an examination of Corneille's verse, but there are two reservations, both more or less theoretical, which should be made. The first is that the view of passion contained in Racine's poetry has become so much a part of our consciousness that we are no longer capable of approaching Corneille with an open mind. And the second is that although the code of honour on which the *Cid* is based may no longer seem valid, the quality of the poetry it once inspired is not affected by changed moral standards.

3

Corneille's poetry has been variously described as a conflict between "love and honour," as a "drama of the will" or as mere stoicism. All these views have been challenged at one time or another; but though it is true that a great poet's work can never be summed up in a single formula, these views may serve as pointers in examining his work so long as they are not too rigidly interpreted. "Love and honour" was a favourite theme in the literature of chivalry and it is interesting to see how Corneille extends its significance. The central fact in the *Cid* is a duel—the single combat between two "men of honour." It has not been sufficiently remarked that far from being a picturesque incident, the duel is a symbol of the whole play and indeed of all Corneille's poetry:

D. RODRIGUE:
    A moi, Comte, deux mots.
LE COMTE:
                    Parle.
D. RODRIGUE:
              Ote-moi d'un doute.
    Connais-tu bien don Diègue?
LE COMTE:
                  Oui.
D. RODRIGUE:
              Parlons bas; écoute.
    Sais-tu que ce vieillard fut la même vertu,
    La vaillance et l'honneur de son temps? le sais-tu? . . .
LE COMTE
             Que m'importe?
D. RODRIGUE:
    A quatre pas d'ici je te le fais savoir.

LE COMTE
    Jeune présomptueux!
D. RODRIGUE:
                    Parle sans t'émouvoir.
    Je suis jeune, il est vrai; mais aux âmes bien nées
    La valeur n'attend point le nombre des années. . . .
LE COMTE:
    Retire-toi d'ici.
D. RODRIGUE:
                    Marchons sans discourir.
LE COMTE
    Es-tu si las de vivre?
D. RODRIGUE
                    As-tu peur de mourir?

In this admirable scene we hear the thrust and parry of the rapiers—the hiss of steel in

            Sais-tu que c'est son sang? le sais-tu?

and we hear it all through the play. It is the duel that is evoked at the height of the drama in Chimène's

            Dedans mon ennemi je trouve mon amant;
            Et je sens qu'en dépit de toute ma colère,
            Rodrigue dans mon cœur combat encor mon père:
            Il l'attaque, il le presse, il cède, il se défend,
            Tantôt fort, tantôt faible, et tantôt triomphant;
            Mais, en ce dur combat de colère et de flamme,
            Il déchire mon cœur sans partager mon âme. . . .

The thrust and parry of the duel merges into the movement of consciousness, into the conflict between *amour* and *devoir* and this gives the play its unity. These passages reflect the movement of all Corneille's verse—a simple movement befitting a simple psychology. We feel it again, for example, in these lines from *Polyeucte* where the "duel" is purely an interior one:

POLYEUCTE:
    C'est peu d'aller au ciel, je vous y veux conduire.
PAULINE
    Imaginations!
POLYEUCTE:
                    Célestes vérités!

PAULINE:
    Étrange aveuglement!
POLYEUCTE
                    Éternelles clartés!

It is possible now to see how Corneille extends the significance of love and honour. The movement of his verse is not a destructive movement and the conflict does not end, as it usually does in tragedy, in the destruction of the characters. Nor is it true to say, as Lemaître and other French critics have said, that Corneille's poetry is simply a glorification of will and power for their own sake. There is always a definite aim in view, a process in which new values are forged, the human material reshaped and given a fresh direction. Honour is not merely a symbol of reason, it stands for the principle of order which has to be imposed on the chaos of unruly desires, on the whole of the instinctive life which Corneille constantly refers to as *les sens*. The real theme of his poetry, therefore, is not a simple clash between duty and inclination, but the subordination of one set of values to another which leads to the creation of a fresh order.

The background of Corneille's drama is aristocratic, the life of the court. In each of his major works the even flow of this life is disturbed by a shock—by a duel in the *Cid*, a conspiracy in *Cinna*, a conversion in *Polyeucte*. The effect of the shock and the conflict thus set up is to reveal the Cornelian hero to himself in a new way. The court life is seen to be conventional and unreal; and it is only when the convention is disturbed that the characters come into contact with the vital experience which is hidden beneath the outer husk, and that the mechanical code of honour is transformed into something living.

Corneille's drama, particularly the *Cid*, is always a drama of initiation. Fresh claims are made on human nature and it undergoes a change. In the opening scene of the *Cid* Chimène says to her *confidente*:

          Dis-moi donc, je te prie, une seconde fois
          Ce qui te fait juger qu'il approuve mon choix.

It is the voice of a child asking to be told over again that her father approves of her young man. In the second act she says to the Infanta:

          Maudite ambition, détestable manie,
          Dont les plus généreux souffrent la tyrannie!

This time it is the voice of the mature woman criticizing the values she is called upon to accept; and the alexandrine registers the change with remarkable delicacy.

The sudden contact with life produces in the Cornelian heroes a peculiar self-knowledge:

> Je *sais* ce que je suis, et que mon père est mort,

cries Chimène.

> Mon père, je suis femme, et je *sais* ma faiblesse,

says Pauline. This clairvoyance—this insight into their own feelings—gives Corneille's characters a poise, a centrality which are perhaps unique in European drama. The hero is always in imminent danger of being betrayed by the uprush of *les sens* which threaten to overturn reason and plunge him into chaos and disaster.

> La surprise des sens n'abat point mon courage,

says one of them, and it is precisely these *surprises* which are the condition of heroic virtue, of the *grand cœur*:

> Une femme d'honneur peut avouer sans honte
> Ces surprises des sens que la raison surmonte;
> Ce n'est qu'en ces assauts qu'éclate la vertu,
> Et l'on doute d'un cœur qui n'a point combattu.

The theme of the *Cid* is the clash between two generations, the dilemma of youth thrown into a world made by its parents and called upon to accept its standards. It is one of the signs of Corneille's maturity that these standards are never accepted passively; his attitude towards them is always critical. Honour is in constant danger of becoming inhuman and mechanical unless it is accompanied by a profound humanity which is always referred to by the word *généreux*. When Don Diègue says:

> Nous n'avons qu'un honneur, il est tant de maîtresses!
> L'amour n'est qu'un plaisir, l'honneur est un devoir.

the cynical slickness of the lines and the facile epigram are certainly ironic. *Honneur* and *devoir* are turned into counters which no longer correspond to any moral experience. For Don Diègue expresses something which is incompatible with the Cornelian view of life.

The combat does not destroy *les sens*, it dominates them in order
to incorporate them into a definite hierarchy—a hierarchy which
would be ruined if they were predominant, but which would be
hollow and incomplete without them, as the world of Don Diègue
and the Horaces is hollow and incomplete.

The criticism in *Horace* is of a far more drastic order. The play
becomes in the person of Camille—one of Corneille's most extraordinary creations—a harsh and angry indictment of the whole
system:

> Rome, l'unique objet de mon ressentiment!
> Rome, à qui vient ton bras d'immoler mon amant!
> Rome qui t'a vu naître, et que ton cœur adore!
> Rome enfin que je hais parce qu'elle t'honore!
> Puissent tous ses voisins ensemble conjurés
> Saper ses fondements encor mal assurés!

The heavy, monotonous verse suggests the terrible machine
remorselessly sacrificing humanity to an empty phantom. It is not
easy to decide how far Corneille ever accepted his own sanctions,
but it seems clear that they were only acceptable as a means to a
richer and fuller life, not as an end in themselves.

The struggle towards a new synthesis produces some of
Corneille's finest and subtlest verse:

> Ma raison, il est vrai, dompte mes sentiments;
> Mais quelque autorité que sur eux elle ait prise,
> Elle n'y règne pas, elle les tyrannise;
> Et quoique le dehors soit sans émotion,
> Le dedans n'est que trouble et que sédition.
> Un je ne sais quel charme encor vers vous m'emporte;
> Votre mérite est grand, si ma raison est forte:
> Je le vois encor tel qu'il alluma mes feux,
> D'autant plus puissamment solliciter mes vœux,
> Qu'il est environné de puissance et de gloire . . .
> Mais ce même devoir qui le vainquit dans Rome,
> Et qui me range ici dessous les lois d'un homme,
> Repousse encor si bien l'effort de tant d'appas,
> Qu'il déchire mon âme et ne l'ébranle pas.[1]

[1] This speech occurs in a meeting between Pauline and Sévère, the admirer
whom she had been obliged to give up in obedience to her father's wish for
her to marry Polyeucte, and who now returns from the wars covered in glory
and the Emperor's favourite.

This passage with its inversions, its verbs deliberately piled at
the end of the lines, is a remarkable example of the pitiless self-
inquisition to which the Cornelian heroes are subjected. There is
a deliberate and calculated clumsiness about the verse which
admirably expresses the immense effort that the speaker is making
to dominate her feelings. The passage gets its life from the constant
alteration of tone, the change from a note of defiance and determination to the half-whispered reflection of lines 6–8. The merits
of Sévère are carefully catalogued and balanced against the claims
of reason until one has the feeling that Pauline is being gradually
engulfed in a vast stream which threatens to dislodge her at any
moment. In the line

> D'autant plus puissamment solliciter mes feux

the hiss of the s's suggests the voluptuous element, the tug of
les sens. Then, at the moment when she seems lost, there is a sudden
shifting of the tension in the victorious

> Repousse encor si bien l'effort de tant d'appas,
> Qu'il déchire mon âme et ne l'ébranle pas.

The Cornelian "will" is not an abstract principle. The *déchire*
and the *ne l'ébranle pas* are both deeply *felt* and express a genuine
tension between two conflicting tendencies. The antithesis, so far
from being an artificial literary device, is dynamic and corresponds
to a deep division in Pauline's mind. When we compare Corneille's
lines with Racine's

> . . . la raison cède à la violence

we see that while in Racine the accent falls on the destructive word
cède, in Corneille it falls unmistakably on the words expressing
opposition and resistance—*repousse* and *ne l'ébranle pas*. The will
to resist temptation and the "inclination" for one's lover are sources
of energy and vitality. Man cannot live without the energy derived
from *amour*, but neither can he resist dissolution and collapse if it
is allowed to become predominant. The conflict thus becomes a
method of psychological revelation.

The dramatic assertion of the will is, as I have already suggested,
one of the most striking characteristics of Corneille's poetry; and
it seems to me that it is here rather than in the famous *Qu'il mourût*
that we detect the authentic heroic note. It is a note that we hear

not once, but many times in every play. It does not lower the tension
or resolve the conflict, but produces a marked increase of life and
vitality that enables the Cornelian hero to "carry on."

From this we may turn to Pauline's speech at the beginning of
Act III:

> Que de soucis flottants, que de confus nuages
> Présentent à mes yeux d'inconstantes images!
> Douce tranquillité, que je n'ose espérer,
> Que ton divin rayon tarde à les éclairer!
> Mille agitations, que mes troubles produisent,
> Dans mon cœur ébranlé tour à tour se détruisent:
> Aucun espoir n'y coule où j'ose persister;
> Aucun effroi n'y règne où j'ose m'arrêter.
> Mon esprit, embrassant tout ce qu'il s'imagine,
> Voit tantôt mon bonheur, et tantôt ma ruine,
> Et suit leur vaine idée avec si peu d'effet,
> Qu'il ne peut espérer ni craindre tout à fait.
> Sévère incessamment brouille ma fantaisie:
> J'espère en sa vertu, je crains sa jalousie;
> Et je n'ose penser que d'un œil bien égal
> Polyeucte en ces lieux puisse voir son rival.

"This is half-way to poetry," remarks a university lecturer
patronizingly.[1] It seems to me to be a good deal more than that.
It seems to me to be not only dramatically effective, but something to which we can hardly refuse the title of great poetry. The
same writer complains that "the metaphors and images are con-
fused," but the confusion does not seem to me to lie in Corneille's
imagery. For the success of the passage depends very largely on
the skill with which the poet presents "a whole of tangled feelings."
The focal point of the passage is the image of the conflicting feelings dissolving into and destroying one another. The words *soucis
flottants, confus nuages, inconstantes images* suggest a state of complete instability which is accompanied by a desperate longing for
the elusive stability promised by *douce tranquillité, persister, arrêter*;
but there is no security anywhere. Whatever Pauline tries to cling
on to dissolves into mere *fantaisie*. For here the words "seem to do
what they say" as surely as in the finest English poetry of the same
period. Pauline's mind is battered into a state of immobility. She

[1] *Poetry in England and France*, by Jean Stewart, London, 1931, p. 52.

C

is acutely aware of what she feels, but in the midst of the tumult of warring impulses she is passive and unable to act. Only a dumb determination to "hang on" persists and gives the poetry its vitality. The tension does not depend, as it does in Racine, on the sickening sense of complete collapse, but on a contrast between the rigid immobility—the numbness between the metal walls of the alexandrine—which prevents action, and the swirl of the rapidly changing feelings.

Although the passages I have discussed come from different plays, they illustrate the stages in the evolution of Corneille's characters which scarcely varies from one play to another. It is evident that this evolution is as different from the one we find in Racine as it could well be. In Racine there is a violent conflict, but it does not end in the creation of fresh moral values or the renewal of life; it ends in the reversal of all moral values. Corneille is inferior to Racine as a psychologist, but he seems to me to reveal a greater range of what is commonly described as "character." Racine concentrates the whole of his attention on the moral crisis and there is nothing in his work which is comparable to the moral growth that takes place in Corneille's characters. We can, I think, sum up the differences between the two by saying that Corneille's characters are people *qui se construisent* and Racine's people *qui se défont*. The "shock," of which I have already spoken, shatters the complacency of Corneille's characters and reveals their own perplexity and confusion to them. But it also reveals the goal towards which they must strive, and by their immense determination they overcome this perplexity and confusion and achieve a new unity.[1] Racine's characters, on the other hand, start their career as unified or apparently unified beings, and the drama lies in the dissolution of that inner unity.

The final change in Corneille's characters, when it does come, appears as a flash of illumination which transcends all the separate acts of the individual and the different phases of the drama which lead up to it. One is Auguste's sudden realization of his place in the existing order:

> Je suis maître de moi comme de l'univers;
> Je le suis, je veux l'être.

[1] The Germans would call them *zielbewusst* or "goal-conscious." It is this more than anything else which gives their creator's outlook its maturity.

Another is the description of a conversion in *Polyeucte*:

> Je m'y trouve forcé par un secret appas;
> Je cède à des transports que je ne connais pas. . . .

I should be shirking a difficulty if I failed to mention the celebrated encounter between Rodrigue and Chimène in Act III. Sc. iv. This scene—too long to set out here—seemed to Corneille's age to be a masterpiece of pathos. M. Schlumberger cannot resist the temptation to quote it and Brasillach subjects it to an enthusiastic analysis. My own opinion is that Corneille was not a master of pathos and that though the scene contains good passages, the most admired parts are tiresome and embarrassing. They are an example of what happens when Corneille ventures outside his limited field. It must, of course, be remembered that his verse was written to be declaimed and that lines which are embarrassing in the study may sound well enough on the stage, and I have myself seen a good company 'carry" what appear to be the weaker parts of this scene. It is one of the shortcomings of the grand manner that it does allow the poet to "fake" emotion, to rely on the sweep of the alexandrine when there is no correspondence between his personal sensibility and the emotion that he is staging.

4

The *Cid* has always been Corneille's most popular play and it possesses the peculiar beauty which belongs to the first work of a great writer's maturity; but the plays which followed also possess a vision, a complexity, that we do not find in the *Cid*. It has been pointed out that the discovery of Rome was an event of the first importance in Corneille's development, but its importance is not always understood. Corneille wrote of Rome at several different periods of her history and his attitude towards her varied, but the most impressive of the Roman plays is perhaps *Cinna*. The *Cid* is the most individualistic, the most "romantic," of his works. It does not possess, that is to say, any coherent view of society. There is simply the life of the Court with its etiquette and con-

ventions. *Cinna* is far from being a faultless play, but there does
emerge from it a definite conception of society, something which
can, I think, not unreasonably be called a social order. We must
not expect to find in French drama the sort of picture of contemporary life that we get in the English drama of the same period.
French tragedy was essentially the product of an intellectual aristocracy. There was no place for *le peuple* whom Corneille regarded as
creatures of instinct in whose life reason played little part. The social
order which emerges from *Cinna* is therefore concerned with the
problems of the ruling class, for it is assumed—not unnaturally—
that reconstruction starts from above. The advance in Corneille's
art is apparent from the great speech of Auguste who in the second
act significantly displaces Cinna as the hero:

> Cet empire absolu sur la terre et sur l'onde,
> Ce pouvoir souverain que j'ai sur tout le monde,
> Cette grandeur sans borne et cet illustre rang,
> Qui m'a jadis coûté tant de peine et de sang,
> Enfin tout ce qu'adore en ma haute fortune
> D'un courtisan flatteur la présence importune,
> N'est que de ces beautés dont l'éclat éblouit,
> Et qu'on cesse d'aimer sitôt qu'on en jouit.
> L'ambition déplaît quand elle est assouvie,
> D'une contraire ardeur son ardeur est suivie;
> Et comme notre esprit, jusqu'au dernier soupir,
> Toujours vers quelque objet pousse quelque désir,
> Il se ramène en soi, n'ayant plus où se prendre,
> Et monté sur le faîte, il aspire à descendre.
> J'ai souhaité l'empire, et j'y suis parvenu;
> Mais en le souhaitant, je ne l'ai pas connu:
> Dans sa possession j'ai trouvé pour tous charmes
> D'effroyables soucis, d'éternelles alarmes,
> Mille ennemis secrets, la mort à tout propos,
> Point de plaisir sans trouble, et jamais de repos.

It is one of the finest examples of Corneille's handling of the
grand style. Without any rhetoric, the *ampleur* of the style and the
regular thud of the end-rhymes contrive to suggest a stable order.
For there are two voices speaking here—the voice of the lonely
harassed individual debating whether or not to give up his throne
and what one may call the public voice. It is no longer simply

matter of coming to terms with oneself or of satisfying accepted standards of honour, but of playing a part in society. *Cinna* is a drama of adjustment. The individual experience has to fit in with the experience of the community and the drama is only complete when this is accomplished. In *Cinna*, therefore, there is a blending of the political and the moral problems. It is not simply that all political problems are seen to involve a moral problem, but that in transforming moral problems into political problems Corneille gives them a wider context and immensely increases the import of his poetry. It is this which makes his approach extremely actual to-day. In the great political discussion at the beginning of Act II one is aware of a straightening out of the emotions, and order, which is so often discussed and so rarely defined, becomes something almost tangible.

Although Corneille's contemporaries thought of him as the author of *Cinna*, many modern critics consider that *Nicomède*—a much later work—is the finest of the political plays. It is not, perhaps, surprising that the Latin mind with its passion for the "well made play" should be more aware of *Cinna's* faults than its virtues, and no doubt some writers have suspected that the defence of absolute monarchy implied a defence of the monstrous injustices associated with it. *Cinna*, however, is not important as a defence of a particular system of government, but for the passion for order which inspires it. The very violence with which the *individual* conspirators are swept into that order shows that Corneille was fully conscious of these difficulties—conscious of them *as a poet*. For his poetry marks the end of an epoch and he may have felt that the order for which he had fought was doomed to destruction by its inherent rigidity and its inability to provide a bulwark against chaos.

Nicomède is an extraordinary ironic *tour de force* which deserves to be better known in England. "Tenderness and passion have no part in it," said Corneille in his Dedication. "My chief aim has been to paint Rome's politics in her relations with other states." He sets his "cool and efficient hero"—the language of the best-seller is somehow appropriate—against the background of political intrigue and proceeds, very skilfully, to "debunk" the large pretensions of Rome and her predatory designs on smaller countries. Nicomède's ruthless sardonic humour gives the play its peculiar flavour.

Ostensibly he is trying to bolster up his father and make him resist
the demands of Rome; but there is an undercurrent of resentment
which spares neither Prusias' inefficiency nor his senile passion for
his second wife.[1]

PRUSIAS:

> Quelle bassesse d'âme,
> Quelle fureur t'aveugle en faveur d'une femme?
> Tu la préfères, lâche! à ces prix glorieux
> Que ta valeur unit au bien de tes aïeux! . . .

NICOMÈDE:

> Je crois que votre exemple est glorieux à suivre . . .
>
> Pardonnez-moi ce mot, il est fâcheux à dire,
> Mais un monarque enfin comme un autre homme expire . . .

He carefully points the contrast between the office of king and
its present occupant. *Expire*, with its suggestions of the funeral
cortège, the vast mausoleum with the appropriate inscriptions,
reveals the fatuity of the person who will be buried there. The wit
reaches its peak in the last act after Prusias' attempted flight:

ATTALE:

> J'ai couru me ranger auprès du Roi mon père . . .
> . . . ce monarque étonné . . .
>
> Avait pris un esquif pour tâcher de rejoindre
> Ce Romain, dont l'effroi peut-être n'est pas moindre.

> *(Prusias entre)*

PRUSIAS:

> Non, non; nous revenons l'un et l'autre en ces lieux
> Défendre votre gloire, ou mourir à vos yeux.

Prusias is a richly comic creation and has a definite place in
Corneille's survey of seventeenth-century society. In the *Cid* and in
Horace he exposed an "honour" which had become mechanical and
inhuman. Through Félix in *Polyeucte* and Prusias in *Nicomède* he
makes the essential criticisms of middle-class complacency, of the
moral corruption which prevents the attainment of Cornelian
honour.[2]

---

[1] *cf.* Prusias' remark to his son: "J'ai tendresse pour toi, j'ai passion pour
elle."

[2] Thus Félix, who decides to sacrifice his son-in-law in order to save his
career, remarks naively:

A word must be said about a more debatable side of Corneille's work—the religious side. Some critics have denied that he is properly speaking a religious poet at all, while others have described *Polyeucte*, which is certainly his greatest play, as a masterpiece of religious poetry. It must be recorded with gratitude that it is refreshingly free from the incorrigibly romantic attitude towards sin that we find in certain living Catholic writers; but in spite of its subject it is neither more nor less religious than any of Corneille's other works. What is religious in all Corneille's best work is not the subject or the setting, but his sense of society as an ordered whole and of man as a member of this hierarchy. If he tried to round off the picture in *Polyeucte* by presenting the natural order in the light of the supernatural, it seems to me that he failed. It is significant that in this play the fable was modified to fit the usual Cornelian formula and we are left with the feeling that the religion was not inevitable, but that any other *motif* might have produced an equally great play. Corneille's world remains a circumscribed world and his religion does not extend the field of his experience as it clearly ought to have done.[1]

> Te dirai-je un penser indigne, bas et lâche?
> Je l'étouffe, il renaît; il me flatte, et me fâche.
> L'ambition toujours me le vient présenter,
> Et tout ce que je puis, c'est de le détester.
> Polyeucte est ici l'appui de ma famille;
> Mais si, par son trépas, l'autre épousait ma fille,
> J'acquerrais bien par là de plus puissants appuis,
> Qui me mettraient plus haut cent fois que je ne suis.
> Mon cœur en prend par force une maligne joie;
> Mais que plutôt le ciel à tes yeux foudroie,
> Qu'à des pensers si bas je puisse consentir,
> Que jusque-là ma gloire ose se démentir!

[1] *cf.* "The museum of masterpieces is there and none of us will ever grow weary of visiting it. It is superfluous and would be impertinent to insist on this point. Nor can it be denied that in the works of the classic writers the author also expresses himself as a man, sometimes in spite of himself, and sometimes by means of that indirect method of which I have just spoken. It is simply a matter of drawing attention to a point which is of capital importance: according to the classic writer's conception and the canons governing classic art, the author, the man and the Christian are three separate persons, so that in his work the fundamental interior unity of the human being, which was the centre of 'all the different parts' of which man 'is composed,' is destroyed." (Charles Du Bos, *Approximations*, 6ième série, Paris, 1934, p. 255.) See, too, Mauriac, *Journal*, III ("La Grâce dans *Polyeucte*").

It should be apparent by now in what sense Corneille is an heroic poet. It has nothing to do with declamation and bombast (though there is plenty of both in his work), or with the misleading theory that his characters are "supermen." It simply means that by a combination of insight and will power the moral values which Corneille derived from close contact with his class are raised in his plays to a high level of poetic intensity. He was a great poet because he expressed something that is permanent in human nature and because he had behind him the whole weight of what was best in contemporary society. One has only to compare him for a moment with Dryden to see the difference. For Dryden's age was not an heroic age and in trying to write heroic plays he was simply going against the spirit of his time. His drama is an example of the false sublime, of the stucco façade which ill conceals the viciousness and corruption beneath.

5

Corneille's later plays have been the subject of considerable controversy. Contemporary apologists like M. Schlumberger take up their stand against the traditional view which regards the later plays, in Lytton Strachey's words, as "miserable failures." Pierre Lièvre's introduction to his admirable edition of the plays[1] is an eloquent plea that Corneille's work should be treated as a whole, as a steady development from the early comedies to the final tragedies. I confess that I find it difficult to accept this view. Plays like *Rodogune* and *Pompée*, which belong to the third period that lasts from 1644 to 1669, contain fine things, but compared with Corneille's best work they seem to me to show a pronounced falling off. There is, perhaps, a greater breadth of characterization, but the poetry is less impressive. The fact that Corneille never stood still and never repeated himself may be the reason for the difficulty. With *Polyeucte* the Cornelian hero is complete and there is no room for further development along those lines. The poet loses interest in his hero who degenerates into a mechanical warrior —*Attila* provides the worst example—and concentrates on the

---

[1] *Théâtre complet* (Bibliothèque de la Pléiade), 2 vols., Paris, 1934. (This is much the most satisfactory edition for "the common reader.")

people who surround him. The main interest of the plays of this period lies in the amazons like Rodogune, Cornélie and the two Cléopâtres. This produces an alteration in the quality of the verse. Corneille develops the vein of rhetoric which is already visible in the *Cid*:

> Paraissez, Navarrois, Mores et Castillans,
> Et tout ce que l'Espagne a nourri de vaillants;
> Unissez-vous ensemble, et faites une armée,
> Pour combattre une main de la sorte animée . . .

In *Rodogune* this becomes the staple of the whole play:

> Serments fallacieux, salutaire contrainte,
> Que m'imposa la force et qu'accepta ma crainte,
> Heureux déguisements d'un immortel courroux,
> Vains fantômes d'État, évanouissez-vous.

There is a natural tendency to rhetoric in French poetry, to use words as mere labels and to rely for the "poetry" on the drive of the alexandrine. Certainly there is no lack of drive in *Rodogune*, but there is a loss of subtlety and a marked coarseness of texture in the verse.[1]

Although M. Schlumberger has apparently abandoned the view that the last plays of all are the crown of Corneille's work, he still

[1] As a vehicle for invective Corneille's later verse has a strange impressiveness, but it should be noticed that invective is often used as a substitute for something different. In *Pertharite*, Rodelinde, speaking of her son says to her suitor:

> Puisqu'il faut qu'il périsse, il vaut mieux tôt que tard;
> Que sa mort soit un crime, et non pas un hasard;
> Que cette ombre innocente à toute heure m'anime,
> Me demande à toute heure une grande victime;
> Que ce jeune monarque, immolé de ta main,
> Te rende abominable à tout le genre humain . . .
> Je t'épouserai lors, et m'y viens d'obliger,
> Pour mieux servir ma haine, et pour mieux me venger,
> Pour moins perdre de vœux contre ta barbarie,
> Pour être à tous moments maîtresse de ta vie,
> Pour avoir l'accès libre à pousser ma fureur,
> Et mieux choisir la place à te percer le cœur.

There are two things that strike us in this passage. One is that moral values are no longer *directly* apprehended and that the poet is using declamation to keep up appearances. The other is that his psychological insight has become blunted. The characters no longer analyse their feelings and turn instead to the denunciation of their enemies. It is in this sense that invective is a clever substitute for the great qualities that have been lost.

C*

gives *Pulchérie* and *Suréna* a high place in it. In these plays there is
a return to the old Cornelian formula which was to some extent
abandoned in the plays of the middle period. He sees in them a
tenderness and serenity which he does not find in any of Corneille's
other work. This may be so, but one cannot help wondering
whether they deserve all the praise they get. Consider, for example,
the opening speech of *Pulchérie*:

> Je vous aime, Léon, et n'en fais point mystère:
> Des feux tels que les miens n'ont rien qu'il faille taire.
> Je vous aime, et non point de cette folle ardeur
> Que les yeux éblouis font maîtresse du cœur,
> Non d'un amour conçu par les sens en tumulte,
> A qui l'âme applaudit sans qu'elle se consulte,
> Et qui ne concevant que d'aveugles désirs,
> Languit dans les faveurs, et meurt dans les plaisirs:
> Ma passion pour vous, généreuse et solide,
> A la vertu pour âme, et la raison pour guide,
> La gloire pour objet, et veut sous votre loi
> Mettre en ce jour illustre et l'univers et moi.

According to Croce this passage marks the summit of Corneille's
poetry and, with a lofty assumption of philosophical detachment,
he proceeds to commend Pulchérie's attitude to physical love. It is
not difficult to see why these lines appeal to one whose criterion is
evidently "simple, sensuous and passionate." It is by no means a
negligible piece of verse, but it owes its charm to a subtle flavour
of dissolution. The difficulty that one feels might be expressed by
saying that honour wins altogether too easily. It is clear from the
looseness of texture, the slackness of the versification, that we are
a long way from the poet of *Polyeucte*. It is the work of an old man,
of a great poet in decline. Nor can one share Croce's enthusiasm for
the content. For who but a survival of nineteenth-century romanti-
cism can feel any sympathy for the bloodless spinster high-mindedly
giving up her love to contract a "chaste" alliance with her father's
aged counsellor?[1]

[1] The same weariness, the same tendency to take a voluptuous pleasure in
suffering, are apparent in his last play, *Suréna*:

> Je veux, sans que la mort ose me secourir,
> Toujours aimer, toujours souffrir, toujours mourir.

> Que tout meure avec moi, Madame; que m'importe
> Qui foule après ma mort la terre qui me porte?

What is to be the final estimate? "Corneille," answers M. Schlumberger, "does not ask the supreme questions, neither does he answer them. If I give him a high place in my æsthetic, there remains a vast region of myself in which I feel the need of other poets besides him." It is clear that he lacks many of the qualities that we have come to expect of poetry. Certain fundamental truths were grasped with the clarity and the tenacity of genius; he was a penetrating critic of the evils of the existing order; but his own vision was partial and incomplete and the order towards which he was striving seems somehow indistinct. Yet his central experience —his sense of society as an ordered whole and of man as a part of that hierarchy—has an important place in European literature and without him it would be incomplete. Of all the great masters Corneille is the most limited, but that he is a master we cannot doubt.

MOLIÈRE

"C'est une étrange entreprise que de faire rire les honnêtes gens"
—La Critique de l'École des Femmes

I. MOLIÈRE AND HIS AGE

1

THE seventeenth century in France is curiously deceptive. On the surface it appears to be simple and uniform. In reality it was complex and multiform. We are faced not with one age, but with several ages; not with a static society, but with a society in a continual process of evolution. The different ages overlap, merge into one another, so that conventional divisions into historical periods are of little assistance. We need fresh standards, and a useful approach is suggested by a passage in M. Pierre Maillaud's admirable book on France:

"Throughout the Classical Age," he writes, "the fundamental object of philosophy, literature, and art remains the study of Man, of his nature, of his passions, of his motives, of his social habits and oddities: man as an individual to whom the existing social order provides only an artistic background, and not man against an existing order, for there is no sign of political reformism among its writers."[1]

The single-minded concentration of the masters of the Classical Age on their subject is one of the main sources of their greatness. When it is looked at as a whole, the work of the philosophers, the moralists and the poets of the seventeenth century is seen to be one of the most searching examinations of human nature that has ever been made. Its completeness depends paradoxically on the acceptance by individual writers of the limitations of their art, on their concentration not simply on man, but on certain facets of his character; and the facets that they chose to reveal were largely determined by social and political changes and by changes in sensibility which were going on beneath the surface of society. We never meet Man in their writings; we meet instead the Rational Man, the Sceptical Man, the Social Man or the Natural Man. Labels are always danger-

[1] *France* (The World To-day), Oxford, 1942, p. 55.

MOLIÈRE
From a drawing by Ronjat, after the painting attributed
to Pierre Mignard

MOLIÈRE
From a drawing by Ronjat, after the painting attributed
to Pierre Mignard

ous, but as long as we realize that there was room for innumerable variations within the individual approach they help us to understand the relations between a particular writer's conception of man and the age in which he wrote. With these reservations, the century can be divided broadly into three ages and the ages named after the three greatest French dramatists—Corneille, Molière, Racine.

Corneille wrote at a time when France had been disrupted by the wars of religion and was trying to set her house in order. His theme is the Man of Honour, the imposition of order—a moral order—on the chaos of human desires. Racine stands at the other extreme. He belonged not to an age of reconstruction, but to an age which had reached its zenith and was beginning to disintegrate from within. His interest lies in the Man of Passion, in the collapse of order before the swirls of unruly desires. Molière occupies a position midway between the two extremes. The centre of his world is the Natural Man and he studies the way in which perverted natural instincts may become a danger to the community. He believed more deeply, perhaps, in his age than either Corneille or Racine. He was the laureate of *la bonne Régence*, of an age when society seemed for a moment to have reached stability, when, in spite of conflicting "philosophies," its structure was not threatened and there was time to examine man's "social habits and oddities," to laugh over his extravagances.

Although a precise clear-cut conception of man emerges from the work of each of the three poets, the change from the Age of Corneille to the Age of Molière, or from the Age of Molière to the Age of Racine, was not the result of any violent upheaval. The changes were gradual, the shades and subtleties almost infinite. They can be detected in a shifting of the focus, in the sounding of a fresh note which was not always perceptible to contemporary readers. Indeed, the cross-currents of the century were so complex that not only the passing of one age but the beginning of the next was sometimes manifested in the work of the same writer. We can see now that in *Nicomède*, which was written in 1651, eight years after the last of the four great tragedies and after a series of imitations of his own style, Corneille not only wrote a masterpiece, but a masterpiece in a new manner. Prusias is an ironic figure in which the possibilities of Félix in *Polyeucte* are exploited and he points the way straight to the Age of Molière.

Yet when Molière tried to do the same thing in 1658 the result was a failure. *Dom Garcie de Navarre* did not fail because Molière was writing against the grain of the age, as one feels that Racine was in *Alexandre le Grand* where the Cornelian phrases stick out jaggedly among the smooth alexandrines. It failed because *Nicomède* was so far in advance of its time that in 1658 Molière was not sufficiently mature to benefit from its discoveries. It was only in the *Misanthrope*, for which Molière significantly lifted some of the best passages from *Dom Garcie*, that *Nicomède* bore its full fruit, and lines which had sounded hollow and unreal in Dom Garcie's mouth are in perfect harmony with Alceste's character. The *Misanthrope* is the meeting-point of three ages. It is the finest flower of the Age of Molière, but it looks back in a healthy sense to the Age of Corneille and forward to the Age of Racine. Compare Auguste's

> Je suis maître de moi comme de l'univers;
> Je le suis, je veux l'être.

with Alceste's

> Je veux qu'on soit sincère, et qu'en homme d'honneur
> On ne lâche aucun mot qui ne parte du cœur.

and you see at once that the times have changed. You notice that the "Man of Honour" has ceased to be a man of *action* and become a man of *words*—an apostle of plain speaking. You notice, too, that there is no genuine volition behind Alceste's *Je veux*. He is incapable of imposing a positive discipline first on himself, then on society, as Auguste does. When faced with the obstacles which Corneille's characters successfully overcome, he simply abdicates:

> Je n'y puis plus tenir, j'enrage, et mon dessein
> Est de rompre en visière à tout le genre humain.

His determination crumbles at once and his energy dissolves in an explosion of useless rage which drives him towards a negative goal —the abandonment of society and the hunt for

> un endroit écarté
> Où d'être homme d'honneur on ait la liberté.

These lines are a forcible illustration of the nature of the changes which had taken place. The heroic age is past; the Cornelian Man of

Honour has become a figure of fun, a windbag who leads an eccentric life outside society. Rodrigue turns into Alceste, Polyeucte into Orgon. The true representatives of the Age of Molière are the *honnêtes hommes* with their reasonable, tolerant outlook, their solid, unheroic virtues.

Alceste is a comic figure, but a comic figure of a new kind, for he is already endowed with the power of introspection, the deadly lucidity of the heroes of Racine, and his

> Mes sens par la raison ne sont plus gouvernés,
> Je *cède* aux mouvements d'une juste colère.

recalls at once Hippolyte's

> Je me suis engagé trop avant.
> Je vois que la raison *cède* à la violence.

In Molière's characters, the energy and drive which in Corneille bring order out of chaos are transformed into a fanaticism which potentially at least is as dangerous to society as the "violence" of Racine.

"In Molière," wrote Sainte-Beuve in one of his memorable over-statements—"in Molière as in Montaigne we meet nature, but nature without any appreciable mixture of what belongs to the *order of Grace*; he was not touched at any period of his life, any more than Montaigne was, by Christianity."[1] Discussions of the relative value of the three writers are fruitless, but Sainte-Beuve's *mot* helps to explain the popularity of Molière in this country— the country of Shakespeare—and the sad neglect of Corneille and Racine. The English reader is disconcerted by the world of France's two greatest tragic poets. He does not know what to make of the booming voices extolling *honneur* and *gloire* and exhorting him to acts of heroic virtue. He is no more at home in Racine's world which threatens to dissolve at any moment and to engulf its inhabitants in their own furious passions.

Molière presents a very different picture. He has his roots deep in the earth and he introduces the English reader to a world where he is on firm ground, a solid, opaque world built in the normal dimensions and filled with the ceaseless noise and bustle of the *quartier*:

[1] *Port-Royal* III, Paris, 1848, p. 198.

> Ces carrosses sans cesse à la porte plantés,
> Et de tant de laquais le bruyant assemblage.

We find it very difficult to visualize the physical appearance of Racine's characters. The whole of the drama is concentrated into the world within; passion glows like a single white-hot filament in the surrounding darkness; and clothes are only mentioned to show that even the flimsiest garment is an intolerable constraint to the vibrating nerves, the tormented bodies:

> Que ces vains ornements, que ces voiles me pèsent!

Molière's characters not only wear clothes like other people, the clothes are a part of the characters. The subtle, flexible style, which faithfully registers the accent of the individual voice—the whine of Orgon, the ranting of Harpagon, the childlike lisp of Agnès—possesses vivid pictorial qualities which place the characters compellingly before our eyes: Tartuffe in his peculiar monkish habit calling on his servant to tighten the hair shirt and Alceste, unforgettable as "l'homme aux rubans verts." "Il a au cœur la tristesse," said Sainte-Beuve of Molière; but though a sombre note runs through some of his greatest plays, our abiding impression is not one of sadness. There is an immense *joie* in the created world, in the world of *pourpoints*, *collets*, *rubans* and *canons*.

As Molière's genius ripens, the panorama of a whole age unfolds before us. He does not confine himself to any one section of the community like Corneille with his warriors or Racine with his princes and princesses. His vision has greater width than theirs; his work is a *comédie humaine* which embraces society from top to bottom, a society of courtiers, *marquis*, doctors, lawyers, prudes, peasants, lacqueys, of amorous old men and lecherous young women.

2

The face which looks down at us from the Mignard portrait of Molière is an impressive one. There is a hint of melancholy and even of suffering in the eyes, but it is not this alone that makes the portrait so arresting. It is rather the expression of wisdom, of a wisdom derived from human experience in which *tristesse* blends with an obvious zest for life that is apparent in the full, sensual lips. When we survey Molière's career as a writer, it is indeed a combination of wisdom, immense determination and an enormous love of life which seems to distinguish it.

"One of the clearest signs of the character of the man and of his creative power," writes M. Maurice Blanchot in an excellent note on Molière, "is his sudden impatient and imperious grasp of things. We are aware in Molière of a power of attack which is apparent not merely in his taste for satire, which is something much more general, so that as soon as he is in contact with his subject he takes possession of it and goes straight for the essential ... Molière shows the same hot-headedness as his own Misanthrope."[1]

It is not difficult to see why this should be so. It is easy to explain too much in terms of heredity and environment, but there can be little doubt that Molière's early life played a part of capital importance in the development of the qualities which M. Blanchot describes and which give his work its immense vitality.

Jean-Baptiste Poquelin, who later became known as Molière, was born in Paris on 15th January 1622, in a house at the corner of the Rue Saint-Honoré and the Rue des Vieilles Étuves which was popularly known as the Maison des Singes from the decorations on the pillars. He came on both sides of solid, middle-class parents and was in the fullest sense of the term *un bourgeois de Paris*. His father, Jean Poquelin, was a *marchand-tapissier* or upholsterer and his mother was Marie Cressé, the daughter of another *marchand-tapissier*. Molière's father was a person of some importance in his profession, and in 1631 he obtained a charge as *tapissier du roi*, a position which has been compared to that of a high official in the Office of Works in our own time.

Molière's childhood and youth are obscured by a mass of legend and speculation. His biographers cannot agree whether or not he was a pupil of the famous Gassendi, and literary critics cannot agree about the influence or supposed influence of that philosopher on his work. A few facts, however, are undisputed. From 1635 to 1641 he was a pupil of the Jesuits at Clermont. It was the custom at

[1] *Faux pas*, Paris, 1943, p. 307.

Jesuit schools for masters and boys to collaborate in the adaptation and production of Latin plays on public occasions, and Molière like Corneille before him may well have acquired his taste for the theatre in this way.

Clermont was a decidedly "smart" school and Molière made one important "contact" there. He met the famous Prince de Conti who became his friend and patron during his years in the provinces. Conti went to Clermont in 1637 and at fifteen he took his "degree." "A little monster of learning," observes one of Molière's biographers.[1] He was soon to become a monster of another kind. For some years he was one of the most notorious *libertins* of the day. Then, with the violence and suddenness which were characteristic of the century, he was converted and, swinging to the other extreme, became a leading *dévot*, renounced the arts, withdrew his patronage from Molière and joined the Compagnie du Saint-Sacrement. "Cet amour de la comédie," observes Allier drily, "était le moindre péché d'un homme qui s'était roulé dans toutes les ordures et qui s'était rongé de débauches."[2]

Molière's father had contrived to have his charge at Court made hereditary and it was in his capacity as *valet-tapissier du roi* that in 1642 the young Molière accompanied Louis XIII on his journey to Narbonne, saw the Midi for the first time and only returned to the capital at the end of the year.

The meeting with Madeleine Béjart the following year was a turning-point in Molière's career. She was the daughter of Joseph Béjart, an official in the Department of Forestry. The Béjarts were a large, picturesque and somewhat disreputable family living on the edge of Bohemia. They had one thing in common—a passion for the theatre. At eighteen Madeleine was writing verses to the dramatist Rotrou. At nineteen she was the mistress of the Comte de Modène and at twenty the birth of a daughter, so far from being considered a scandal, was celebrated by a handsome christening at which the Comte's paternity was publicly acknowledged. The child's godparents were her natural grandmother and the legitimate son of her own illegitimate father.

In one of those peculiar distinctions at which the French excel, Ramon Fernandez has described Molière's relations with Madeleine

[1] John Palmer, *Moliere: His Life and Works*, London, 1930, p. 16.
[2] *La Cabale des dévots*, Paris, 1902, p. 393.

as an "amitié sexuelle autant que morale."[1] No doubt he is right, but the rest is speculation. What is certain is that her influence on his future as a writer was decisive. After a struggle with his father he abandoned his charge at Court, entered into partnership with Madeleine and founded the Illustre Théâtre. The enterprise was not a success and in 1646 Molière with Madeleine and the company set out on a tour of the French provinces where he spent the next twelve years as an actor-playwright. Critics have drawn fanciful pictures of the weary actors trapesing from place to place with their stage properties and putting up in barns, and one writer has hinted salaciously at happy promiscuity in the warm hay. Life under such conditions was very different from Corneille's uneventful youth at Rouen or Racine's monkish, cloistered childhood among the "solitaries" at Port-Royal and his visit to his uncle's comfortable rectory at Uzès, where he waited impatiently for the *bon bénéfice* which never turned up. It left a lasting impression on Molière's work, for it was during the *wanderjahre* that he came into close contact with the people and acquired the habit of acute, humorous observation of his fellow-men.

The formative influences were the old French farces, the Commedia dell'Arte and direct experience. His earliest plays, in which faithless wives plant the horned cap well and truly over the ears of their elderly husbands or send the unfortunate husbands to market trussed up in sacks like pigs, in which *coups de bâton* and *pots de chambre* abound, are pure slapstick. They do not seem particularly funny to-day, but they treat of themes which are deeply rooted in the consciousness of the race and which appeal directly to primitive instincts—laughter, mockery, hatred, envy. They may seem far from the famous *réalisme comique* of his greatest work, but in reality there is a direct connection between the two. Although Molière abandoned these crude methods, he retained many of his early themes and his appeal was always to natural human feelings which are stifled beneath the conventions of civilization. The light-hearted farce of *la Jalousie du barbouillé* and *l'Étourdi* develops into the grim farce of parts of the *École des femmes* and *George Dandin*. One of the chief means of getting a laugh in the early farces was repetition. In the mature comedies the repetition of phrases like *Le pauvre homme!* and *Sans dot!* which reminds one

[1] *La Vie de Molière* (Vies des Hommes Illustres No. 32), Paris, 1929, p. 19.

of a gramophone needle which has got stuck in the same groove, becomes a skilful device for revealing the characters' state of mind. The whole trend of Molière's art was away from the comedy of situation to the comedy of character. We can see how the comic exaggerations of his early work are transformed into the strange manias which possess Arnolphe, Orgon and Alceste, and a German critic has coined the word *durchpsychologisierung*[1] to describe the process.

3

In 1658 Molière and his troupe returned to Paris. The following year he produced the *Précieuses ridicules*. It is generally recognized that this play is a landmark in his work. The farces are a thing of the past. Molière has found his vocation. The *Précieuses ridicules* is a brilliantly satirical picture of one section of French society and the two disguised *marquis* show how much Molière had profited from the traditional French farces. The play has, however, a deeper purpose which can be illustrated by two brief extracts. When one of the *précieuses* remarks:

"Mais de grâce, monsieur, ne soyez pas inexorable à ce fauteuil qui vous tend les bras il y a un quart d'heure; contentez un peu l'envie qu'il a de vous embrasser"

—we are not being asked to laugh at a simple misuse of language. The distortion of language reflects a psychological distortion. For words and gestures which express human emotions are used of inanimate things. There is an inclination to rob words of a certain sexual connotation by misapplying them to things and to lower people by raising things. This intention becomes more apparent when we turn back to Cathos' words in the preceding scene:

"Pour moi, mon oncle, tout ce que je vous puis dire, c'est que je trouve le mariage une chose tout à fait choquante. Comment est-ce qu'on peut souffrir la pensée de coucher contre un homme vraiment nu?"

The *précieuses* may be only a pair of silly, affected girls playing at being "high society," but the trend is evident, and it leads to the

[1] There is no English equivalent. It means to fill in the characters' psychology, to "psychologize" the characters.

attitude towards marriage which is attacked in *les Femmes savantes*. There is a flight from natural human feelings, a morbid horror of what is *vraiment nu*. Preciosity is seen to be a form of defence mechanism, a method of neutralizing the life of our normal instincts by robbing them of their vitality. It leads straight to psychological perversion, to the obsessions which are studied with marvellous insight in Molière's greatest plays.

It must not be thought that Molière's work is merely a gallery of eccentrics. His starting-point is always the individual man or woman, but his characters are all representative, are all rooted in the society of their time, and he goes on to make an anatomy of this society in which some of the deepest as well as some of the most controversial problems are debated. The *Précieuses ridicules* with its frontal attack on preciosity was his first serious essay in social criticism and its effectiveness is proved by the storm that it created. The main line runs thence through the two *Écoles*, reaches its summit in his three greatest plays—*Tartuffe*, *Dom Juan* and *le Misanthrope*—and moves on to its logical conclusion in *George Dandin* and *le Malade imaginaire*. In these plays he examined the position of women, the state of religious belief, and the nature and place of medicine in society. It was because his vision transcended the limits of his age that his characters are symbols of universal significance which belong to all time.

II. *L'ÉCOLE DES FEMMES*

The year 1662 was an important one in Molière's life. It was the year of his marriage to Armande Béjart. This event has been a gift to the gossip-writer and to critics who delight in discovering autobiographical references in his plays. We cannot say with any certainty who Armande Béjart was but it seems probable that she was a younger sister of Molière's friend and partner, Madeleine Béjart. Molière's enemies took a different view and it was not long before they were accusing him "d'avoir épousé la fille et d'autrefois

avoir couché avec la mère." At the time of his marriage Molière
was forty and his wife eighteen. It is not altogether surprising that
enemies and critics alike should have regarded *l'École des maris* and
l'École des femmes as attempts to solve personal problems—the
problems of the middle-aged man who marries a young girl—and
already in his own time people were saying that in begetting his
own wife Molière had begun her education even earlier than
Arnolphe.

A great imaginative writer naturally draws on his own experience
for his work, but there is no evidence for the view that in the
École des maris Molière was attempting to explore the prospects of
his forthcoming marriage or that Arnolphe in the *École des femmes*
is "a portrait of the artist." In both plays the emphasis falls on
école, on education for marriage. The *École des maris* is a charming
comedy in which Molière contrasts two different ways of bringing
up young women—the narrow, jealous method of Sganarelle which
leads to deception and disaster, and the tolerant and reasonable
spirit of Ariste who lets Léonor go her own way, marries her with
her own consent and no doubt lived happily ever after.

L'École des femmes is not among Molière's supreme achievements,
but it marks an immense step forward. For here in essentials and
for the first time we find the mature Molière. The maturity is
nowhere more apparent than in the transformation of Sganarelle
into Arnolphe, the first of the great comic characters. When
Arnolphe declares:

> J'ai suivi sa leçon sur le sujet d'Agnès,
> Et je la fais venir dans ce lieu tout exprès,
> Sous prétexte d'y faire un tour de promenade,
> Afin que les soupçons de *mon esprit malade*
> Puissent sur le discours la mettre adroitement,
> Et, lui sondant le cœur, s'éclaircir doucement.

he not only sounds a fresh note, he also looks forward to Cléante's
warning to Alceste:

> Non, tout de bon, quittez toutes ces incartades.
> Le monde par vos soins ne se changera pas;
> Et puisque la franchise a pour vous tant d'appas,
> Je vous dirai tout franc que *cette maladie*
> Partout où vous allez, donne la comédie.

The critical words are *mon esprit malade* and *cette maladie*. For all Molière's principal comic characters are *malades*. More than any other great comic writer of the time he realized that comedy is essentially a serious activity. His work is a study of some of the chief social maladies not merely of his own, but of all time, seen against the background of a stable order. In this play it is jealousy, in *Tartuffe* religious mania and in *le Malade imaginaire* the cult of ill-health. The ravages of the *maladie* are very extensive. It undermines the natural human faculties and encloses the victim in a private world of his own disordered imagination. One of the fundamental traits of the *malade* is a fanatical desire to impose the standards of this private world on society, as Alceste tries to "change the world" and Arnolphe tries to bring up Agnès according to his own unbalanced theories:

> Dans un petit couvent, loin de toute pratique,
> Je la fis élever selon ma politique,
> C'est-à-dire ordonnant quels soins on emploierait
> Pour la rendre idiote autant qu'il se pourrait.

This sinister declaration, this open attempt to destroy a woman's natural faculties, shows to what extent the *malade* has become a menace to the community. The remedy lies in collective action, in the destruction of the anti-social tendencies by laughter and the introduction of sane values into the comic world. This brings us to the *honnête homme* who makes his first appearance in the *École des femmes*. Chrysalde is not of the stature of Cléante or Philinte, and his view that it doesn't matter whether you are a *cocu* or not as long as you take your misfortune like a gentleman is crude in comparison with their urbane, polished discourses on *la juste nature* and *la parfaite raison*; but in spite of his shortcomings he does stand for a norm of tolerance and good sense.

I have never felt convinced by the theory of certain French critics that Molière's characters are in some sense abstractions, that he shows us the Jealous Man, the Hypocrite, the Misanthrope or the Miser, while a modern novelist like Balzac shows us a particular miser in a particular French province in the nineteenth century. There is a clear distinction between Shakespearean comedy and Jonson's "comedy of humours." It seems to me that Molière is closer to Shakespeare than he is to Jonson, and that so far from probing more deeply into human nature than Molière, Balzac bears a striking resemblance to Jonson. Classical comedy certainly imposed limitations, but what is remarkable is that in spite of these limitations Molière managed to present such a comprehensive study of the complexities and contradictions of human nature. Argan is not merely a *malade imaginaire*, he is mean and cruel and cheerfully prepared to sacrifice his daughter's happiness in order to secure free medical advice for himself. In the *Femmes savantes* what really interests us in Armande is not her ridiculous intellectual pretensions, but the angry frustration of the sexually acquisitive woman.

The *École des femmes* is primarily a study of jealousy, but Arnolphe is no more a simple case than Molière's other characters. The originality of Molière's approach is well brought out by Ramon Fernandez when he suggests that the point of the play lies in the transformation of the *homme-père* into the *homme-mari*. It is true that Arnolphe loves his ward as a husband while she can only love him as a father, but this is not the whole of the problem. It must not be thought that the prominence given to cuckoldry is a light-hearted borrowing from traditional French farce or that Molière's treatment of it has anything in common with Wycherley's in his crude adaptation of the play. Arnolphe's anxiety to "create" a wife who will be faithful to him springs from a primitive but deep-seated fear of being a cuckold. There is no need to dwell on the psychological implications of this fear which is so pervasive that it turns jealousy into a form of sexual mania. When Arnolphe declares:

> Je veux pour espion, qui soit d'exacte vue,
> Prendre le savetier du coin de notre rue.
> Dans la maison toujours je prétends la tenir,
> Y faire bonne garde, et surtout en bannir
> Vendeuses de ruban, perruquières, coiffeuses,
> Faiseuses de mouchoirs, gantières, revendeuses,
> Tous ces gens qui sous main travaillent chaque jour
> A faire réussir les mystères d'amour.

the crux of the passage lies in the lurid *mystères d'amour*, and the words gain their effect from the contrast with the normal life of the *quartier* which Molière evokes with his characteristic skill. For in Arnolphe's disordered imagination the whole of this world is undermined by the subterranean activities of the purveyors of love,

as the whole of his personality is undermined by his mania. When
in another place he cries:

> Et cependant je l'aime, après ce lâche tour,
> Jusqu'à ne me pouvoir passer de cet amour.
> Sot, n'as-tu point de honte? Ah! je crève, j'enrage,
> Et je souffletterais mille fois mon visage.

there is no mistaking the voice. It is the voice of all Molière's great
comic characters, the voice of impotent, exasperated denunciation
of a world which they cannot "change" and in which they have no
place.

The voice also explains one of the secrets of Molière's art. "His
characters," wrote Paul Bourget, "are, so to speak, composed in
two layers. The first consists of the peculiarities which make them
ridiculous, the second of the authentic human material. . . . At
certain moments in the play, the first layer bursts apart and reveals
the second."[1]

Although this comment suggests that there is something a little
mechanical about the construction of Molière's characters and under-
estimates, perhaps, the extent to which their peculiarities are rooted
in their personality, it underlines one important factor. In the
central passages in the comedies there is a sudden eruption of subterranean instincts into the world of everyday experience, and it is
this that gives Molière's work its special resonance. At such
moments the mind of the spectator is suspended between two
impulses—pity and laughter—which superficially appear to exclude
one another, and comedy is felt to be a continual oscillation between
what one writer has lately called *la vie tragique* and *la vie triviale*.
It is not, however, an alternation between tragic and comic emotions. The two are fused into a single new emotion which differs
from them both and is proper to comedy. Life is suddenly perceived under a twofold aspect and this is the core of the comic poet's
experience.

It is not the tranquil homilies of Chrysalde which place Arnolphe's
maladie in its true perspective, but the simple words of Agnès, as
she speaks of her love for Horace:

> Il jurait qu'il m'aimait d'une amour sans seconde,
> Il me disait des mots les plus gentils du monde,

---

[1] *Œuvres complètes: II. Critique, études et portraits*, Paris, 1900, p. 271.

Des choses que jamais rien ne peut égaler,
Et dont, toutes les fois que je l'entends parler,
La douceur me chatouille et là-dedans remue
Certain je ne sais quoi dont je suis toute émue.

In these lines, in which we seem to catch the very tone of the girl's voice and which derive much of their force from the contrast with Arnolphe's overwrought declarations, we see the healthy, natural human feelings asserting themselves, expressing themselves in spite of a lack of adequate concepts on the part of the speaker. It is the ruin of Arnolphe's horrifying *politique*.

III. *TARTUFFE*

1

"When Molière wrote his *Tartuffe*," said a contemporary, "he read the first three acts to the king. This play pleased His Majesty who spoke much too well of it not to arouse the jealousy of Molière's enemies and above all of the *cabale des dévots*. M. de Péréfixe, Archbishop of Paris, placed himself at their head and spoke to the king against this comedy. The king, who was continually under pressure on all sides, told Molière that one must not annoy the *dévots* who were implacable and that he ought not to perform his *Tartuffe* in public. His Majesty thought it sufficient to speak to Molière in this way without ordering him to suppress the play. It is for this reason that Molière took the trouble to read it aloud to his friends."

This, broadly speaking, is the story of one of the bitterest of all the literary controversies of the seventeenth century. *Tartuffe* was given its première on 12th May 1664. Five days later the storm broke with a frontal attack in the *Gazette de France* which declared roundly that the play was "extremely harmful to religion and likely to have a most dangerous effect." It was useless for Molière to change the title to *l'Hypocrite*, to protest that he was only attacking the *faux dévots* or to say that one of the functions of the theatre was to correct human vices. The pious world was thoroughly roused. The denunciation in the *Gazette de France* was followed by other attacks. In a tract called *le Roy glorieux au monde*, Pierre Roullé, the parish priest of Saint-Barthélmy, described Molière as "un homme, ou plutôt un démon vêtu de chair et habillé en homme, et le plus signalé impie et libertin qui fût jamais dans les siècles passés." Bourdaloue, who at this time was the fashionable preacher at Notre-Dame, took part in the battle, and years after Molière's death Bossuet spoke of him with a depth of bitterness which shows how profoundly the *bien pensants* had been shaken.

The heaviest blow of all came from the Archbishop of Paris who forbade the faithful to be present at a performance of *Tartuffe* under pain of excommunication. Although the King, who was clearly on Molière's side, was advised by an eminent canon lawyer that the ban was probably invalid, he did not intervene. For five years the play led an underground existence in constantly altering versions.[1] It was read, apparently with approval, before the Papal Nuncio and his suite, in the salons and at the home of Ninon de Lenclos; but it was not until 1669, when the King had composed his differences with the Holy See, that he removed the obstacles and *Tartuffe* was played to packed houses while Molière's enemies retired discomforted.

Tartuffe was closely bound up with the religious situation in the seventeenth century and we must glance at one of the chief manifestations—the Compagnie du Saint-Sacrement or, as its enemies called it, *la cabale des dévots*—if we are to appreciate the play to the full. In May 1627, a devout nobleman, Henri de Levis, duc de Ventadour and a peer of the realm, had conceived the idea of founding a pious association for the furtherance of the Catholic religion in France. From modest beginnings the redoubtable Compagnie du Saint-Sacrement arose with affiliated branches which extended all over the country. Its membership was large and varied. It included bishops, prelates, simple parish priests, members of the aristocracy—some of them among the most famous names in France—and, inevitably, a vast number of pious busybodies. Its activities were manifold. It did good work in the mission field, in the fields of prison reform, social welfare and what is now called the *protection de la jeune fille*. Not all its activities were equally

[1] The original version had only three Acts.

creditable. It undoubtedly developed into a powerful religious secret society with an efficient police system, denouncing and persecuting heretics, informing husbands of the debauchery and infidelity of wayward wives and interfering in the dioceses of lazy bishops. Its ultimate downfall and destruction were brought about by its campaign against duelling which annoyed the nobility and led to the personal intervention of Mazarin.

The *Compagnie* was formally suppressed in 1660, but its power remained virtually intact for some years to come and there is no doubt that it was largely reponsible for keeping *Tartuffe* off the stage for five years. That such a society should have been founded at all, that it should have reached such dimensions and have fought so bitterly against Molière, is an illuminating comment on the religious situation in the seventeenth century. Although the Catholic Church in France had emerged victorious from the wars of religion, the faith had been deeply disturbed by the upheavals of the sixteenth century.

"Let us have no illusions about the state of religious belief in this seventeenth century which people always choose to see in a blaze of glory . . ." wrote Sainte-Beuve. "Madame du Deffand says somewhere that she cannot think of anyone in the seventeenth century except M. de La Rochefoucauld who really was a free-thinker. This remark merely shows how ill each age knows the one that immediately preceded it. When we examine the seventeenth century from a particular angle, we perceive unbelief running all the way through it *in a direct unbroken tradition*. The reign of Louis XIV is thoroughly undermined by it."[1]

Debauchery and unbelief were rife. There was certainly plenty to occupy the faithful, but their methods were not always happily chosen nor were their aims invariably to be commended. We may admire a St. Vincent de Paul (whose attitude towards the *Compagnie* was highly circumspect) or a Bérulle, but the grim spirit of persecution and spying which distinguished the *dévots*, and their suspicious attitude towards anything which could be interpreted as an attack on religion, were a clear sign of weakness. They felt that the Church was threatened, but the methods used to meet the threat betray not merely a sense of impotency, but an absence of true spirituality on the part of those who practised them.

Port-Royal, III, pp. 229–30 (italics Sainte-Beuve's).

2

Although these events took place nearly three hundred years ago, *Tartuffe* has remained a battleground. The debate, which began with Bourdaloue and Bossuet, echoes down the centuries, disturbing peaceful academic backwaters and ruining the objectivity of literary critics. Sainte-Beuve propounded a tempting theory that the play was a subtle apologia for *la morale des honnêtes gens* and Brunetière, while still a champion of free-thought, published a long essay on "La Philosophie de Molière" in which he demonstrated gleefully that Molière was an exponent of "la philosophie de la nature" and the forerunner of the materialist philosophers of the eighteenth century.[1] To-day *Tartuffe* is still a scandal to the devout and a stick with which the free-thinkers try to belabour the *bien pensants*. Ramon Fernandez has alleged mischievously that Orgon is a representative Christian, and M. François Mauriac leaves us with the impression that, in the eyes of the author of *Destins*, only Molière's Christian death excuses him for having written *Tartuffe*.

The doctrinaire approach has done much to prevent a true appreciation of one of the greatest masterpieces of the French theatre. The misunderstandings and misrepresentations have been so grave that the time has come to declare roundly that there is no attack, direct or indirect, on religion in the play, that there is little to support Sainte-Beuve's theory and nothing at all to excuse Brunetière's fanciful views of Molière's philosophy. Molière was not a deeply religious man certainly, but in spite of constant persecution by the *dévots* there is no reason for supposing that he was anything but a believing Christian. In *Tartuffe* he dealt with one of the burning questions of the time; but though he could not resist baiting the *dévots*, he approached a serious question with the seriousness and detachment of a great artist.[2]

Tartuffe is first and foremost a sociological study of the corrosive

[1] A few years later a converted Brunetière repeated the same arguments in another of those interminable volumes on the history of French literature, but his satisfaction had disappeared and Molière's "philosophy" was the subject for schoolmasterly reproach.

[2] He was partly to blame for the trouble. His provocative reference to "les célèbres originaux du portrait que je voulais peindre" was an opportunity for his enemies and a temptation to literary critics to forget the text in order to indulge in fruitless detective work.

influence, not of religion, but of a decadent religiosity on the life of the community, and as such it seems to me to be unsurpassed in European literature. Molière does not study its effect on the community as a whole; he selects a particular unit—the family. He draws, with that incomparable colour and vitality which have placed him among the great European masters, a prosperous middle-class French family in the reign of Louis XIV. There are the middle-aged husband and his young and rather worldly second wife, the two children of his first marriage—the headstrong Damis and the timid, wilting Marianne who is in love with Valère—the crusty puritanical mother-in-law, the urbane and reasonable brother-in-law and the magnificent *bonne*.

Brunetière declared that Orgon is as much the centre of the play as Tartuffe and there is a good deal of truth in this observation. Tartuffe himself is a superbly comic creation; he possesses the same life and vitality as the Wife of Bath or Falstaff and his character is perhaps more varied. He is a composite figure. He represents all the main varieties of contemporary religious abuse and is the channel through which they infect the sane, balanced life of the family and almost bring it to disaster. This is also the real reason for the attacks on Molière. The abuses that Molière was attacking were so widespread and were perceived with such clarity that nearly all the devout felt that the blows were aimed at them, and instead of searching their hearts, they tried to allay their sense of guilt by violent attacks on their critic.

Tartuffe is a good deal more besides. "Tartuffe," wrote Edmond Jaloux, in a valuable note on the play,

"Tartuffe is greedy, lazy, licentious and self-seeking, but he is only these things at certain times and, so to speak, spasmodically. He has no intention of hiding his real self behind the mask of hypocrisy. *It is his real self that is hypocritical.* . . . We can be sure that when he is alone in his room, he is far from laughing over the gullibility of the good Orgon, but that he piously says his rosary, not without interrupting his devotions from time to time to sigh regretfully over Elmire."[1]

Tartuffe is not a purely religious figure. He is a scoundrel, the eternal "confidence man." Since the society which produced him was in the main a Christian one, nothing was more natural than to choose religion as the means of cheating the gullible Orgon

[1] *L'Esprit des livres*, 1ère série, Paris, 1923, pp. 6 and 7 (italics mine).

out of his possessions and seducing his wife. In other ages he employs other means. Tartuffe is the sham clergyman who collects for a non-existent charity, or the sham soldier who sells bogus news about your son who has been reported missing at the front; but he is also the soap-box orator and the editor of the small sectarian paper, whether political or religious; he is even the political leader with his smooth assurances and promises. For the crux of the matter is that, in spite of his viciousness, Tartuffe is in his way genuine—genuine in that his hypocrisy is an integral part of his character—and deceives himself as well as other people. It is, indeed, his soft corruption—admirably brought out by Molière in the language used by Tartuffe and Orgon—which makes him such a menace to the community.

Our starting-point is the description of Tartuffe which Orgon gives his brother:

> Ha! si vous aviez vu comme j'en fis rencontre,
> Vous auriez pris pour lui l'amitié que je montre.
> Chaque jour à l'église il venait, d'un air doux,
> Tout vis-à-vis de moi se mettre à deux genoux.
> Il attirait les yeux de l'assemblée entière
> Par l'ardeur dont au Ciel il poussait sa prière;
> Il faisait des soupirs, de grands élancements,
> Et baisait humblement la terre à tous moments;
> Et, lorsque je sortais, il me devançait vite
> Pour m'aller à la porte offrir de l'eau bénite.
> Instruit par son garçon, qui dans tout l'imitait,
> Et de son indigence et de ce qu'il était,
> Je lui faisais des dons; mais, avec modestie,
> Il me voulait toujours en rendre une partie.
> "C'est trop, me disait-il, c'est trop de la moitié;
> Je ne mérite pas de vous faire pitié."
> Et quand je refusais de le vouloir reprendre,
> Aux pauvres à mes yeux, il allait le répandre.
> Enfin le Ciel chez moi me le fit retirer,
> Et, depuis ce temps-là, tout semble y prospérer . . .
> Mais vous ne croiriez point jusqu'où monte son zèle:
> Il s'impute à péché la moindre bagatelle;
> Un rien presque suffit pour le scandaliser,
> Jusque-là qu'il se vint l'autre jour accuser
> D'avoir pris une puce en faisant sa prière,
> Et de l'avoir tuée avec trop de colère.

This passage, with its brilliantly comic ending, is a masterly portrait of a type who is always with us. It is also an excellent example of the vivid pictorial qualities of Molière's style and his power of seizing on the essential gestures of his characters—the *air doux*, "se mettre à *deux* genoux," the sighs, the humble kissing of the ground, the offering of holy water. Molière's characters are in no sense caricatures. He has a firm hold on the world of common experience which makes his slight deviations from it the more effective and explains why his characters are so convincing and so durable. Molière's irony is a two-edged weapon. In this passage he is able to attack the exaggerated and unhealthy devotion of the day in Tartuffe and, at the same time, by presenting Tartuffe through Orgon's eyes, to show exactly how he himself is corrupted by it. Orgon was undoubtedly a deeply religious man before meeting Tartuffe. The change is, therefore, from a deep but healthy piety to an unhealthy devotion which is apparent in the tone of cringing admiration in which he speaks of Tartuffe. This is how Dorine describes Tartuffe's influence on him:

> Nos troubles l'avaient mis sur le pied d'homme sage,
> Et pour servir son prince il montra du courage;
> Mais il est devenu comme un homme hébété,
> Depuis que de Tartuffe on le voit entêté.
> Il l'appelle son frère et l'aime dans son âme
> Cent fois plus qu'il ne fait mère, fils, fille et femme.
> C'est de tous ses secrets l'unique confident
> Et de ses actions le directeur prudent . . .

The focal word is *hébété*. Instead of enriching the personality by building on the natural, human qualities, this sort of religiosity has the reverse effect. It corrodes and undermines what is sane and healthy, and this is the basis of Molière's criticism. Dorine's views are reinforced by Orgon's naïve admission:

> Oui, je deviens tout autre avec son entretien:
> Il m'enseigne à n'avoir affection pour rien,
> De toutes amitiés il détache mon âme,
> Et je verrais mourir frère, enfants, mère et femme,
> Que je m'en soucierais autant que de cela.

Cléante makes the appropriate rejoinder:

> Les sentiments humains, mon frère, que voilà!

It draws attention to the obvious point—*les sentiments humains* which suffer such violence and perversion. Orgon is a type who is well known to us. He is what a contemporary writer has called in another context a *rat de bénitier*; but in his case the malady has become radical and dangerous. His attitude is not one of Christian resignation; it is the reverse of Christian. It simply cuts straight across all Christian teaching and is entirely contrary to charity.

This absurd and dangerous devotion produces one of the great comic scenes of the play:

ORGON:
      Tout s'est-il, ces deux jours, passé de bonne sorte?
      Qu'est-ce qu'on fait céans? comme est-ce qu'on s'y porte?

DORINE:
      Madame eut avant-hier la fièvre jusqu'au soir,
      Avec un mal de tête étrange à concevoir.

ORGON:
      Et Tartuffe?

DORINE:
                  Tartuffe? Il se porte à merveille,
      Gros et gras, le teint frais, et la bouche vermeille.

ORGON:
      Le pauvre homme!

DORINE:
            Le soir, elle eut un grand dégoût
      Et ne put au souper toucher à rien du tout,
      Tant sa douleur de tête était encor cruelle!

ORGON:
      Et Tartuffe?

DORINE:
          Il soupa, lui tout seul, devant elle,
      Et fort dévotement il mangea deux perdrix
      Avec une moitié de gigot en hachis.

ORGON:
      Le pauvre homme!

DORINE:
             La nuit se passa tout entière
      Sans qu'elle pût fermer un moment la paupière;
      Des chaleurs l'empêchaient de pouvoir sommeiller,
      Et jusqu'au jour près d'elle il nous fallut veiller.

ORGON:
      Et Tartuffe?

D

DORINE:

> Pressé d'un sommeil agréable,
> Il passa dans sa chambre au sortir de la table,
> Et dans son lit bien chaud il se mit tout soudain,
> Où sans trouble il dormit jusques au lendemain.

ORGON:

> Le pauvre homme!

From the time of the earliest comedies, the repetition of words and phrases had been one of the commonest of Molière's comic devices. He developed it until it became, as it is here, a subtle method of probing the minds of his characters. For Orgon's folly is not merely described: the identity of word and action is complete. His inability to understand what is said to him reveals the grotesque effects of his perverse devotion. He does not notice that Tartuffe's gluttony cuts straight across his austere principles. He does not see that his own indifference to the physical welfare of his family is incompatible with his solicitude for Tartuffe's well-being, that his preoccupation with Tartuffe—with the superficial appearance of piety—is actually becoming, in theological language, an obstacle to his salvation. Orgon's state of mind, indeed, bears a marked resemblance to Alceste's during his *emportement* against the customs of society. He has entered a world of private mania and his contact with the actual world is only intermittent. This is apparent from his failure to understand what is being said to him. In Dorine's description of Tartuffe devouring partridges and swilling wine the words do not register because there is a gulf between Orgon and the world of common experience. He sees only the miserable, ragged, indigent Tartuffe of the first meeting which for psychological reasons has fixed itself in his subconscious mind, refusing to allow the real Tartuffe to enter the world of private fantasy.

The effects of his inhibition are far-reaching. They lead to a decline which is at once intellectual, moral and emotional. He does not scruple to break his promise to allow his daughter to marry Valère, and plays the part of the tyrannical father in order to force her to marry Tartuffe. He makes over his possessions to Tartuffe without considering the claims of his family, turns a secret entrusted to him by a friend into an absurd *cas de conscience* and finishes by betraying the confidence to Tartuffe. In other words, he is hypnotized by Tartuffe and this leads to a complete disruption of all values.

In order to exhibit to the full the ravages of false religion, Molière provides his principal characters with two foils—Cléante and Dorine—who both represent his own point of view.

Cléante has been the subject of considerable controversy and dons have debated his religious views in learned footnotes.[1] Brunetière considered that the part was superfluous, but one suspects that this was because his religious opinions were contrary to the professor's theories about "the philosophy of Molière." Allier and Michaut felt that Cléante is the pivot of the play and that he represents Molière's own religious position. It seems to me that the second view is in the main the true one, but the part is perhaps more important than these critics allow. Cléante is like Philinte in the *Misanthrope*, the urbane, cultured man of the world, tirelessly expounding the philosophy of the *juste milieu*:

> Les hommes, la plupart, sont étrangement faits!
> Dans la juste nature on ne les voit jamais;
> La raison a pour eux des bornes trop petites;
> En chaque caractère ils passent ses limites;
> Et la plus noble chose, ils la gâtent souvent
> Pour la vouloir outrer et pousser trop avant.

This is the voice of true civilization, of a society in which it was natural to speak of measure and proportion. But if this were all, Cléante might still be, as Brunetière alleged, a *porte-parole* who was designed to mislead the public about Molière's personal opinions and who was not essential to the action of the play. His importance lies precisely in the fact that in the pattern of the play he stands for the incorruptible intellect cutting remorselessly through Orgon's mental confusions, stripping away the subterfuges of the *dévots* and revealing them in their true light. His eulogy of *la juste nature* is followed immediately by a frontal attack on hypocrisy:

> Je ne suis point, mon frère, un docteur révéré,
> Et le savoir chez moi n'est pas tout retiré.
> Mais, en un mot, je sais, pour toute ma science,
> Du faux avec le vrai faire la différence.
> Et, comme je ne vois nul genre de héros
> Qui soient plus à priser que les parfaits dévots,

[1] "Une petite question indiscrète: ce Cléante fait-il ses Pâques? je le crois. Certainement, cinquante ans plus tard il ne les fera plus!" (Sainte-Beuve, *Port-Royal*, III, p. 215 *n*.)

Aucune chose au monde et plus noble et plus belle
Que la sainte ferveur d'un véritable zèle,
Aussi ne vois-je rien qui soit plus odieux
Que le dehors plâtré d'un zèle spécieux,
Que ces francs charlatans, que ces dévots de place,
De qui la sacrilège et trompeuse grimace
Abuse impunément et se joue à leur gré
De ce qu'ont les mortels de plus saint et sacré;
Ces gens qui, par une âme à l'intérêt soumise,
Font de dévotion métier et marchandise,
Et veulent acheter crédit et dignités
A prix de faux clins d'yeux et d'élans affectés;
Ces gens, dis-je, qu'on voit d'une ardeur non commune
Par le chemin du Ciel courir à leur fortune,
Qui, brûlants et priants, demandent chaque jour,
Et prêchent la retraite au milieu de la cour,
Qui savent ajuster leur zèle avec leurs vices,
Sont prompts, vindicatifs, sans foi, pleins d'artifices,
Et pour perdre quelqu'un couvrent insolemment
De l'intérêt du Ciel leur fier ressentiment . . .

Cléante does not make any great claims for himself. He is not, he assures Orgon, *un docteur révéré*. He does not pretend to be a deeply spiritual man, but is content to admire the devotion of the saints from a respectful distance. He merely claims to be able to distinguish true devotion from false, and this passage leads up to the famous plea for a decent, human piety:

On ne voit point en eux ce faste insupportable,
Et leur dévotion est humaine, est traitable . . .

Cléante's intellectualism is important because intellectual confusion—an inability to distinguish true piety from the sham which is so effectually denounced here—is at the root of Orgon's own corruption. It is left to Dorine to deal with some of the other consequences of this perversity. She is very different from Cléante, but it is a sign of Molière's wide and generous humanity that her role is not less important. She is the peasant, the voice of the earth. She is guided not by careful distinctions or elaborate arguments, but by sound instinct, by a natural wisdom which belongs to her class. The clue to her part in the play is the description of the prude in the first scene:

Il est vrai qu'elle vit en austère personne;
Mais l'âge dans son âme a mis ce zèle ardent,
Et l'on sait qu'elle est prude à son corps défendant.
Tant qu'elle a pu des cœurs attirer les hommages,
Elle a fort bien joui de tous ses avantages;
Mais, voyant de ses yeux tous les brillants baisser,
Au monde, qui la quitte, elle veut renoncer,
Et du voile pompeux d'une haute sagesse
De ses attraits usés déguiser la faiblesse.
Ce sont là les retours des coquettes du temps.
Il leur est dur de voir déserter les galants.
Dans un tel abandon, leur sombre inquiétude
Ne voit d'autre recours que le métier de prude,
Et la sévérité de ces femmes de bien
Censure toute chose et ne pardonne à rien;
Hautement d'un chacun elles blâment la vie
Non point par charité, mais par un trait d'envie,
Qui ne saurait souffrir qu'une autre ait les plaisirs
Dont le penchant de l'âge a sevré leurs désirs.

This passage is an example of Molière's style at its best. It shows
the vitality with which he could hit off the portraits of the types
who surrounded him. It is also a brilliant exposition of his views on
the life of the senses and an illustration of the way in which these
views are dissolved into the play. In spite of their difference of
approach, Cléante and Dorine are complementary. A healthy piety
—a devotion that is *humaine* and *traitable*—is perfectly compatible
with the normal life of the senses. Dorine's attack on the false prude
is very similar in intention to Cléante's on the *faux dévots*. She
attacks the prude because her austerity is not genuine, because it
does not spring from true spirituality but from sexual frustration.
The "zèle ardent" is the result of a debilitated body, a body worn
out by the empty coquetry of her youth which is criticized by
implication. The positives and negatives are balanced with considerable felicity: *zèle ardent, corps défendant; attraits usés, sombre
inquiétude; l'âge a sevré leurs désirs.* In Molière's world the life of
the senses, when properly developed, is the stable element which
binds humanity together; but the prude through her lack of moderation has transformed herself into an empty shell; her sexual frustration has changed into a bitter censorious devotion that cuts
her off from the rest of humanity, and we seem, in the last phrase,

to hear Time's scythe cutting remorselessly through the withered *désirs*.

The same sturdy common sense is apparent in Dorine's *rapports* with her master. When Orgon, speaking of the marriage of his daughter with Tartuffe, remarks:

> Cet hymen de tous biens comblera vos désirs,
> Il sera tout confit en douceurs et plaisirs.
> Ensemble vous vivrez, dans vos ardeurs fidèles,
> Comme deux vrais enfants, comme deux tourterelles . . .

we not only detect the senile whining note of the *dévot*, we see that the *désirs* and *plaisirs*, which in Dorine are healthy and vigorous, have become twisted and perverted. There is something about those *désirs* and those *ardeurs fidèles* which makes the flesh creep. Dorine has already stated the proper view:

> . . . laissons sa noblesse . . .
> Sachez que d'une fille on risque la vertu,
> Lorsque dans son hymen son goût est combattu,
> Que le dessein d'y vivre en honnête personne
> Dépend des qualités du mari qu'on lui donne,
> Et que ceux dont partout on montre au doigt le front
> Font leurs femmes souvent ce qu'on voit qu'elles sont.

The feeble and *fainéante* Marianne, who talks of retiring to a convent or of committing suicide if she is made to marry Tartuffe, produces a violent reaction in Dorine:

> Fort bien. C'est un recours où je ne songeais pas;
> Vous n'avez qu'à mourir pour sortir d'embarras.
> Le remède sans doute est merveilleux. J'enrage
> Lorsque j'entends tenir ces sortes de langage.

The whole of Molière's belief in life is crowded into these four lines, his intense belief that life is good, that the senses are good provided that one follows *la juste nature* and avoids the inhibitions of a narrow puritanism or frittering one's life away in a series of empty *affaires*.

3

Tartuffe himself does not make his appearance until the third Act, but the way has been well prepared. We have already seen the

ravages that he has caused in the family and when he does appear
the relation between a false piety and an unhealthy sexuality is
very clearly brought out. His entry is one of the high lights of the
play:

> Laurent, serrez ma haire avec ma discipline,
> Et priez que toujours le Ciel vous illumine.
> Si l'on vient pour me voir, je vais aux prisonniers
> Des aumônes que j'ai partager les deniers.

The accent falls ostensibly on the disciplining of unruly desires;
but instead of being genuinely disciplined, these desires are driven
underground, are "prisoners" and prisoners of a very dangerous
and subversive nature. With an absurdly exaggerated gesture, he
throws his handkerchief over Dorine's breasts:

TARTUFFE:

> Couvrez ce sein que je ne saurais voir;
> Par de pareils objets les âmes sont blessées,
> Et cela fait venir de coupables pensées.

The description of the breasts as "de pareils objets" at
once strikes a perverse, unhealthy note and Dorine's reaction is
characteristic:

> Vous êtes donc bien tendre à la tentation,
> Et la chair sur vos sens fait grande impression?
> Certes, je ne sais pas quelle chaleur vous monte;
> Mais à convoiter, moi, je ne suis point si prompte,
> Et je vous verrais nu du haut jusques en bas,
> Que toute votre peau ne me tenterait pas.

This onslaught strikes exactly the right note. It is a gust of fresh
air which for a moment dissipates the stuffy erotic mist that surrounds Tartuffe. The language possesses the crude, racy vitality
of the peasant living in close contact with the earth. Dorine is a
symbolical figure. Her voice is a primitive voice; it represents the
primitive folk-element which is present in nearly all the greatest
art down to the seventeenth century, and it is the absence of this
element from the slick, cynical comedies of Molière's English contemporaries which makes them shallow and empty and explains
the thinness and poverty of their language.[1] Dorine joins hands with

[1] Compare *l'École des femmes* with Wycherley's English adaptation of it—
The Country Wife.

Shakespeare's peasants. She stands for the norm on which a great civilization was founded. It was because Molière himself believed so firmly in the life of the senses that sexual intrigue, which is a deviation from the norm, is given such prominence in his work.

Tartuffe's encounter with Dorine is followed by the magnificent scene in which he attempts the seduction of Elmire. What is strikingly original in these scenes is the way in which Molière explores the connection between a debased religion and the sexual instinct. The handling of his medium is triumphantly successful, and the verse has a subtlety and brilliance which are not surpassed in any of his other plays:

> Que le Ciel à jamais par sa toute bonté
> Et de l'âme et du corps vous donne la santé,
> Et bénisse vos jours autant que le désire
> Le plus humble de ceux que son amour inspire!

The key-words are *âme*, *corps* and *santé*. For the scene is precisely a conflict between *âme* and *corps*. The *santé* for which Tartuffe prays is something very different from norm represented by Dorine. Tartuffe's own gestures, which are described in the sinister stage directions: "Il lui met la main sur le genou," "Maniant le fichu d'Elmire," are indeed a denial of true *santé*. This is the real Tartuffe, the disgusting, libidinous old man pawing the wife of his protector while aspiring to the hand of the daughter. It leads to the first of the great speeches:

> L'amour qui nous attache aux beautés éternelles
> N'étouffe pas en nous l'amour des temporelles.
> Nos sens facilement peuvent être charmés
> Des ouvrages parfaits que le Ciel a formés.
> Ses attraits réfléchis brillent dans vos pareilles;
> Mais il étale en vous ses plus rares merveilles.
> Il a sur votre face épanché des beautés
> Dont les yeux sont surpris et les cœurs transportés;
> Et je n'ai pu vous voir, parfaite créature,
> Sans admirer en vous l'auteur de la nature,
> Et d'une ardente amour sentir mon cœur atteint,
> Au plus beau des portraits où lui-même il s'est peint.
> D'abord j'appréhendai que cette ardeur secrète
> Ne fût du noir esprit une surprise adroite,

Et même à fuir vos yeux mon cœur se résolut,
Vous croyant un obstacle à faire mon salut.
Mais enfin je connus, ô beauté toute aimable,
Que cette passion peut n'être point coupable,
Que je puis l'ajuster avecque la pudeur,
Et c'est ce qui m'y fait abandonner mon cœur.

These lines sometimes remind one of the speech beginning "Good morning to the day" in *Volpone*, but the resemblance is a superficial one. Molière's method is very different from Jonson's. He does not create a fantastic world by exaggeration and distortion; his method is more directly satiric, more realistic, and his aims are perhaps more varied. The Christian believes that human beauty is a reflection of the Divine beauty, and that it is because of the limitations of human language and human concepts that he must describe God in human terms. In this passage and in the passages that follow the process is inverted. Tartuffe contrives by an adroit mingling of the clichés of devotional and erotic writing to transform Elmire into a being who is partly saint and partly mistress and whom he proceeds to invoke. When he says

Nos sens facilement peuvent être charmés
Des ouvrages parfaits que le Ciel a formés

or

D'abord j'appréhendai que cette ardeur secrète
Ne fût du noir esprit une surprise adroite

or

J'aurai toujours pour vous, ô suave merveille,
Une dévotion à nulle autre pareille

we detect in the alternation of the hissing s's and the liquid l's and m's the sudden intake of the breath, the sudden catching back of the saliva as desire rises. For the movement of sexual desire, which he refers to furtively as *cette ardeur secrète* and *un feu discret*, follows the movement of the invocation like an insidious undercurrent, wrapping itself round and round the strange fantastic Elmire whom he has created, fretting and nibbling at her in the attempt to undermine her resistance and stifle her scruples.

It is both invocation and argument; content and movement are welded into one. The problems presented are specious and are

D*

"solved" by a series of sleights of hand, by the pretence of sudden illumination:

> ... même à fuir vos yeux mon cœur se résolut,
> Vous croyant un obstacle à faire mon salut.
> Mais enfin je *connus*, ô beauté toute aimable,
> Que cette passion peut n'être point coupable ...

It is the undercurrent of sexual desire, which is carefully maintained, that gives the passage and indeed the whole scene its unity. When Elmire objects that such language is unbecoming in a *dévot*, Tartuffe repeats the same formulas with more vehemence:

> Ah! pour être dévot, je n'en suis pas moins homme;
> Et lorsqu'on vient à voir vos célestes appas,
> Un cœur se laisse prendre, et ne raisonne pas.
> Je sais qu'un tel discours de moi paraît étrange;
> Mais, Madame, après tout, je ne suis pas un ange,
> Et, si vous condamnez l'aveu que je vous fais,
> Vous devez vous en prendre à vos charmants attraits.

The famous line

> Ah! pour être dévot, je n'en suis pas moins homme ...

is one of the focal points of the play. It is a restatement, from another point of view, of Cléante's

> Les hommes, la plupart, sont étrangement faits!
> Dans la juste nature on ne les voit jamais ...

Tartuffe is indeed a man, but a man whose natural instincts have been warped and perverted because he has strayed from the norm. For this reason he is an object of satire, is one of the varieties of perversion which are studied in this and in the other plays.

There is one other aspect of this scene which calls for comment. It is not merely an attack on religious hypocrisy in general; it is directed in particular against the casuists and the famous method known as *la dévotion aisée*. When Molière makes Tartuffe say of his passion for Elmire

> ... je puis l'ajuster avecque la pudeur

he is attacking precisely the same abuse as Pascal in *les Provinciales* —the method of juggling with conscience which had become fashionable and which was attributed to the Jesuits. This line of attack is only concluded in the second scene between Tartuffe and Elmire:

ELMIRE:
>Mais comment consentir à ce que vous voulez,
>Sans offenser le Ciel, dont toujours vous parlez?

TARTUFFE:
>Si ce n'est que le Ciel qu'à mes vœux on oppose,
>Lever un tel obstacle est à moi peu de chose,
>Et cela ne doit pas retenir votre cœur.

ELMIRE:
>Mais des arrêts du Ciel on nous fait tant de peur!

TARTUFFE:
>Je puis vous dissiper ces craintes ridicules,
>Madame, et je sais l'art de lever les scrupules.
>Le Ciel défend, de vrai, certains contentements;
>(*C'est un scélérat qui parle.*)
>Mais on trouve avec lui des accommodements.
>Selon divers besoins, il est une science
>D'étendre les liens de notre conscience,
>Et de rectifier le mal de l'action
>Avec la pureté de notre intention.

The trite, banal rhythm provides the appropriate comment on this form of intellectual perversion. The last five lines, however, are not merely a caricature of the methods of the casuists; there is a serious purpose behind them. For Molière these methods, as surely as the piety of Orgon and the hypocrisy of Tartuffe, are a deviation from the norm. What he does is to demonstrate that this sort of intellectual and moral dishonesty leads straight to crime. So far from being a forerunner of eighteenth-century materialism, he seems to me in this play to be a serious critic of an abuse which went a very long way towards undermining the authority of the Church in France and preparing the way for the secularization of French culture. There is something ominous about the lines which follow:

>Enfin votre scrupule est facile à détruire:
>Vous êtes assurée ici d'un plein secret,
>Et le mal n'est jamais que dans l'éclat qu'on fait.
>Le scandale du monde est ce qui fait l'offense,
>Et ce n'est pas pécher que pécher en silence.

In this whispered confidence we have a sinister vision of a great and gracious civilization whose foundations are already threatened by the subversive activities of warring *cabales*, whose moral fibre is profoundly undermined by people who in all seriousness could sponsor such views.

For the sake of completeness one must turn back a few pages to the scene where Elmire explains to her husband why she did not want her stepson to reveal the first assault on her virtue:

> Est-ce qu'au simple aveu d'un amoureux transport
> Il faut que notre honneur se gendarme si fort?
> Et ne peut-on répondre à tout ce qui le touche
> Que le feu dans les yeux et l'injure à la bouche?
> Pour moi, de tels propos je me ris simplement,
> Et l'éclat là-dessus ne me plaît nullement.
> J'aime qu'avec douceur nous nous montrions sages,
> Et ne suis point du tout pour ces prudes sauvages
> Dont l'honneur est armé de griffes et de dents
> Et veut au moindre mot dévisager les gens;
> Me préserve le Ciel d'une telle sagesse!

The attitude behind these lines has been variously interpreted. Some writers have regarded Elmire as a mean opportunist, others as an ally of her brother, as an upholder of the golden mean. Their importance seems to me to lie in the fact that this is the reverse of the heroic attitude, that the reference to "le feu dans les yeux et l'injure à la bouche" is a deliberate parody of the Cornelian honour which marks the passing of an age. It is the attitude of an astute, sensible middle-class woman who is responsible for outwitting Tartuffe.

With the unmasking of Tartuffe at the end of Act IV Molière arrives at the last stage of his journey, but before following him further it is worth glancing at what has already been accomplished. The study is clearly a twofold one. There is a psychological study of the influence of a false conception of religion on the character of a group of individuals, and the sociological study of its consequences or possible consequences for a middle-class family. The group divides roughly into two parties. In Tartuffe, Orgon and Madame Pernelle religion produces a marked deterioration of character and fosters weaknesses which are inherent in their personalities. In Cléante and Dorine it produces the reverse effect; it causes the healthy organism to react vigorously, to apply itself to the expulsion of the intruder and to the mitigation of the damage already caused. The reactions of Elmire are of a severely practical nature like Dorine's. She is not interested in theory, but simply in averting the catastrophe which threatens her home and her children. Her role is, therefore, to expose Tartuffe, and there is no conflict between her skilful action and her disparaging comments on honour. The two children are caught between the contending parties. Damis is headstrong and simply wants to see Tartuffe thrown out, and Cléante has to try to exercise a moderating influence on him. Marianne is inclined to give in and it needs all Dorine's vitality to prop her up, to stimulate a healthy reaction to the situation.

Although Tartuffe has been unmasked the tribulations of the family are by no means over. It is now threatened with complete ruin through the foolish actions committed by Orgon under the influence of Tartuffe. The last scene, where the Exempt steps in and marches him off to prison, has been regarded as a *deus ex machina* and a graceful tribute to King Louis. One editor, indeed, has even suggested that the Exempt's speech is so ill-written that it must be an interpolation. These arguments seem to me to miss the point. The conclusion is perfectly logical and in spite of *négligences*, which are by no means uncommon in Molière's work, the last long speech is completely convincing. Not simply a single family, but the whole of society is menaced by the extravagances of the *dévots*, and salvation is only to be found in a vigorous community life under a discerning monarch. This is precisely what Louis XIV was for Molière. Whatever may be said of the rest of the speech, no one can mistake the immense confidence behind

Nous vivons sous un Prince ennemi de la fraude.

It not only carries immediate conviction; it is not too much to say that the whole weight of the play is behind this single line. No one criticized contemporary abuses more vigorously than Molière, and no one was more conscious of the dangers of the various abuses which threatened to cloud men's minds, warp their senses and seduce them from *la juste nature*. No one was more conscious than he that the majority of his fellows were indifferent to the maxims of "Reason," but this did nothing to undermine his own belief in the fundamental decency and sanity of the existing order. We may feel that he judged it too lightly, but that is not relevant in a study of *Tartuffe*. What matter are the brilliance and penetration of the play and the unity and coherence of the poet's vision.

IV. *DOM JUAN*

1

Financially, the suppression of *Tartuffe* was a serious blow to Molière. He was already at work on *le Misanthrope*, but in order to keep his company together it was imperative to produce a new play at once. *Dom Juan* had its première in February 1665. The theme was a popular one in the seventeenth century and the new play was a success. It is not surprising—particularly when one recalls that a fresh attack on the *dévots* was provocatively put into the mouth of Dom Juan himself—that it should have added fuel to the flames, and though it escaped the drastic fate of *Tartuffe* it, too, became a battle-ground and has continued to be the subject of acrimonious controversy down to our own time.

In the nineteenth century earnest free-thinkers hailed *Dom Juan* as "un intrépide représentant de la libre pensée," and the play as a text-book which had anticipated their own views by two hundred years and stated them with a power and persuasiveness to which they could scarcely pretend. It was incredible, they thought, that anyone who was not blinded by superstition could still doubt that Dom Juan was Molière's own spokesman. If one is determined to have a "message" at all costs, *Dom Juan* can be used to prove almost anything. It would not be difficult, for example, to make out a case for a Marxist Molière born out of due time by pretending that he was really on the side of "the people" against the corrupt aristocrat and writing off the supernatural as a concession to popular superstition.

The truth seems to me to be rather different. *Dom Juan* is a companion piece to *Tartuffe* in which Molière subjects the problem of extreme incredulity to the same searching examination as the problem of extreme credulity in the earlier play. He was an artist, not a pamphleteer trying to make proselytes, but there is nothing in the play to suggest that he intended to hold his principal character up to admiration. His attacks are directed against both the *libertins* and the *dévots*:

"Vous savez ce que vous faites, vous, et, si vous ne croyez rien, vous avez vos raisons; mais il y a certains petits impertinents dans le monde, qui sont libertins sans savoir pourquoi, qui font les esprits forts parce qu'ils croient que cela leur sied bien . . ."

"L'hypocrisie est un vice à la mode, et tous les vices à la mode passent pour vertus. . . . Tous les autres vices des hommes sont exposés à la censure, et chacun a la liberté de les attaquer hautement; mais l'hypocrisie est un vice privilégié, qui de sa main ferme la bouche à tout le monde et jouit en repos d'une impunité souveraine."

The first of these comments belongs to Sganarelle, the second to Dom Juan; but though there is bitter personal feeling behind the onslaught on hypocrisy, there is no reason to doubt that Sganarelle's remarks about *certains petits impertinents* are meant to be taken at their face value. Molière drew for his material in this play on the *libertins* as surely as he had drawn on the *dévots* in *Tartuffe*.

"The lack of prudence which Molière displays in *Dom Juan*," writes M. Blanchot, "is like a series of uncontrolled movements which are provoked by annoyances that have become too persistent. In trying to drive off the hornets buzzing round his head which infuriate him, he strays to the edge of the forbidden zone. His impatience carries him further than he realized, and by an impulse which is contrary to his natural inclination, he identifies himself with an extreme example of the spirit of rebellion and anti-conformity."

"In his greatest plays," continues the same critic, "Molière does not show the slightest interest in speculative questions. His morality is in no sense based on indulgence and compromise. If it tends to relax the bonds of convention and make rules more flexible, it is not on account of a taste for something which is flat and flabby. On the contrary, it springs from Molière's hostility to artificial restrictions, to conventions which stifle the growth of genuine vitality and put the brake on his natural impatience."[1]

M. Blanchot makes two important points here. Molière's exasperation may have led him too far at times—this must remain a

[1] *op. cit.*, p. 308.

matter of opinion—but it is a sign of his immense vitality and a great positive force in his work. The second point is his complete lack of interest in speculative problems which is well illustrated by Sganarelle's opening speech:

"Quoi que puisse dire Aristote et toute la Philosophie, il n'est rien d'égal au Tabac; c'est la passion des honnêtes gens, et qui vit sans tabac n'est pas digne de vivre. Non seulement il réjouit et purge les cerveaux humains, mais encore il instruit les âmes à la vertu, et l'on apprend avec lui à devenir honnête homme. Ne voyez-vous pas bien, dès qu'on en prend, de quelle manière obligeante on en use avec tout le monde, et comme on est ravi d'en donner à droit et à gauche, partout où l'on se trouve?"

This passage provides a clue to the whole play. It strikes, to be sure, a farcical note but the intention is serious. Molière is pointing the contrast between the claims of abstract thought, of "Philosophy," and the simple pleasure-life symbolized by "Tobacco." For he was not interested in the philosophical system on which the *libertins* based their outlook any more than he was interested in the particular doctrines on which the *dévots* founded their claims to interfere with other people's business or the theories of medicine which led doctors to behave in such a peculiar and dangerous manner. He was interested in the concrete and particular, in the attitude of mind and the conduct of those who took it upon themselves to upset the simple, tobacco-loving *honnêtes gens* or to bleed perfectly healthy people to death with their appalling *saignées*.

This attitude is maintained consistently throughout the play and frequently brings Molière to the edge of what M. Blanchot calls *les gouffres interdits*. Sganarelle's "defence" of religion is one of the best examples:

SGANARELLE:
Mon raisonnement est qu'il y a quelque chose d'admirable dans l'homme, quoi que vous puissiez dire, que tous les savants ne sauraient expliquer. Cela n'est-il pas merveilleux que me voilà ici, et que j'aie quelque chose dans la tête qui pense cent choses différentes en un moment et fait de mon corps tout ce qu'elle veut? Je veux frapper des mains, hausser le bras, lever les yeux au ciel, baisser la tête, remuer les pieds, aller à droit, à gauche, en avant, en arrière, tourner . . .

(*Il se laisse tomber en tournant*)

DOM JUAN:
   Bon! voilà ton raisonnement qui a le nez cassé.

This was one of the scenes which most scandalized the devout in the seventeenth century as it no doubt elated the sceptics in the nineteenth century. There are no real grounds for scandal or, apart from its intrinsic funniness, for elation. Molière is not ridiculing the simple soul whose outlook is deliberately contrasted with Dom Juan's. He is tilting at *raisonnement*, at abstract thought as such, and when we reach the end of the play we find that none of the fashionable systems has escaped without a "broken nose."

I think that we should add that every form of dogmatism, everything which could be called a "system," was fundamentally abhorrent to Molière because he saw that they all led to the fanaticism and intolerance which he was always criticizing in his plays. In *Dom Juan* the main onslaught appears to be directed against the *libertins*, or what Lenin was contemptuously to describe much later as "the bourgeois free-thinkers' movement"; but Arnolphe's *politique* and Orgon's religious mania were both manifestations of "philosophy" and hateful for the same reasons. They are the "artificial restrictions . . . which stifle the growth of genuine vitality and put the brake on his natural impatience." The attack in *Dom Juan* is a twofold one because, as Stendhal pointed out, Don Juanism can exist only in a society which is riddled with hypocrisy. It is dislike of hypocrisy that explains one of Dom Juan's most striking traits—a psychological need to outrage public opinion. Molière would probably have been the first to admit that one of the principal evils of hypocrisy was the fact that it drove the Natural Man to abandon measure and proportion and to "stray to the edge of the forbidden zone," to become a victim of the exaggerations against which Molière himself was fighting.[1]

It must be emphasized, however, that Molière was primarily concerned with states of mind, with the repressive impulses which inspired the followers of "Philosophy" and regarded the particular tenets of the warring sects as a matter of very minor importance. These impulses are still with us and that is one of the reasons why Molière's work has lost none of its vitality in the two and a half centuries which have passed since it was written. If he had lived

[1] See Stendhal's interesting discussion of the play at the beginning of the story called "Les Cenci" in *Chroniques et nouvelles*.

in the twentieth century, we can be sure that he would have been among the most ruthless and amusing critics of Marxism, Fascism and the other forms of political despotism which are so clearly at variance with *la parfaite raison* and such an intolerable nuisance to the pleasure-loving *honnête homme*. Whether he would have escaped as lightly as he did at the hands of the *dévots* is another matter.

2

In *Dom Juan* Molière abandoned the usual pattern; there are no *honnêtes hommes* to prod us in the ribs or pluck our sleeve when the author is about to speak; but it seems clear that we are intended to sympathize with at least four characters in whom Dom Juan's career arouses horror and disgust—Done Elvire, Dom Carlos, Dom Louis and "le Pauvre"—and they provide a more varied commentary than the usual spokesmen. They stand, broadly speaking, for the virtues of Faith, Hope, Charity, Chivalry and Simplicity which are outraged by Dom Juan.

Molière took his Dom Juan from legend and transformed him into a serious study which has little in common with the heroes of contemporary plays on the subject or with the Don Juan of the Romantic Movement. The result is a superb example of *durchpsychologisierung!*

Sganarelle provides a useful hint towards the interpretation of his character when he remarks in the opening scene:

"Mais un grand seigneur méchant homme est une terrible chose."

This comment is echoed by Dom Juan's father towards the end of the play when he says:

"Apprenez enfin qu'un gentilhomme qui vit mal est un monstre dans la nature, que la vertu est le premier titre de noblesse, que je regarde bien moins au nom qu'on signe qu'aux actions qu'on fait, et que je ferais plus d'état du fils d'un crocheteur qui serait honnête homme, que du fils d'un monarque qui vivrait comme vous."

Dom Juan's high estate is a factor of the greatest importance in the interpretation of his character. He is essentially an aristocrat, a member of the ruling class. It is his rank that gives him his immense

power for evil-doing, for harming the simple people for whom
Sganarelle speaks. Dom Louis' indictment follows the same lines,
but he looks at his son from a different angle. There is genuine
fear behind Sganarelle's "un grand seigneur méchant homme est
une terrible chose"; but Dom Louis is primarily concerned with
his son's abuse of his privileges. In his world privileges imply
duties, but instead of setting a good example Dom Juan has outraged
all the canons of this world and not least the code of chivalry by
using his great position to do evil, has become in fact "un monstre
dans la nature." When Dom Louis goes on to observe: "La vertu
est le premier titre de noblesse" and "Je regarde bien moins au
nom qu'on signe qu'aux actions qu'on fait," he is asserting standards of honesty and decency which Molière himself would have been
the first to endorse, as he would assuredly have endorsed the
primacy of "virtue" over "rank."

Earlier in the opening scene Sganarelle has observed to Gusman:

"Tu vois en Dom Juan, mon maître, le plus grand scélérat que la
terre ait jamais porté, un enragé, un chien, un diable, un Turc, un
hérétique, qui ne croit ni Ciel, ni Enfer, ni loup-garou, qui passe cette
vie en véritable bête brute, un pourceau d'Épicure, un vrai Sardanapale,
qui ferme l'oreille à toutes les remontrances qu'on lui peut faire et traite
de billevesées tout ce que nous croyons. Tu me dis qu'il a épousé ta
maîtresse: crois qu'il aurait plus fait pour sa passion, et qu'avec elle il
aurait encore épousé toi, son chien et son chat. Un mariage ne lui coûte
rien à contracter; il ne se sert point d'autres pièges pour attraper les
belles, et c'est un épouseur à toutes mains. Dame, demoiselle, bourgeoise,
paysanne, il ne trouve rien de trop chaud ni de trop froid pour lui; et
si je te disais le nom de toutes celles qu'il a épousées en divers lieux, ce
serait un chapitre à durer jusques au soir. Tu demeures surpris et changes
de couleur à ce discours; ce n'est là qu'une ébauche du personnage, et,
pour en achever le portrait, il faudrait bien d'autres coups de pinceau."

This is written with all Molière's incomparable comic verve,
but the intention is serious. It is a portrait of Dom Juan as he
appears to "the little man," but Sganarelle possesses a shrewd
common sense. He sees very clearly that Dom Juan's amorous
exploits and his unbelief are inseparable and are the key to his
character. The main emphasis, however, properly falls on the
distance between "him" and "us." "All that *we* hold with is just a
lot of mumbo-jumbo to *him*. Thorough old ram too. Fair goes off

his head at the sight of a skirt. Makes no difference whether it's a decent girl or a tart: they're all the same to him. A gent who goes on like that's a menace to the lot of us. We're none of us safe when he's around."

All this, adds Sganarelle, is only "une ébauche du personnage," and it is precisely the "bien d'autres coups de pinceau" that the rest of the play provides. Molière worked on a large canvas in *Dom Juan*. The unities of time and place were properly jettisoned to enable him to exhibit the principal character in all his complexity. The play is singularly rich in local colour, and outside Shakespeare it is difficult to think of anything comparable to the peasant scenes or some of the exchanges between Sganarelle and Dom Juan. It is rich, too, in incidents, but each incident—each *coup de pinceau*— is carefully selected to illustrate a particular trait of Dom Juan's character. It is only when we have studied his treatment of Elvire, the peasants, "le Pauvre," his tailor, his reactions to his father and to the Commander that we can be said to know the character, to have the finished portrait in front of us.

The scene in which Sganarelle appears disguised as a doctor shows how closely knit the play is. There is an extremely funny moment when he tries to excuse himself for hiding behind a bush when his master is attacked by remarking: "Je crois que cet habit est purgatif"; but it is not merely an attack on doctors. Its intention is to illustrate the completeness of Dom Juan's scepticism:

DOM JUAN:
Et quels remèdes encore leur as-tu ordonnés?

SGANARELLE:
Ma foi, monsieur, j'en ai pris par où j'en ai pu attraper; j'ai fait mes ordonnances à l'aventure, et ce serait une chose plaisante si les malades guérissaient et qu'on m'en vînt remercier.

DOM JUAN:
Et pourquoi non? Par quelle raison n'aurais-tu pas les mêmes privil-lèges qu'ont tous les autres médecins? Ils n'ont pas plus de part que toi aux guérisons des malades, et tout leur art est pure grimace. Ils ne font rien que recevoir la gloire des heureux succès, et tu peux profiter comme eux du bonheur du malade, et voir attribuer à tes remèdes tout ce qui peut venir des faveurs du hasard et des forces de la nature.

SGANARELLE:
Comment, monsieur! vous êtes aussi impie en médecine?

DOM JUAN:

   C'est une des grandes erreurs qui soit parmi les hommes.

SGANARELLE:

   Quoi! vous ne croyez pas au séné, ni à la casse, ni au vin émétique?

DOM JUAN:

   Et pourquoi veux-tu que j'y croie?

SGANARELLE:

   Vous avez l'âme bien mécréante. Cependant vous voyez depuis un temps que le vin émétique fait bruire ses fuseaux. Ses miracles ont converti les plus incrédules esprits, et il n'y a pas trois semaines que j'en ai vu, moi qui vous parle, un effet merveilleux.

DOM JUAN:

   Et quel?

SGANARELLE:

   Il y avait un homme qui depuis six jours était à l'agonie; on ne savait plus que lui ordonner, et tous les remèdes ne faisaient rien; on s'avisa à la fin de lui donner de l'émétique.

DOM JUAN:

   Il réchappa, n'est-ce pas?

SGANARELLE:

   Non, il mourut.

DOM JUAN:

   L'effet est admirable.

SGANARELLE:

   Comment! il y avait six jours entiers qu'il ne pouvait mourir, et cela le fit mourir tout d'un coup. Voulez-vous rien de plus efficace?

DOM JUAN:

   Tu as raison.

Molière strikes a fresh note in this scene. There had been criticism of doctors in his earlier plays, but the seriousness behind this criticism is something new. I shall have more to say about this later; for the moment I merely wish to point out how carefully Molière's plays must be read in order to be sure that we have understood the tone and intention of a particular scene. Although Molière does not seem to me to identify himself with his principal character, Dom Juan is clearly the most intelligent character in the play and Molière does not scruple to use him as his mouthpiece when making his most radical criticisms of contemporary abuses.

Sganarelle is one of Molière's most remarkable creations and he is one of the key-figures in the play. He is to some extent a chorus commenting on the action, but he is also a symbolical figure who seems at times to represent poor erring humanity. He disapproves of many of his master's actions and though he is in the main too cowardly to stand up to him, he does criticize him openly on occasion. On such occasions he resembles the King's fool and enjoys the same sort of immunity. One of the things which most outraged the *dévots* was that Molière should have entrusted the defence of Christianity to a buffoon. Sganarelle is certainly no theologian; he thinks that belief in heaven and hell and in *le moine bourru* or *le vin émétique* is equally important; but from an artistic point of view, it is precisely his inadequacy as a theologian which gives his simple, muddled *raisonnement* the stamp of truth. The discussion on medicine quoted above leads logically to the discussion of religious belief. "What do you believe in?" asks Sganarelle later in the same scene.

DOM JUAN:
> Je crois que deux et deux sont quatre, Sganarelle, et que quatre et quatre sont huit.

SGANARELLE:
> La belle croyance et les beaux articles de foi que voilà! Votre religion, à ce que je vois, est donc l'arithmétique?

The laugh does not seem to me to be at the expense of religion, but of Dom Juan. For Sganarelle's method is the only one for dealing with this solemn, humourless profession of unbelief.

Dom Juan is the rootless intellectual aristocrat whose powers are bent on destruction. When he remarks:

> "Quoi qu'il en soit, je ne puis refuser mon cœur à tout ce que je vois d'aimable; et, dès qu'un beau visage me le demande, si j'en avais dix mille, je les donnerais tous. Les inclinations naissantes, après tout, ont des charmes inexplicables, et tout le plaisir de l'amour est dans le changement"

—it sounds at first like a passage from an early work by M. André Gide, but this impression is misleading. Dom Juan is a *libertin* and he must be seen in his historical setting. M. Blanchot rightly describes him as "une image extrême de la rébellion et de l'anti-conformisme." The *libertins* mark a break with tradition. They inaugurate what M. Denis de Rougemont calls the "secularization of the myth."[1] Love is stripped of its glamour, ceases to be some-

[1] See pp. 165–70 below.

thing sacrosanct as it had been in the past and becomes a purely biological function. Dom Juan's feeling for women—it is this that makes him a representative *libertin*—is shorn of any emotional attraction and has far more in common with the *volupté* of the eighteenth century than with the *amour* of the seventeenth. He is really an eighteenth-century figure and the immediate ancestor of Casanova and Valmont.[1]

The destructiveness of Dom Juan's mind is apparent in the peasant scene:

"Jamais je n'ai vu deux personnes être si contents l'un de l'autre et faire éclater plus d'amour. . . . Oui, je ne pus souffrir d'abord, de les voir si bien ensemble; le dépit alarma mes désirs, et je me figurai un plaisir extrême à pouvoir troubler leur intelligence et rompre cet attachement dont la délicatesse de mon cœur se tenait offensée."

At the root of his corruption and his nihilism is intellectual pride. He is the eternal gambler who cannot bear to admit defeat. He is not really interested in the two peasant girls, but he cannot tolerate the thought that either of them should prefer another man to himself, any more than he could tolerate the idea that Done Elvire might prefer fidelity to her vows to marriage with him. He might have said of her life in the religious community as he says here of Charlotte and Pierrot:

"Je ne pus souffrir d'abord, de les voir si bien ensemble; le dépit alarma mes désirs."

It is a revealing phrase which tells us a lot about his psychology. His actions are not governed by the positive *désirs*, but by the negative *dépit*, the irritation caused by a happiness in which he has no part, by the thought that anyone can be happy without being dependent on him. This is strikingly illustrated by his encounter with "le Pauvre":

DOM JUAN:
    Il ne se peut donc pas que tu ne sois bien à ton aise?
LE PAUVRE:
    Hélas! monsieur, je suis dans la plus grande nécessité du monde.

[1] The new attitude was certainly fostered by the philosophical materialism implicit in Descartes' *Traité des passions de l'âme.*

DOM JUAN:

Tu te moques: un homme qui prie le Ciel tout le jour ne peut pas manquer d'être bien dans ses affaires.

LE PAUVRE:

Je vous assure, monsieur, que le plus souvent je n'ai pas un morceau de pain à mettre sous les dents.

DOM JUAN:

Voilà qui est étrange, et tu es bien mal reconnu de tes soins. Ah! ah! je m'en vais te donner un louis d'or tout à l'heure, pourvu que tu veuilles jurer.

LE PAUVRE:

Ah! monsieur, voudriez-vous que je commisse un tel péché?

DOM JUAN:

Tu n'as qu'à voir si tu veux gagner un louis d'or ou non. En voici un que je te donne, si tu jures. Tiens, il faut jurer.

LE PAUVRE:

Monsieur! . . .

DOM JUAN:

A moins de cela tu ne l'auras pas.

SGANARELLE:

Va, va, jure un peur, il n'y a pas de mal.

DOM JUAN:

Prends, le voilà; prends, te dis-je; mais jure donc.

LE PAUVRE:

Non, monsieur, j'aime mieux mourir de faim.

DOM JUAN:

Va, va, je te le donne pour l'amour de l'humanité.

The speech opens in a tone of raillery and Dom Juan pretends to be incredulous when he hears that anyone who spends his life in prayer is "dans la plus grande nécessité." He is prepared to relieve the Pauvre's material needs, but only at the price of upsetting the harmony of this life, this world from which he is excluded. The hermit's refusal to swear in order to win the *louis d'or* is incomprehensible to him. When he persists in his refusal, a note of perplexity and irritation creeps into Dom Juan's voice. The refusal is a challenge to his pride and he is faced with defeat through his failure to trouble this life. The firmness of the "Non, monsieur, j'aime mieux mourir de faim" shows him that he has met his match and to save his face he gives the money with the sardonic: "Va, va, je te le donne pour l'amour de l'humanité" and at once tries to retrieve

his position by going to the rescue of Dom Carlos who has been
attacked by bandits:

"Mais que vois-je là? Un homme attaqué par trois autres? La partie
est trop inégale, et je ne dois pas souffrir cette lâcheté."

The accent falls on "*Je* ne dois pas souffrir." He will compensate
himself by making someone far grander than "le Pauvre" dependent
on him. It remains to add that Sganarelle's "Va, va, jure un peu,
il n'y a pas de mal" reveals the touch of a master. It is weak and
wayward humanity always ready to compromise principles in the
interests of immediate necessity.

The encounter with the Statue is really the final stage in the
revelation of Dom Juan's character. When the Statue nods, he is
plainly disconcerted and says hurriedly:

"Allons, sortons d'ici."

Sganarelle emphasizes his discomfort:

"Voilà des mes esprits forts, qui ne veulent rien croire."

The words seem intended to reduce his master to the level of
"certains petits impertinents . . . qui font les esprits forts parce
qu'ils croient que cela leur sied bien."

Dom Juan has certainly been badly shaken and his irritation is
evident from the next scene:

"Quoi qu'il en soit, laissons cela: c'est une bagatelle, et nous pouvons
avoir été trompés par un faux jour, ou surpris de quelque vapeur qui
nous ait troublé la vue."

When Sganarelle retorts:

"Eh! monsieur, ne cherchez point à démentir ce que nous avons vu
les yeux que voilà."

Dom Juan loses his temper and threatens to beat him unless he
drops the matter altogether.

Dom Juan's pride is the decisive factor in his downfall. The
Statue has made a breach in his philosophy. As a thoroughgoing
pragmatist he cannot deny the evidence of his senses, but his pride
prevents him from admitting that what he has seen is proof of any
supernatural intervention. He is certainly not lacking in physical
courage, and in spite of the warnings of the Statue, of Done Elvire

and the phantom, he simply persists in his refusal to repent and goes
stoically down to damnation:

"Il y a bien quelque chose là-dedans que je ne comprends pas; mais,
quoi que ce puisse être, cela n'est pas capable, ni de convaincre mon
esprit, ni d'ébranler mon âme. . . ."

Molière's contemporaries were profoundly shocked by the final
scene where fire comes down from heaven and the earth opens and
swallows Dom Juan. They said that the clumsy stage properties
made this representation of the Divine wrath ridiculous and unseemly and were, indeed, intended to do so. This criticism seems
to me to reveal a complete misunderstanding of Molière's purpose.
The number of different spokesmen that he used enabled him to
show Dom Juan's character in a constantly changing light, but the
general effect depends very largely on the contrast between the
haughty, disdainful aristocrat and the delightful and ridiculous
Sganarelle. *The last episode is seen through Sganarelle's eyes.* For
him the annihilation of the arrogant Dom Juan is at once bewilder-
ing, terrifying and comic, and his final words: "Mes gages, mes
gages, mes gages," which had to be omitted from seventeenth-
century productions, strike exactly the right note. It is not, as
contemporary critics alleged, impious farce, but a very serious and
sombre farce.

V. *LE MISANTHROPE*

1

Le Misanthrope is by common consent the greatest of Molière's
plays, but attempts to discover the nature of its peculiar excellence
have sometimes led critics into unprofitable paths. The Romantic
critics found in it the main support for their theory of "the tragic
Molière"; Ramon Fernandez, the stern champion of "philosophical
criticism," has spoken of "cette comédie où le principe même de
la comédie est mis en péril"[1]; and a German writer has used it to

[1] *op. cit.*, p. 189.

propound a theory of "the diabolical element in great comedy."[1]
These theories have one factor in common. They suggest that the
Misanthrope is in some way "deeper," more "profound," more
"serious" than Molière's other works, overlooking perhaps the
fact that comedy is essentially a serious activity.[2] Compare it with
Tartuffe and the dangers of such a criterion are at once apparent.
It is not difficult to see in what sense the *Misanthrope* and *Tartuffe*
are more "serious" than *les Femmes savantes* or *l'Avare*, but we
should be on very uncertain ground in claiming that the *Misanthrope* is more serious than *Tartuffe*. Indeed, it would be less difficult
to prove the contrary. *Tartuffe* has obvious affinities with primitive
comedy. The most striking of them is the sacrificial element.
Tartuffe is the scapegoat whose chastisement provides a release
for the audience's primitive desires and emotions, and Molière
knew very well what he was about when he underlined the sexual
propensities of his victim. The play appeals to some of the deepest,
though not the most admirable, of human instincts, and it has a
ferocity which is unparalleled in Molière's work. "My opinion of
Tartuffe," wrote Baudelaire in his diary, "is that it is not a comedy,
but a pamphlet." This is an over-statement, but it helps us to understand the limitations of that masterpiece and the superiority of the
Misanthrope.

The *Misanthrope* in the seventeenth century was the connois-
seur's play and a contemporary described it with felicity as "une
pièce qui fait rire dans l'âme." Its pre-eminence lies not in greater
depth or profundity, but in a greater variety of tone, a wider social
reference, more complex and more delicate shades of feeling. It is
one of the most personal of Molière's plays. *Tartuffe* was a magnificent onslaught on a narrow, vindictive puritanism which had all
but succeeded in driving comedy from the stage. The *Misanthrope*
was written during a personal crisis and is certainly coloured by

---

[1] Curt Sigmar Gutkind in *Molière und das Komische Drama* (Halle, 1928).
It is only fair to add that the point is not unduly stressed and that the chapter
on the *Misanthrope* seems to me to be the best study of the play that I have
come across in any language.

[2] How little this has been understood in France, where the distinction
between tragedy and comedy is much more definite than in England, can be
seen from Brunetière's "*Le Misanthrope* and *Tartuffe* are already middle-class
tragedies which Molière tried in vain to fit into the framework of comedy."
"Les Époques de la Comédie de Molière" in *Études critiques sur l'histoire
de la littérature française*, VIII, 3ième éd., Paris, 1922, pp. 116-17.)

Molière's own domestic difficulties. We must be careful not to read too much into the play, but those critics who have found its laughter "sad" are on the right track; there is no doubt that personal suffering helped to give Molière the astonishing insight into the human heart which he displays in the *Misanthrope* and which contributes to its richness and maturity.[1]

2

"He did not set out to write a comedy full of incidents," said Visé in a commentary which is believed to have been published with Molière's approval, "but simply a play in which he could speak against the manners of the age."

There is one striking difference between the *Misanthrope* and Molière's other plays. He does not confine himself to the study of the psychology of an individual seen against the background of a stable society. His irony is turned on society as well as on Alceste, and the play ends, as we shall see, not with the restoration of order, but with something that is very like a mark of interrogation.

The theme is presented by means of a triple conflict—the conflict between Alceste and social convention, Alceste and justice, Alceste and Célimène. It is the constant shifting of the focus from one to the other and the way in which Molière plays on our divided sympathies that give the *Misanthrope* its variety, so that it calls for a greater effort of attention from the reader than any of the other comedies.

Mr. L. C. Knights has suggested that a close examination of the tone and intention of each line in the first scene is the best way of discovering how the play as a whole should be read.[2] The opening scene is so carefully constructed and the theme stated with such clarity and force that almost everything which follows is a development of hints and suggestions contained in it.

PHILINTE:
    Qu'est-ce donc? Qu'avez-vous?
ALCESTE (*assis*):
                    Laissez-moi, je vous prie.

[1] When the play was originally produced, Alceste was played by Molière, Célimène by his wife, Éliante by his mistress and Arsinoé by Mlle du Parc who had repulsed his advances!

[2] In *Determinations*, London, 1934, p. 118.

PHILINTE:

Mais encor, dites-moi, quelle bizarrerie . . .

ALCESTE:

Laissez-moi là, vous dis-je, et courez vous cacher.

PHILINTE:

Mais on entend les gens, au moins, sans se fâcher.

ALCESTE:

Moi, je veux me fâcher, et ne veux point entendre.

PHILINTE:

Dans vos brusques chagrins je ne puis vous comprendre,
Et, quoique amis, enfin, je suis tout des premiers . . .

ALCESTE (*se levant brusquement*):

Moi, votre ami? Rayez cela de vos papiers.
J'ai fait jusques ici profession de l'être;
Mais après ce qu'en vous je viens de voir paraître,
Je vous déclare net que je ne le suis plus,
Et ne veux nulle place en dès cœurs corrompus.

The play opens as usual on a note which sounds uncommonly
like farce, but the intention is serious. There is something wrong
with Alceste and most of the play is devoted to discovering what
it is. It makes his behaviour so unreasonable that he becomes
incomprehensible to the tolerant and reasonable Philinte. The
violent tone is characteristic of Alceste and an understanding of it
leads to an understanding of the *motifs* behind it. The *cacher* and
the *brusques chagrins* are important clues—the unobtrusive stage
direction, *se levant brusquement*, illustrates the close connection
between word and gesture in Molière—and their recurrence in the
play emphasizes the closeness of its texture.

The dialogue that follows explains the origin of Alceste's *chagrin*,
but before examining it in detail, I wish to jump eighty lines and
look at the next use of the word:

ALCESTE:

Mes yeux sont trop blessés, et la cour et la ville
Ne m'offrent rien qu'objets à m'échauffer la bile;
J'entre en une humeur noire, en un chagrin profond,
Quand je vois vivre entre eux les hommes comme ils font . . .

PHILINTE:

Ce chagrin philosophe est un peu trop sauvage.
Je ris des noirs accès où je vous envisage . . .

It is clear that for Alceste the *humeur noire* and the *chagri.*
profond are a matter of deadly seriousness, but it is also clear fror.
the change of tone and the ironical *chagrin philosophe* that they hav
a different value for Philinte, for the ordinary, reasonable man
It is characteristic of the peculiar ambiguity of the play, and c
Philinte's place in it, that we feel doubtful at this point whethe
the *chagrin* is or is not a laughing matter. There is still room fo
doubt when he goes on four lines later:

> Non, tout de bon, quittez toutes ces incartades.
> Le monde par vos soins ne se changera pas;
> Et puisque la franchise a pour vous tant d'appas,
> Je vous dirai tout franc que cette maladie,
> Partout où vous allez, donne la comédie . . .

Philinte drops the tone of easy banter and proceeds to give
serious warning. The *chagrin* is now described as *cette malad*
and we are meant to take the word at its face value, but it is sti'
a *maladie* which in the eyes of the world *donne la comédie*. Ther
is a conflict of values. The *chagrin* has a different significance fo
different individuals. The doubt lies in deciding what importanc
should be attached to the respective valuations of Alceste, Philint
and *le monde*. Are they all right or all wrong, or partly right an
partly wrong?

This doubt is really the crux of the whole play, and it is interestin
to glance at the use of this and similar words—the *désert* and th
endroit écarté—in other contexts:

> 1. Têtebleu! ce me sont de mortelles blessures
>   De voir qu'avec le vice on garde des mesures;
>   Et parfois il me prend des mouvements soudains
>   De fuir dans un *désert* l'approche des humains.
>   (I. i.)
>
> 2. C'est que jamais, morbleu! les hommes n'ont raison,
>   Que *le chagrin contre eux* est toujours de saison . . .
>   (II. iv.)
>
> 3. Elle tâche à couvrir d'un faux voile de prude
>   Ce que chez elle on voit *d'affreuse solitude*.
>   (*Célimène of Arsinoé*, III. iii.)

4. Allez-vous en la voir, et me laissez enfin
   Dans ce petit coin sombre, avec *mon noir chagrin*.

   (v. i.)

5. Pourvu que votre cœur veuille donner les mains
   Au dessein que j'ai fait de fuir tous les humains,
   Et que dans mon *désert*, où j'ai fait vœu de vivre,
   Vous soyez, sans tarder, résolue à me suivre . . .

   (v. iv.)

6. Trahi de toutes parts, accablé d'injustices,
   Je vais sortir d'un *gouffre* où triomphent les vices,
   Et chercher sur la terre *un endroit écarté*,
   Où d'être homme d'honneur on ait la liberté.

   (v. iv.)

It is tempting but dangerous to compare Alceste's *chagrin* with Pascal's vision of *l'abîme*[1] or even with Baudelaire's *spleen*, because in doing so we run the risk of serious misinterpretation. Alceste is painfully conscious of his perplexity and frustration, but it is evident from these examples that his attitude is a *personal* one. It does not spring from a vision which transcends the deceptive appearances of everyday life. It is largely negative, is directed *contre [les hommes]*; and in the fourth example, where he caricatures himself, he seems for a moment to be aware that there is something a little absurd about his *chagrin*. There is a burlesque note, too, in the fifth and sixth examples. Alceste strikes a pose. He renounces the world and goes off to play at being a "man of honour" in the "desert." Now the "desert" is both objective and subjective, and has certain affinities with Arsinoé's *affreuse solitude* which are suggested by a passage in M. Mauriac's interesting essay on the play:

"In a world where a decent man and a Christian has so many reasons not for protest, at least for examining his own conscience, Alceste only attacks the most harmless practices, those 'lies' which do not take anyone in but which are necessary if social life is to go on at all. He is indignant over slanders which only affect people indirectly, which do not penetrate the hidden vices and merely provoke laughter. In a world where injustice is rife, where crime is everywhere, he is up in arms against trivialities. He feels no horror for what is really horrible—beginning with himself. All his attacks are directed to things outside himself; he

[1] See Sainte-Beuve's interesting, but to my mind misleading, discussion of Pascal and Molière in *Port-Royal*, III, pp. 201 *et seq.*

only compares himself with other people in order to demonstrate hi own superiority."[1]

M. Mauriac's criticism of Alceste seems to me to be unduly severe and there is, perhaps, a tendency to simplify the issues; bu it does illuminate one side of his character. A good deal of hi *chagrin contre les hommes* springs from a psychological need t distract his attention from his own sense of frustration, fron "what is horrible" in his own nature, and in this he is representativ of the society that he is attacking. For all the characters on whom Molière turns his irony are in a greater or lesser degree aware o their own interior emptiness, of an *affreuse solitude* from which they are trying to escape. This explains their restless activity, thei desperate preoccupation with gossip and *galanterie*. While the strug gle to escape from themselves by losing themselves in the world c minor social events is one of the principal themes of the play, i must be emphasized that Molière's study of their vacancy an fatuity is not a tragic one. The *Misanthrope* is pre-eminently comedy; it is not a *tragédie bourgeoise* in the manner of *l'Éducatio sentimentale*.

3

It is time to turn to a consideration of the individual character and their place in the pattern of the play, and to the sources c Alceste's *chagrin*. His first long speech is a denunciation of soci convention:

> Je vous vois accabler un homme de caresses,
> Et témoigner pour lui les dernières tendresses;
> De protestations, d'offres et de serments
> Vous chargez la fureur de vos embrassements;
> Et quand je vous demande après quel est cet homme,
> A peine pouvez-vous dire comme il se nomme;

[1] *Journal*, II, Paris, 1937, pp. 147–8.
As a corrective to this, compare Stendhal's view of Alceste: "His man for hurling himself against whatever appears odious, his gift for close ar accurate reasoning and his extreme probity would soon have led him in politics or, what would have been much worse, to an objectionable ar seditious philosophy. Célimène's salon would at once have been compromis and soon have become a desert. And what would a coquette find to do in deserted salon?" (*Racine et Shakespeare*, II ed., P. Martino, Paris, 192 p. 177.)

Votre chaleur pour lui tombe en vous séparant,
Et vous me le traitez, à moi, d'indifférent.
Morbleu! c'est une chose indigne, lâche, infâme,
De s'abaisser ainsi jusqu'à trahir son âme;
Et si par un malheur j'en avais fait autant,
Je m'irais, de regret, pendre tout à l'instant.

The tone of nervous exasperation, the taste for extremes, signified by *accabler, dernières tendresses, fureur de vos embrassements*, and the piled up adjectives rising to a crescendo—*indigne, lâche, infâme* —is peculiar to Alceste, and there is an obvious disproportion between the language used and the "most harmless practices" which he is attacking. He uses precisely the same tone in speaking of his lawsuit and his love affair:

Quoi! contre ma partie on voit tout à la fois
L'honneur, la probité, la pudeur, et les lois;
On publie en tous lieux l'équité de ma cause,
Sur la foi de mon droit mon âme se repose;
Cependant je me vois trompé par le succès:
J'ai pour moi la justice, et je perds mon procès!
Un traître, dont on sait la scandaleuse histoire,
Est sorti triomphant d'une fausseté noire!
Toute la bonne foi cède à sa trahison!
Il trouve, en m'égorgeant, moyen d'avoir raison!
Le poids de sa grimace, où brille l'artifice,
Renverse le bon droit et tourne la justice!

.   .   .

J'ai ce que sans mourir je ne puis concevoir;
Et le déchaînement de toute la nature
Ne m'accablerait pas comme cette aventure.
C'en est fait . . . Mon amour . . . Je ne saurais parler.

The uniformity of tone shows that he reacts in precisely the same way to three different situations, that he places the same valuation on his campaign against convention, his lawsuit and his love affair. There is certainly a connection between the three, but they are very far from being of the same importance. His cult of sincerity is a fetish. If his principles were adopted, social intercourse would come to an end, and it is perhaps because he is a threat to a brittle society that his attitude is unpopular. There is more to be

E

said for his other preoccupations. Philinte admits that he has a grievance over the unfortunate lawsuit, and Célimène confesses that she has treated him badly. But though they sympathize with him, they are at one in protesting against the violence of his denunciation and the extravagance of his remedies. "I agree with all you say," remarks Philinte,

> ... je tombe d'accord de tout ce qu'il vous plaît:
> Tout marche par cabale et par pur intérêt;
> Ce n'est plus que la ruse aujourd'hui qui l'emporte,
> Et les hommes devraient être faits d'autre sorte.
> *Mais est-ce une raison que leur peu d'équité*
> *Pour vouloir se tirer de leur société ?*[1]

In short, Alceste's attitude betrays a confusion of values, an extraordinary lack of discrimination, which alone would make him ludicrous. Minor mishaps are the pretext for wild generalizations about human nature; the perfidy of a shallow, frivolous society woman assumes the proportions of a universal catastrophe in his disordered imagination, and his denunciation peters out in a strangled cry:

> C'en est fait ... Mon amour ... Je ne saurais parler.

The more we study his pronouncements, the more evident it becomes that his attitude is the reverse of disinterested. When he declares:

> Je veux qu'on soit sincère, et qu'en homme d'honneur
> On ne lâche aucun mot qui ne parte du cœur

we may feel that though this is a counsel of perfection, it is not altogether unreasonable. A few lines later, however, his real objections to the insincere enthusiasm with which people greet one another emerge very clearly:

> Je refuse d'un cœur la vaste complaisance
> Qui ne fait de mérite aucune différence;
> Je veux qu'on me distingue, et, pour le trancher net,
> L'ami du genre humain n'est point du tout mon fait.

There is a strong element of vanity in his protests. He is determined that people shall be made to distinguish *him* from his fellows.

[1] Italics mine.

and the lines betray a sense of insecurity, a need of psychological affirmation. When Philinte suggests in the first scene that he should visit some of the judges who will try his suit, he refuses angrily:

> Non; j'ai résolu de n'en pas faire un pas.
> J'ai tort ou j'ai raison.

The second line is a curious illustration of the rigidity of Alceste's mind which prevents any compromise with society; but it is interesting for another reason. It has not always been understood by contemporary readers who have felt that his attitude is commendable and have compared it favourably with Célimène's assiduous "touting" in *her* lawsuit. Now it must be remembered that in the seventeenth century the practice of visiting one's judges was universal and was not regarded as being in any way improper. The explanation of Alceste's refusal is to be found in his reaction to Philinte's suggestion that he should appeal against the decision when he loses his case:

> Non; je veux m'y tenir.
> Quelque sensible tort qu'un tel arrêt me fasse,
> Je me garderai bien de vouloir qu'on le casse:
> On y voit trop à plein le bon droit maltraité,
> Et je veux qu'il demeure à la postérité
> Comme une marque insigne, un fameux témoignage
> De la méchanceté des hommes de notre âge.
> Ce sont vingt mille francs qu'il m'en pourra coûter;
> Mais pour vingt mille francs j'aurai droit de pester
> Contre l'iniquité de la nature humaine,
> Et de nourrir pour elle une immortelle haine.

These are not the words of a fighter or a reformer. Alceste is convinced that there has been a miscarriage of justice; but instead of trying to set it right, he is delighted at the loss of his suit because he feels that it gives him a *right* to fulminate against human nature, and this right seems cheap at twenty thousand francs. This is characteristic of his general behaviour. He is always on the look-out for some abuse that he can attack or someone with whom he can pick a quarrel, and the slightest excuse is sufficient to set the machinery of excited denunciation in motion. "Quoi!" cries the horrified Philinte,

> Quoi! vous iriez dire à la vieille Émilie
> Qu'à son âge il sied mal de faire la jolie,
> Et que le blanc qu'elle a scandalise chacun?

ALCESTE:
  Sans doute.

PHILINTE:
                A Dorilas, qu'il est trop importun,
  Et qu'il n'est, à la cour, oreille qu'il ne lasse
  A conter sa bravoure et l'éclat de sa race?

ALCESTE:
  Fort bien.

This suggests that his attitude is to a certain extent *voulu*. While it is true that denunciation is a form of self-indulgence, a substitute for *action*, this does not exhaust the question. It is noticeable that in most of the plays the *honnête homme* treats this heated denunciation as the danger point. It is the point at which the normative influence of society ceases to be effective and the comic character's hysterical mood may well lead to some desperate act. It is for this reason that Philinte's warnings are nearly always directed against Alceste's *tone* and not against what he says. Now Alceste's violence deserves a closer examination than it has perhaps received. In some of the lines lifted from *Dom Garcie de Navarre* Alceste denounces Célimène's perfidy:

> Que toutes les horreurs dont une âme est capable
> A vos déloyautés n'ont rien de comparable;
> Que le sort, les démons, et le Ciel en courroux
> N'ont jamais rien produit de si méchant que vous.

Again:

> Je ne suis plus à moi, je suis tout à la rage:
> Percé du coup mortel dont vous m'assassinez,
> Mes sens par la raison ne sont plus gouvernés,
> Je cède aux mouvements d'une juste colère. . . .

At such moments we have the illusion that we are listening to a Cornelian *tirade*, but it is an illusion. Alceste is not, even at these moments, a tragic figure. His denunciation, though undeniably serious, belongs peculiarly to comedy, and there is an interesting passage at the beginning of the play which helps us to appreciate why this is so:

Non, je ne puis souffrir cette lâche méthode
Qu'affectent la plupart de vos gens à la mode;
Et je ne hais rien tant que les contorsions
De tous ces grands faiseurs de protestations,
Ces affables donneurs d'embrassades frivoles,
Ces obligeants diseurs d'inutiles paroles,
Qui de civilités avec tous font combat,
Et traitent du même air l'honnête homme et le fat.

What is striking about these lines is a curious air of unreality, the sense that we are watching a Punch-and-Judy show. This is no accident. The violence and the jerkiness have a different function here. The focal word is *contorsions* and it colours the rest of the passage. The element of caricature is deliberate. This is not abstract denunciation of real people; it is society as it appears to Alceste. We feel ourselves looking at it through his eyes and seeing a world of grinning, gesticulating marionnettes, going through their grotesque performance as some unseen showman pulls the strings. For Alceste's violence leads to a state of hysteria—Molière's word for it is *emportement*—in which the actual world is transformed into a comic nightmare, reminding us a little oddly of a Disney cartoon. The nightmare is in Alceste's mind, and the contrast between his distorted outlook and unreasonable behaviour and the humdrum world in which he lives makes him at once a comic and a moving figure. Our response to this passage, and indeed to the whole play, is a balance between two impulses which superficially appear to exclude one another—the impulse to laugh at Alceste's absurdity and the impulse to pity the obvious waste of his gifts. The art of the comic writer depends on preserving this nice balance between two apparently contradictory emotions, on the continual switch from one set of feelings to another and back again without ever allowing the balance to tip over to the extremes of tragedy or farce. There are moments when he takes us to the brink of tragedy. George Dandin will go to the edge of the water and will stand there gazing at his own reflection, wondering whether to throw himself in or not; but in the end he will turn his back on it and return slowly homewards, will return to the cultivation of his farm and to the problem of finding a *modus vivendi* with his impossible wife—as Molière himself did. In the same way, Alceste reaches the point at which reason totters, but he too will retreat into the world of words and harmless denunciation. It is not the least of the dramatist's achievements that he establishes this feeling of confidence in his audience and convinces us that it will be so.

It is the failure to understand this that has led to many of the attempts to turn the *Misanthrope* into a tragedy. Fernandez, for example, has suggested that in the course of the play Alceste's character undergoes a radical change and that the man who departs for the "desert" as the curtain falls is no longer the same man as the fiery reformer of Act I. The change is supposed to lie in the collapse of the will. It is an entertaining theory, but I can find no evidence for it in the text of the play. It is true that Alceste is always using expressions of great determination—"Je veux qu'on me distingue," "Je veux m'y tenir"—but, as I have already suggested, there is no real volition behind the words which are a sort of smoke screen used to hide a complete absence of determination. The Alceste of Act V is identical with the Alceste of Act I. His *physical* exile is the logical outcome of the *psychological* exile—the retreat into a private world—which is studied with such profound insight in the course of the play.

I stress this point because Fernandez' theory seems to me to rest on a misunderstanding of Molière's method of presentation in this play. Alceste is constructed partly by direct statement and partly by his action on other characters. Certain essential traits are presented in the opening scene and driven home by deliberate repetition all through the play. Once he has sketched the outlines, Molière proceeds to fill in the details. A series of impressions of Alceste as he appears to other characters is superimposed one on another. These impressions add to our knowledge both of Alceste and of the other characters. They are not always in agreement and sometimes, as we shall see, they qualify or contradict one another. This is a point of considerable importance and it is one of the things that force the reader to follow the dialogue with such minute care, to decide what weight must be attributed to the constant shift and change of tone.

This brings us to a consideration of Philinte's role in the play. In one of the central passages he declares:

> Il faut, parmi le monde, une vertu traitable;
> A force de sagesse on peut être blâmable;

La parfaite raison fuit toute extrémité,
Et veut que l'on soit sage avec sobriété.
Cette grande roideur des vertus des vieux âges
Heurte trop notre siècle et les communs usages;
Elle veut aux mortels trop de perfection:
Il faut fléchir au temps sans obstination,
Et c'est une folie à nulle autre seconde
De vouloir se mêler de corriger le monde.
J'observe, comme vous, cent choses tous les jours,
Qui pourraient mieux aller, prenant un autre cours;
Mais, quoi qu'à chaque pas je puisse voir paraître,
En courroux, comme vous, on ne me voit point être;
Je prends tout doucement les hommes comme ils sont,
J'accoutume mon âme à souffrir ce qu'ils font;
Et je crois qu'à la cour, de même qu'à la ville,
Mon flegme est philosophe autant que votre bile.

We recognize this passage, which recalls Cléante's plea for a
devotion which is *humaine* and *traitable*, as the familiar statement of
Molière's positives. It is also a good example of the patterned movement of his verse. It is not a mere catalogue of "the great abstractions." There are life and warmth in his *sagesse, parfaite raison* and
sobriété. They have behind them centuries of European civilization
which is vividly felt. The *roideur des vieux âges* underlines the peculiar and disabling rigidity of Alceste's outlook and, at the same time,
reflects a delicate appreciation of the graciousness of contemporary
civilization which exists in spite of human imperfection. The passage closes on a personal note; precept merges into practice and
one becomes aware of the urbanity and good sense of the civilized
man. Philinte's tone is intended to act as a foil to Alceste's, to
moderate his transports. When Alceste cries

Et parfois il me prend des mouvements soudains
De fuir dans un désert l'approche des humains,

Philinte replies:

Mon Dieu, des mœurs du temps mettons-nous moins en peine,
Et faisons un peu grâce à la nature humaine.

The sharp *soudains-humains* creates a sense of physical constriction
and the relief provided by *peine-humaine* is palpable. The *grâce* and
the *douceur* prolong the process on the logical plane. It is not without

significance, however, that Philinte's attempts to moderate Alceste's transports are seldom successful. The very gentleness of tone seems to heighten his exasperation, and he reserves some of his bitterest shafts for his friend. In these exchanges his tactics vary and he is decidedly *rusé*. When he retorts:

> Mais ce flegme, monsieur, qui raisonne si bien,
> Ce flegme pourra-t-il ne s'échauffer de rien?

raisonne is balanced against *s'échauffer*. He feels instinctively that *flegme* puts the brake on his *emportement* and he tries to discredit it by suggesting that it is an excuse for tolerating injustice. There is a curious eagerness to brush aside obstacles. The verse stumbles and almost comes to a halt over the repeated *flegme*, then moves breathlessly forward to the word *s'échauffer* which is sufficient to set the machinery of denunciation in motion.

"Je sais," he begins with icy politeness in another place,

> Je sais que vous parlez, monsieur, le mieux du monde;
> En beaux raisonnements vous abondez toujours;
> Mais vous perdez le temps et tous vos beaux discours.
> La raison, pour mon bien, veut que je me retire:
> Je n'ai pas sur ma langue un assez grand empire;
> De ce que je dirais je ne répondrais pas,
> Et je me jetterais cent choses sur les bras.

In order to keep up the appearance of rational behaviour, he pretends that his proposal to retire to the desert is a reasoned one, but there is a world of difference between the *beaux raisonnements* attributed to Philinte and Alceste's *raison*. "Reason" ceases to be universal and becomes a private and very misleading label that he attaches to the demon which is driving him into the desert. The last three lines are double-edged. It is because he is unreasonable and not because society is unreasonable that he is likely to find himself in trouble if he remains where he is.

I have already spoken of the peculiar ambiguity of the play and of Philinte's place in it. In the *Misanthrope* there is a skilful modification of the pattern of Molière's comedies which becomes more subtle and more varied. Although Philinte is certainly Molière's spokesman in many places and certainly helps to provide the background of reason and sanity which contributes largely to

the poise of the play, his role is a shifting one. We do not feel, as
we do with Cléante, that the whole of the play is behind his words,
and the explanation is to be found in Éliante's observations on
Alceste in Act IV. Sc. i:

> Dans ses façons d'agir il est fort singulier;
> Mais j'en fais, je l'avoue, un cas particulier,
> Et la sincérité dont son âme se pique
> A quelque chose en soi de noble et d'héroïque.
> C'est une vertu rare au siècle d'aujourd'hui,
> Et je la voudrais voir partout comme chez lui.

Éliante is the only wholly sympathetic character in the play. It
would not be accurate to say that she represents Molière's own
point of view more completely than Philinte, but her role is of
the first importance. In the *Misanthrope*, as in *Tartuffe*, Molière
felt the need of two spokesmen; but the function of Éliante and
Philinte goes beyond that of Dorine and Cléante. Dorine and
Cléante complete one another, but Éliante qualifies the role of
Philinte and it is this that gives the play a mellowness which is
unique in Molière's work. For Éliante's words display a fresh attitude
towards the comic hero. Arnolphe, Harpagon and Orgon (in spite
of his conversion to a *dévotion traitable*) are and remain completely
unsympathetic; but Alceste awakens the sympathies of the audience
to a degree which is exceptional in seventeenth-century and indeed
in all comedy.

Éliante minimizes Alceste's peculiarities and by placing the
emphasis on his "rare virtue" she corrects Philinte. Alceste is not
a buffoon in the same sense as Molière's other comic characters.
There is always a foundation of good sense behind his criticisms
and, in spite of their exaggeration, this is true of his attacks on
convention. In the scene where Oronte's sonnet is criticized, which
is significantly placed immediately after the exposition of the
principal theme of the play in Scene i, his good taste and sound
judgment obviously compare favourably with Philinte's flattery.[1]
There is a less obvious but more impressive example towards the

---

[1] For a more orthodox interpretation of Philinte's role and of this scene,
see Michaut's chapter on the play in *les Luttes de Molière* (Paris, 1925).
Although I do not feel able to accept this interpretation, I should like to commend Michaut's writings on Molière which are the best kind of literary
scholarship and are of inestimable value to the literary critic.

E*

end of the play when, after commiserating with Alceste on the loss of his lawsuit, Philinte proceeds to expound the virtues of his own philosophy:

> Tous ces défauts humains nous donnent dans la vie
> Des moyens d'exercer notre philosophie;
> C'est le plus bel emploi que trouve la vertu;
> Et si de probité tout était revêtu,
> Si tous les cœurs étaient francs, justes et dociles,
> La plupart des vertus nous seraient inutiles . . .

Philinte's logic may be unexceptionable, but is not the attitude that he is defending in danger of becoming abstract and unreal? Is there not a gap between life and thought, a gap which can only be closed by the more human and more generous approach of Éliante? Does not his attitude overlook the fact that the ordinary man is not a mere logician and that "the exercise of our philosophy" cannot impose order on the tangled feelings and desires which Molière perceived as clearly as Racine? The neat maxims which appealed so much to the reasonable seventeenth century are useless in solving the central problem of the play—the conflict between what Gutkind calls with true Teutonic violence "the pert, frivolous, fickle, coquettish young widow and Alceste, the heavy-blooded man who is eaten up by his passion and who is fighting for his love."[1]

The conclusion seems to me to be unmistakable. In this play Molière criticizes his own standards. The urbanity and moderation of the *honnête homme* are felt to be insufficient. When Éliante speaks of "quelque chose en soi de noble et d'héroïque," she is referring to the potentialities of Alceste's character; but these potentialities are prevented from realizing themselves by his lack of balance and his impatience of all restraint. His virtues are converted into negation, into the *haines vigoureuses* of one passage and the *immortelle haine* of another; his violence leads him away from the world of common experience into a world of private mania where, deprived of the normative influence of society, he thunders against wildly exaggerated abuses in the void. This makes him a comic figure, but it is the consciousness of his potential virtues and of his profound humanity which gives the play its peculiar resonance.

[1] *op. cit.*, p. 125.

4

The triple conflict represents the three points of contact between Alceste and society. The continual switching from one to the other and back again enables Molière to present both Alceste and society in a perpetually changing light until, as the play moves towards its climax, the three blend and give it its cumulative force. The direct conflict with convention underlines Alceste's absurdity and prevents comedy from turning into tragedy; the lawsuit redresses the balance and seems at times to justify his violence; the affair with Célimène is the richest and most serious of all and in a way contains them both. Alceste's rage over convention and his lawsuit is the point at which he separates himself from his fellow men and his love affair is the point at which he rejoins them. It stands for normality; it is the side of his character by which (in Mauriac's words) "il nous devient fraternel." "Je m'étonne, pour moi," remarks Philinte:

> Je m'étonne, pour moi, qu'étant, comme il le semble,
> Vous et le genre humain si fort brouillés ensemble,
> Malgré tout ce qui peut vous le rendre odieux,
> Vous ayez pris chez lui ce qui charme vos yeux;
> Et ce qui me surprend encore davantage,
> C'est cet étrange choix où votre cœur s'engage.
> La sincère Éliante a du penchant pour vous,
> La prude Arsinoé vous voit d'un œil fort doux:
> Cependant à leurs vœux votre âme se refuse,
> Tandis qu'en ses liens Célimène l'amuse,
> De qui l'humeur coquette et l'esprit médisant
> Semble si fort donner dans les mœurs d'à présent.

Alceste replies at once, with his curious mixture of arrogance and perspicacity, that he has no illusions about the shortcomings of Célimène:

> Non, l'amour que j'ai pour cette jeune veuve
> Ne ferme point mes yeux aux défauts qu'on lui treuve,
> Et je suis, quelque ardeur qu'elle m'ait pu donner,
> Le premier à les voir, comme à les condamner.
> Mais, avec tout cela, quoi que je puisse faire,
> Je confesse mon faible, elle a l'art de me plaire;

> J'ai beau voir ses défauts, et j'ai beau l'en blâmer,
> En dépit qu'on en ait, elle se fait aimer;
> Sa grâce est la plus forte, et sans doute ma flamme
> De ces vices du temps pourra purger son âme.

Célimène's importance is twofold. She is the complete representative of the society that Alceste and through him Molière is
attacking. When some of her retainers tell Alceste that he should
blame her and not them for the spiteful remarks that she is making
about acquaintances and friends, he retorts acutely:

> Non, morbleu! c'est à vous; et vos ris complaisants
> Tirent de son esprit tous ces traits médisants.

Part of his problem is to "convert" Célimène, to carry her away
from the vicious circle in which she lives; but the problem remains
unsolved because of Alceste's eccentricity, because he can only
convert her by transporting her into his own world, by carrying
her off with him into the "desert" to which he eventually retires.
What distinguishes him from Molière's other characters is an extraordinary insight into his own feelings. There are moments when he
suddenly forgets his grievances against society, drops the tone of
violent denunciation and sees himself as he really is—not a reformer,
but a man sadly perplexed by his passion for a woman who is unworthy of him. It is at such moments that we become aware of his
immense superiority over the brittle society that is trying to laugh
him out of criticisms which are felt to be a threat to it:

PHILINTE:
> Pour moi, si je n'avais qu'à former des désirs,
> La cousine Éliante aurait tous mes soupirs.
> Son cœur, qui vous estime, est solide et sincère,
> Et ce choix plus conforme était mieux votre affaire.

ALCESTE:
> Il est vrai: ma raison me le dit chaque jour;
> Mais la raison n'est pas ce qui règle l'amour.

In the last two lines *raison* is used in its normal sense, which is
not the sense of

> La raison, pour mon bien, veut que je me retire.

Célimène stands for the tangled feelings and desires which, as I
have already suggested, the seventeenth century tried in vain to

enclose in its neat formulas. It is at this point that the "systems" of both Alceste and Philinte break down. The obstinate fanaticism of the one and the philosophical maxims of the other are alike impotent to solve the problems of life. For in this play Molière explores regions in which conventional formulas have no validity, and the insight with which he does so gives the *Misanthrope* its exceptional place in French comedy. Nor must we overlook the irony of *solide et sincère* which is echoed later in the play by Alceste's

> Enfin, quoi qu'il en soit, et sur quoi qu'on se fonde,
> Vous trouvez des raisons pour souffrir tout le monde.

Alceste, Célimène and Éliante form a triangle. Alceste places himself at a point outside society; Célimène is entirely absorbed in it; Éliante occupies an intermediate position. She is of society, but is wholly uncontaminated by it. *Alceste's contact with the world of common experience is seen to be intermittent.* He is continually rebounding from its polished surface into the world of his private mania. The victory of either Alceste or Célimène in the tug-of-war would fail to solve the problem. For Alceste the only solution, the only way back to the norm of sanity and common sense, lies in marriage with Éliante and he refuses it. This is true of nearly all the characters in their different ways. They are all looking for something *solide et sincère*, for some philosophy on which to base their lives, but they meet with disappointment at every turn. Custom, justice and love prove equally hollow and unreal and they suddenly find themselves face to face with the void.

A large part of the play is thus taken up with the tug-of-war between Alceste and Célimène as each tries to draw the other into his or her own sphere. Célimène is shallow and frivolous but she too is dimly conscious of her shortcomings, and it is only because she is not beyond redemption that she provides Alceste with an adequate foil. From time to time the glitter and polish of the exchanges between them are disturbed by a deeper note:

ALCESTE:
> Mais moi, que vous blâmez de trop de jalousie,
> Qu'ai-je de plus qu'eux tous, madame, je vous prie?

CÉLIMÈNE:
> Le bonheur de savoir que vous êtes aimé.

This note only occurs at rare intervals. Célimène's normal tone bears a marked similarity to Philinte's. She answers Alceste's over-wrought declarations either in a mood of light banter or with mild surprise which lowers the tension:

ALCESTE:

Morbleu! faut-il que je vous aime!
Ah! que si de vos mains je rattrape mon cœur,
Je bénirai le Ciel de ce rare bonheur!
Je ne le cèle pas, je fais tout mon possible
A rompre de ce cœur l'attachement terrible;
Mais mes plus grands efforts n'ont rien fait jusqu'ici
Et c'est pour mes péchés que je vous aime ainsi.

CÉLIMÈNE:

Il est vrai, votre ardeur est pour moi sans seconde.

ALCESTE:

Oui, je puis là-dessus défier tout le monde.
Mon amour ne se peut concevoir, et jamais
Personne n'a, madame, aimé comme je fais.

CÉLIMÈNE:

En effet, la méthode en est toute nouvelle,
Car vous aimez les gens pour leur faire querelle;
Ce n'est qu'en mots fâcheux qu'éclate votre ardeur,
Et l'on n'a jamais vu un amour si grondeur.

ALCESTE:

Mais il ne tient qu'à vous que son chagrin[1] ne passe.
A tous nos démêlés coupons chemin, de grâce,
Parlons à cœur ouvert, et voyons d'arrêter . . .

This illustrates very well the constant change of tone. Alceste begins in a mood of deadly seriousness. The turns and twists of the dialogue reflect the turns and twists of the trapped animal—"the heavy-blooded man who is eaten up by his passion and who is fighting for his love"—to escape the *attachement terrible*, and recalls ironically Philinte's

Cependant à leurs vœux votre âme se refuse,
Tandis qu'en ses liens Célimène l'*amuse*.

For Alceste's struggle is no laughing matter, and the gravity of Célimène's

Il est vrai, votre ardeur est pour moi sans seconde

[1] This use of the word *chagrin* illustrates the way in which, as I have already said, Alceste's love affair "contains" the conflict with convention and justice.

shows that she is impressed in spite of herself, is faced with something which is outside her experience. But when Alceste continues
in the same tone, her mood changes and she comments light-
heartedly on the "new method" of making love. The reference
to his notorious ill-humour not only lowers the tension of the
scene, it brings Alceste back to his usual level—the comic figure
who is at odds with society. The relief, however, is only momentary,
and the scene closes with something that sounds like a cry for
mercy. "Coupons chemin, de grâce"—Alceste's arrogance vanishes
and he knows that he has been defeated in the encounter.

5

With Act II. Sc. ii the work of exposition is complete. The stage
is cleared and Molière brings his batteries to bear on the procession
of vain, empty, frivolous courtiers who have nothing better to do
than engage Célimène in malicious chatter or attend some small
function at Court.

ACASTE:
       A moins de voir Madame en être importunée,
       Rien ne m'appelle ailleurs toute la journée.
CLITANDRE:
       Moi, pourvu que je puisse être au petit couché,
       Je n'ai point d'autre affaire où je sois attaché.

It is noticeable that almost every word uttered by these people
about their friends or in the bitter exchanges between themselves
is double-edged. It returns like a boomerang to the speaker. Acaste
remarks complacently:

       Parbleu! je ne vois pas, lorsque je m'examine,
       Où prendre aucun sujet d'avoir l'âme chagrine.

The implication is that the game of self-deception is so successful,
that he is so shallow and empty, that he is incapable of perceiving
his shortcomings or experiencing the torment which infects Alceste.
This becomes clearer in the brilliant portrait of the fop which
emerges innocently as the speech continues:

> Pour le cœur, dont sur tout nous devons faire cas,
> On sait, sans vanité, que je n'en manque pas,
> Et l'on m'a vu pousser, dans le monde, une affaire
> D'une assez vigoureuse et gaillarde manière.
> Pour de l'esprit, j'en ai sans doute, et du bon goût
> A juger sans étude et raisonner de tout,
> A faire aux nouveautés, dont je suis idolâtre,
> Figure de savant sur les bancs du théâtre,
> Y décider en chef, et faire du fracas
> A tous les beaux endroits qui méritent des Has.
> Je suis assez adroit; j'ai bon air, bonne mine,
> Les dents belles surtout, et la taille fort fine.
> Quant à se mettre bien, je crois, sans me flatter,
> Qu'on serait mal venu de me le disputer.
> Je me vois dans l'estime autant qu'on y puisse être,
> Fort aimé du beau sexe, et bien auprès du maître.
> Je crois qu'avec cela, mon cher Marquis, je crois
> Qu'on peut, par tout pays, être content de soi.

The small, flat words contrast with the solemnity of the performance. When he uses a word like *vigoureuse* the thin, mincing lilt of the line robs it of its power and gives it a grotesque air. When we come to the *juger sans étude*, there is a note of fatuity which is heightened by the eulogy of his teeth and his waist which are given the same importance as his skill as a critic. And with a final pirouette he turns to survey the admiring world of his peers. The brittle, artificial style reflects the poverty of experience of all these people.

One of the best demonstrations of the vigour and subtlety of Molière's style occurs in the great scene between Célimène and Arsinoé which is one of the high-lights of the play. Thus Célimène:

> Oui, oui, franche grimace;
> Dans l'âme elle est du monde, et ses soins tentent tout
> Pour accrocher quelqu'un, sans en venir à bout.
> Elle ne saurait voir qu'avec un œil d'envie
> Les amants déclarés dont une autre est suivie;
> Et son triste mérite, abandonné de tous,
> Contre le siècle aveugle est toujours en courroux.
> Elle tâche à couvrir d'un faux voile de prude
> Ce que chez elle on voit d'affreuse solitude,
> Et, pour sauver l'honneur de ses faibles appas,
> Elle attache du crime au pouvoir qu'ils n'ont pas.

Cependant un amant plairait fort à la dame,
Et même pour Alceste elle a tendresse d'âme;
Ce qu'il me rend de soins outrage ses attraits,
Elle veut que ce soit un vol que je lui fais,
Et son jaloux dépit, qu'avec peine elle cache,
En tous endroits, sous main, contre moi se détache.

The more one studies Molière's style, the more impressed one is by its concrete particularity. It is possible to argue, as some critics have done, that his prose is superior to his verse and that the alexandrine was on occasion too rigid an instrument for his purpose. This may be true, but it can be seen in this play that the verse registers the changing expressions of his characters with remarkable vividness and that, without seeming to do so, the words do an immense amount of work. Words almost invariably issue in action and the actions of the characters mirror conflicting feelings. There was nothing absurd or discreditable about the *métier de prude* in the seventeenth century. A prude was simply an austere and rather puritanical woman; it was only later that the word acquired its present-day suggestion of affectation and insincerity. Molière's prudes, however, are all "false prudes" and they are used as negative symbols—as symbols of a hypocritical rejection of the life of the senses in which Molière himself believed so firmly. So it is here. *Grimace* sets the tone of the passage and it is sufficient to give us a picture of the stiff, puritanical old maid, trying to hide her lack of success behind a mask; but it is a *franche grimace*, a mask which hides nothing and simply draws attention to her hypocrisy. For in spirit she belongs to the world of Célimène and Acaste, accepts its values and does her best to "hook" or "angle" for a husband. We see the prude stretching out her hand furtively, but she misses the mark. She is left looking enviously at the procession of gallants who pass her by, without so much as a glance, in the train of some other beauty. She is the withered old maid—this is the cruel sense of *triste mérite*—completely abandoned in a world, in an age, in which favours are only too lightly distributed. The *faux voile de prude* reinforces the *franche grimace*, makes it more explicit, more pictorial. It is a veil which she puts between herself and the world, a veil which she uses vainly to cover the *affreuse solitude*, the terrible, consuming sexual frustration of the ageing spinster. But her deception extends further than that. It is used to conceal her intrigues and it is also a weapon which she uses to attack other women who are more successful than herself. The hand which is stretched out, pathetically, to "hook" a gallant is now stretched out to stab Célimène as a relief to her bitterness. The image of the "veil" is caught up and developed in the encounter between Célimène and Arsinoé which follows. Célimène is pretending to quote some unfavourable comments on Arsinoé's deportment which she has overheard in someone's drawing-room:

> A quoi bon, disaient-ils, cette mine modeste,
> Et ce sage dehors que dément tout le reste?
> Elle est à bien prier exacte au dernier point;
> Mais elle bat ses gens et ne les paye point.
> Dans tous les lieux dévots elle étale un grand zèle;
> Mais elle met du blanc et veut paraître belle.
> Elle fait des tableaux couvrir les nudités;
> Mais elle a de l'amour pour les réalités.

The procedure is the same as in the earlier passage. We see life going on simultaneously on different sides of a "veil," the contrast between the public and private life of a false prude. The *mine modeste* is the mask which hides, or is intended to hide, an interior disorder. She is exact in carrying out her religious duties; we see her sink to her knees and rise to her feet in church; but behind the locked doors of her house, the pious gestures merge into the savage rise and fall of the whip as she thrashes her servants. She gives alms, but has no money to pay her servants their just wages. She is the centre of attention at the cenacle where the pious meet, ostentatiously crossing herself; but in the fastness of her boudoir the pious gestures are replaced by the hand painting the face in a vain effort to repair its *triste mérite*. The last two lines are one of the glories of the play. The prude solemnly hangs a veil over some heavy classical painting of nude figures to hide them from a shocked world, but it is another subterfuge, another attempt to hide her own frustration. The *réalités* convey an extraordinary sense of hot, guilty intimacy, a morbid brooding over the intimate details of sexual relations, and the spiteful Célimène is only too conscious of the bitterness of the shaft.

I have dwelt on these passages not only because of their intrinsic merits, but also because the image of the "veil" and the "mask" explains the intention behind the play. It is to an even greater extent than *Tartuffe* a comedy of unmasking, but the unmasking is a game in which author and characters all take part. Alceste tries to abolish conventional politeness because he feels that it encourages insincerity and prevents him from seeing into the human heart. He attacks his opponent in the lawsuit because he is accepted at his face value and is able to secure an unjust decision:

> Au travers de son *masque* on voit à plein le traître;
> Partout il est connu pour tout ce qu'il peut être,
> Et ses roulements d'yeux et son ton radouci
> N'imposent qu'à des gens qui ne sont point d'ici.

In another place:

> . . . on devrait châtier sans pitié
> Ce commerce honteux de *semblants d'amitié*.

Célimène is busy stripping the mask from Arsinoé and from other members of her circle in order to reveal their hypocrisy and absurdity, but at the end of the encounter with Arsinoé she makes a far more damaging admission than she realizes:

> Madame, on peut, je crois, louer et blâmer tout,
> Et chacun a raison suivant l'âge ou le goût.
> Il est une saison pour la galanterie;
> Il en est une aussi propre à la pruderie.
> On peut, par politique, en prendre le parti,
> Quand de nos jeunes ans l'éclat est amorti:
> Cela sert à couvrir de fâcheuses disgrâces.
> Je ne dis pas qu'un jour je ne suive vos traces:
> L'âge amènera tout, et ce n'est pas le temps,
> Madame, comme on sait, d'être prude à vingt ans.

For here Molière himself takes a hand. The fragile prettiness of the verse reflects the fragile values by which Célimène lives. She accepts them absolutely and uncritically, and the future holds out little for her beyond Arsinoé's own fate.

The characters enter wholeheartedly into the game of unmasking which reaches its climax with the reading of Célimène's letter in the last Act; but as with Arsinoé they only do it as a distraction, as a means of "veiling" their own interior emptiness from themselves. Now the game is of the utmost seriousness when played by

Alceste and Célimène. They are doubtful about their feelings for
one another. Alceste *thinks* that he is madly in love with Célimène,
but the very violence of his protestations betrays an element of
doubt. He is not at all sure that she loves him, and he sets to work
to find out because it distracts him from his doubts about his own
feelings. The play enters on its last phase when Arsinoé undertakes
to prove to Alceste that Célimène is not in love with him:

> Oui, toute mon amie, elle est et je la nomme
> Indigne d'asservir le cœur d'un galant homme,
> Et le sien n'a pour vous que de feintes douceurs.

Alceste bridles at this:

> Cela se peut, madame: on ne voit pas les cœurs;
> Mais votre charité se serait bien passée
> De jeter dans le mien une telle pensée.

The "on ne voit pas les cœurs" is a defence mechanism: it
describes exactly what Alceste wants to know and directs his attention uncomfortably back to his own doubts. The damage is done
in spite of his protests:

> Non; mais sur ce sujet, quoi que l'on nous expose,
> Les doutes sont fâcheux plus que toute autre chose;
> Et je voudrais, pour moi, qu'on ne me fît savoir
> Que ce qu'avec clarté l'on peut me faire voir.

Arsinoé gleefully undertakes the job—on condition that he goes
home with her:

> Là je vous ferai voir une preuve fidèle
> De l'infidélité du cœur de votre belle;
> Et si pour d'autres yeux le vôtre peut brûler,
> On pourra vous offrir de quoi vous consoler.

She is extremely successful in giving Célimène away, but not
in replacing her. In the last two acts Molière rings the changes so
rapidly, the feelings are so complex, that one is doubtful whether
"comic," "moving" or "horrible" is the proper description of some
of the scenes.

"The whole misfortune of Alceste," writes M. Mauriac, "of that
Alceste who is in all of us, lies in a psychological need of the absolute
that we bring to love which is the most relative of human feelings.

Alceste angrily brushes aside all false appearances; he is determined to advance on firm ground into this *pays du Tendre* which is essentially the home of fickleness and change; and it is precisely because it is the home of fickleness and change that it is the domain of Célimène."[1]

Alceste's

> Non; j'ai résolu de n'en pas faire un pas.
> J'ai tort ou j'ai raison,

of which I have already spoken, has its parallel in the story of his love affair. When he remarks

> Plus on aime quelqu'un, moins il faut qu'on le flatte:
> A ne rien pardonner le pur amour éclate,

his *pur amour* is the absolute love described by Mauriac, the absolute necessity of fixing his love in a formula and compelling the loved one to conform to it. It is here that he fails with Célimène. He feels that he is in the *domaine du mouvant*, that the ground is shifting under his feet, threatening to plunge him into chaos at any moment. When he discovers the letter to Oronte, he loses all control over himself; the whole universe rocks:

> . . . le déchaînement de toute la nature
> Ne m'accablerait pas comme cette aventure.

Éliante comes to the rescue with her moderate and reasonable

> Avez-vous, pour le croire, un juste fondement?

recalling the *solide et sincère* and the desperate hunt for a sound foundation of earlier scenes. This produces an extraordinary reaction in Alceste who suddenly sees in her a refuge against the devouring doubt. "You must avenge me, madame," he cries. "Avenge you, but how?"

> En recevant mon cœur.
> Acceptez-le, madame, au lieu de l'infidèle ;
> C'est par là que je puis prendre vengeance d'elle.

When we recall that Éliante is Alceste's one chance of salvation, we can appreciate the grimness of Molière's irony here.

It becomes clearer as the play draws towards its conclusion that

---

[1] *Journal*, II, pp. 151–2.

Célimène is a means to an end, that Alceste's chief preoccupation is deliverance from his own obsession, is a need to achieve a startling success to rehabilitate himself in the eyes of the world and to make himself feel that he is rooted in society:

> Ah! rien n'est comparable à mon amour extrême,
> Et, dans l'ardeur qu'il a de se montrer à tous,
> Il va jusqu'à former des souhaits contre vous.
> Oui, je voudrais qu'aucun ne vous trouvât aimable,
> Que vous fussiez réduite en un sort misérable,
> Que le Ciel, en naissant, ne vous eût donné rien,
> Que vous n'eussiez ni rang, ni naissance, ni bien,
> Afin que de mon cœur l'éclatant sacrifice
> Vous pût d'un pareil sort réparer l'injustice,
> Et que j'eusse la joie et la gloire, en ce jour,
> De vous voir tenir tout des mains de mon amour.

This shows to what extent Alceste lives in a private world, how impossible it is to prevent the "quelque chose en soi de noble et d'héroïque" from being swamped and destroyed by his eccentricities. For he is obliged to invent a situation, in which he can repair imaginary injustices by imaginary sacrifices, to convince himself not merely of the reality of his own feelings, but of his very existence.

While Alceste is hunting desperately to discover some sure foundation in the *domaine du mouvant*, Célimène is clinging no less tenaciously to her shifting, changing world. For her whole existence depends on maintaining a state of doubt—doubt about her own feelings, doubt in the minds of her retainers about her feelings for them. When Alceste and Oronte deliver their ultimatum—"Choose between us two"—it is she who assumes the role of a trapped animal, or perhaps of the trapped butterfly, struggling desperately to avoid a commitment:

> Mon Dieu! que cette instance est là hors de saison,
> Et que vous témoignez, tous deux, peu de raison!
> Je sais prendre parti sur cette préférence,
> Et ce n'est pas mon cœur maintenant qui balance:
> Il n'est point suspendu, sans doute, entre vous deux,
> Et rien n'est si tôt fait que le choix de nos vœux.
> Mais je souffre, à vrai dire, une gêne trop forte
> A prononcer en face un aveu de la sorte:

Je trouve que ces mots, qui sont désobligeants,
Ne se doivent point dire en présence des gens;
Qu'un cœur de son penchant donne assez de lumière,
Sans qu'on nous fasse aller jusqu'à rompre en visière;
Et qu'il suffit enfin que de plus doux témoins
Instruisent un amant du malheur de ses soins.

Finally, when she can no longer avoid making a choice, she discovers that she does not love Alceste enough to follow him into his desert, and his vanity is too great to allow of any compromise:

La solitude effraye une âme de vingt ans;
Je ne sens point la mienne assez grande, assez forte,
Pour me résoudre à prendre un dessein de la sorte . . .

6

I have already spoken of the differences between the *Misanthrope* and Molière's other plays. When the curtain comes down on the *École des femmes*, *Tartuffe*, *l'Avare* and *les Femmes savantes*, the audience is left in no doubt about the author's intentions. It is able to "determine . . . exactly what attitude is broken down and what takes its place." In *Tartuffe* religious mania is satirized, a criminal is brought to book and the play closes with the triumph of society.

The same cannot be said of the *Misanthrope*. Molière has richly fulfilled his intention of speaking *contre les mœurs du siècle*; but the doubt, which is an integral part of our experience, persists. We are, perhaps, able to determine what attitude is broken down, but it is less easy to decide what takes its place. It is idle to pretend that order is re-established and that a chastened buffoon is brought back to the norm of sanity. At the close of the play society, in the persons of Célimène and her retainers, leaves by one exit and Alceste abandons society by another, leaving an empty stage. The line that echoes in the mind is not profession of belief, but a profession of complete disbelief, is not Philinte's

La parfaite raison fuit toute extrémité,

but Alceste's

Mais la raison n'est pas ce qui règle l'amour.

Indeed, so far from ending in another triumph for *la parfaite raison*, it is *la parfaite raison* which dissolves into Alceste's

> Mes sens par la raison ne sont plus gouvernés.

Ramon Fernandez seems to put his finger on the point when, in the course of his stimulating but highly erratic study of Molière, he remarks that Molière lived in an age of intellectual scepticism. For when one considers the play as a whole, it is difficult not to feel that Molière had come to share Alceste's own scepticism. The *honnête homme* no doubt contributes to the poise of each of the plays in which he appears, but his urbane, polished discourses never succeed in converting anyone; and even in *Tartuffe* conversion is brought about by a sudden change of situation—the intervention of the "great Prince"—and not by Cléante. In the *Misanthrope*, more than in any of the other plays, the *honnête homme* is a symbolical figure and Molière is particularly careful to avoid the appearance of imposing a solution. The most that he does is to suggest that a blending of the virtues of Philinte and Éliante may have some bearing on the complicated situation which he has created. In no other play does he reveal such variety and complexity of feelings, but in no other does he show such reluctance to judge the individual or so marked a tendency to call in question all accepted standards and formulas. It is a masterly exploration of the motives behind social behaviour; feelings are tracked down, as surely as in Racine, to the moment of their formation; but judgment on them is suspended. There is in truth no formal ending to the play. The cartharsis lies in the clarifying of our feelings, in the perception that social adjustment is a personal matter where in the last resort no facile slogan or philosophical system can help us; and the "message," if we must have one, is that we must have the courage to create our own "order," whatever the cost, instead of yielding to the temptation of an easy escape.

VI. THE LAST PHASE

1

Le Misanthrope was produced in 1666, but though it was on the whole well received it was not the brilliant success that Molière had hoped. He seems to have divined the reasons and he was not slow to take the hint. He wrote fifteen plays after the *Misanthrope*, but though *George Dandin, l'Avare, le Bourgeois Gentilhomme, les Femmes savantes* and *le Malade imaginaire* are clearly the work of a master at the height of his powers and possess all Molière's wit and gaiety and his zest for demolishing middle-class complacency, there is for the most part an unmistakable change in the quality. He must have perceived that in the *Misanthrope* he had written something which was "above the heads" of many of his audience. In the last plays we have the impression that he is deliberately avoiding the depths which he had explored in *Tartuffe* and the *Misanthrope*, that he is keeping near the surface, and the introduction of a ballet into some of the plays seems to me to be the sign of a desire to please his audience and to ensure that his plays were a popular success.

George Dandin, which was produced in 1668, is one of the most curious of Molière's works. It is the story of a *déclassement*, of the decent, prosperous peasant who has married into a family which is socially above him. The sub-title of the play is "le Mari confondu," and though Molière exposes the snobbish pretentiousness of the urban middle classes with all his old skill, it is privilege which wins in the end. There is a bitterness and a depth of feeling beneath the brittle gaiety of the play which suggest that Molière drew heavily on his personal experience. Outwardly George Dandin bears very little resemblance to his creator, but it is worth noticing that he is a completely sympathetic figure and that the satirical quality which we find in the portraits of Arnolphe and Argan is absent. When he declares in the closing lines of the play:

"Ah! je la quitte maintenant, et je n'y vois plus de remède. Lorsqu'on a, comme moi, épousé une méchante femme, le meilleur parti qu'on puisse prendre, c'est de s'aller jeter dans l'eau la tête la première"

—it is the greyness of death and despair which suddenly, incongruously, breaks through into the comic world.

In the *Femmes savantes* Molière deals effectively with intellectual pretentiousness. Philaminte is a brilliant study of the *bas bleu*, of the woman who two hundred years later will develop into the nineteenth-century "progressive" and, later still, into the suffragette and the apostle of sex reform. The attack on the pedants is deadly, but it leaves us with the impression that Molière is, perhaps, playing down to his audience. In the exposure of the folly and conceit of Trissotin and Vadius we miss the assertion of positive standards that we find in the scene in the *Misanthrope* in which Alceste disposes of Oronte's sonnet and provides us with an excellent piece of literary criticism. It is only in the character of Armande, of which I have already spoken, that Molière forgets his resolution and lets himself go.

L'Avare, which had been produced four years earlier, leaves us with a similar impression. Harpagon is a monster, but Molière takes care to make him a comic monster, and the comment on his horses by one of the servants turns something which is potentially horrible into pure comedy:

"Vos chevaux, monsieur? Ma foi, ils ne sont point du tout en état de marcher. Je ne vous dirai point qu'ils sont sur la litière: les pauvres bêtes n'en ont point, et ce serait fort mal parler; mais vous leur faites observer des jeûnes si austères, que ce ne sont plus rien que des idées ou des fantômes, des façons de chevaux."

The high light of *l'Avare* is the great scene at the end of Act IV where Harpagon discovers the loss of his money, which is one of the most impressive that Molière ever wrote:

HARPAGON (*Il crie "Au voleur!" dès le jardin, et vient sans chapeau*):
    Au voleur! au voleur! à l'assassin! au meurtrier! Justice, juste
    Ciel! Je suis perdu, je suis assassiné, on m'a coupé la gorge, on m'a
    dérobé mon argent. Qui peut-ce être? Qu'est-il devenu? Où est-il?
    Où se cache-t-il? Que ferai-je pour le trouver? Où courir? Où ne
    pas courir? N'est-il point là? N'est-il point ici? Qui est-ce? Arrête.
    Rends-moi mon argent, coquin. . . . (*Il se prend lui-même le bras.*)
    Ah! c'est moi. Mon esprit est troublé, et j'ignore où je suis, qui je
    suis, et ce que je fais. Hélas! mon pauvre argent, mon pauvre argent,
    mon cher ami! on m'a privé de toi; et puisque tu m'es enlevé, j'a

perdu mon support, ma consolation, ma joie; tout est fini pour moi, et je n'ai plus que faire au monde! Sans toi, il m'est impossible de vivre. C'en est fait, je n'en puis plus; je me meurs, je suis mort, je suis enterré. N'y a-t-il personne qui veuille me ressusciter, en me rendant mon cher argent, ou en m'apprenant qui l'a pris? Euh? que dites-vous? Ce n'est personne. Il faut, qui que ce soit qui ait fait le coup, qu'avec beaucoup de soin on ait épié l'heure; et l'on a choisi justement le temps que je parlais à mon traître de fils. Sortons. Je veux aller quérir la justice, et faire donner la question à toute ma maison: à servantes, à valets, à fils, à fille, et à moi aussi. Que de gens assemblés! Je ne jette mes regards sur personne qui ne me donne des soupçons, et tout me semble mon voleur. Eh! de quoi est-ce qu'on parle là? De celui qui m'a dérobé? Quel bruit fait-on là-haut? Est-ce mon voleur qui y est? De grâce, si l'on sait des nouvelles de mon voleur, je supplie que l'on m'en dise. N'est-il point caché là parmi vous? Ils me regardent tous, et se mettent à rire. Vous verrez qu'ils ont part, sans doute, au vol que l'on m'a fait. Allons vite, des commissaires, des archers, des prévôts, des juges, des gênes, des potences et des bourreaux. Je veux faire pendre tout le monde; et si je ne retrouve mon argent, je me pendrai moi-même après.

Harpagon's voice is heard before he appears on the stage, and the long-drawn-out vowel sounds of *Au voleur!* give the impression of a dirge. There is a sudden change to the short i's as he arrives on the stage, and the dirge becomes an hysterical scream. The conjunction of "on m'a coupé la gorge, on m'a dérobé mon argent" betrays a complete confusion of values and marks the point at which the real world changes into the world of the comic nightmare. The confusion of mind grows with "Où courir? Où ne pas courir?" The disintegration of language and the tendency of words to lose their rational meaning reflect the disintegration of the world of common experience in Harpagon's mind. The scene takes on a sinister, macabre aspect when he suddenly grasps his own arm, thinking that he has caught the thief—"Rends-moi mon argent, coquin." There follows one of those lucid moments which always come to Molière's great comic characters at the height of the *délire* and which intensify its effect: "Ah! c'est moi. Mon esprit est troublé." This moment, when the comic character suddenly sees himself from the standpoint of the normal person, is one of the clearest signs of Molière's genius. The glimpse is only momentary and the tone sinks to a senile, blubbering wail: "Hélas! mon pauvre argent, mon pauvre argent, mon cher ami, on m'a privé de toi. . . ." The money has clearly usurped the place of family and friends, and we recall that his cruelty to his children is one of the miser's most hateful traits. The seriousness of his condition is heightened by the fantasy of

"Je me meurs, je suis mort, je suis enterré. N'y a-t-il personne qui veuille me ressusciter, en me rendant mon cher argent . . ."

The irony lies in the fact that it is his money which is destroying him, eating up his life; its return can only enclose him more firmly in a private world, and this is what happens at the end of the play.

Harpagon is clearly the victim of persecution mania, and he imagines that he is surrounded by a vast number of people who are all guilty in some way of the theft of his money. He strikes the macabre note again when he proceeds to address the silent, motionless figures of the nightmare.

"Que de gens assemblés . . . De grâce, si l'on sait des nouvelles de mon voleur, je supplie que l'on m'en dise."

Suddenly the silent throng seems to come to life:

"Ils me regardent tous, et se mettent à rire"

—he imagines himself in the midst of a laughing, jeering crowd of thieves.

The passage reaches its climax in the immense exaggeration of:

"Allons vite, des commissaires, des archers, des prévôts, des juges, des gênes, des potences et des bourreaux. Je veux faire pendre tout le monde; et si je ne retrouve mon argent, je me pendrai moi-même après."

His private misfortune becomes a universal catastrophe. In his delirium, he assembles the shadow armies of justice to execute the phantoms that he imagines in front of him and proposes to commit suicide afterwards.

No one can doubt the impressiveness of this scene, but it knocks the rest of the play sideways.[1]

[1] It is well known that the play is an adaptation of Plautus's *Aulularia*, but Gutkind's comparison between this passage and the original on which it was based emphasizes the brilliance of the achievement. (V. *op. cit.*, p. 38.)

2

In 1665 Molière suffered a serious breakdown in health and placed himself under the care of M. de Mauvillain. He became more or less of an invalid, was shortly afterwards put permanently on a milk diet and was never really out of the doctors' hands until his death in 1673.

It seems at first surprising that a writer who so consistently poked fun at doctors, who in *Dom Juan* had denounced their art as *pure grimace* and professed a belief in nature's power to bring about her own cures without the aid of medicine, should have entrusted himself to doctors at all and should have been on excellent terms with his own physician. The explanation is probably to be found in a scene of the *Malade imaginaire* where Béralde declares:

"Ce ne sont point les médecins qu'il [Molière] joue, mais le ridicule de la médecine."

It was the same argument that he had used when he was accused of attacking religion in *Tartuffe* and it seems to me to be equally convincing.

The outcome of Molière's illness was obvious. He was a man of wide culture and took a lively interest in every aspect of social life. It was only natural that his personal contact with doctors should have stimulated his interest in medicine, and that he should have introduced what was after all one of the "burning questions" of the day into his plays.

The doctor, in his tall pointed hat and long black cloak riding round on a mule to visit his patients, was one of the stock figures of seventeenth-century comedy which had inherited it from the Commedia dell' Arte. He makes his appearance in Molière's early plays, but he bears only a superficial resemblance to the doctors in *l'Amour médecin* and *le Malade imaginaire*. The doctor in *la Jalousie du barbouillé*, for example, is none other than the stage Pedant who was a perennial figure of fun in the old farces. It is his long pompous speeches with their endless Latin tags which make him funny; the fact that he is a doctor is a matter of secondary importance. It is far otherwise in the last plays where Molière treats the abuses of the profession with the same seriousness that he had treated other abuses in his earlier plays.

Medical science has advanced so rapidly since the seventeenth century that we are in danger of missing the implications of Molière's criticism and of mistaking his plays about doctors for good-humoured skits. They are far from being that. The conference of doctors in *l'Amour médecin* and the consultation in *le Malade imaginaire* are in no way burlesque. They erred if anything on the side of leniency. The state of the profession was something which is scarcely credible to us to-day. A gullible public was impressed by the elaborate ceremonial and the air of learning assumed by the profession, and treated the pronouncements of doctors with the same uncritical respect that we give to those of scientists in our own time. Their confidence, however, was rudely shaken by a series of scandals. In 1666 Paris had been profoundly shocked by a series of notorious bedside disputations at which eminent doctors had differed violently over the nature of the illness and its treatment while the unfortunate patients lay dying. Desfourgerais, one of the King's physicians, was openly accused by Bussy Rabutin of practising abortion. Guénot, another of them, who had a passion for antimony, was charged with having killed his wife, daughter, nephew, two sons-in-law and a host of other patients with his famous remedy. He attended Mazarin in his last illness, and it is reported that when he was caught in a traffic jam on his way home, a carter who recognized him shouted cheerfully to the assembled crowd: "Way, there, for his honour. It's the good doctor who killed the Cardinal." Still another of the royal physicians, Vallot, was a few years later publicly credited with the death of Queen Henrietta of England.

"Public opinion as to the value of medicine," wrote Palmer, "wavered between blind faith and nervous mockery. Louis XIV might laugh at a travesty of his physicians in ordinary, but he was obliged to entrust his life into their hands, and they got him at last. . . .

"Louis XIV was tortured and misused by a succession of doctors whose proceedings would have been incredible to posterity—had they not left a minute record of their grotesque proceedings. The curious may still read the *Journal de la Santé du Roi* in which Vallot, Daquin and Fagon in turn exhibit with a dreadful complacency the wonders of their science. It is clear from the *Journal* that the King, apart from the fact that he

uffered from worms—a circumstance which made the royal appetite the
wonder and envy of the realm—had a magnificent constitution, and
could only with the greatest difficulty be reduced and kept by his doctors
n the condition of a chronic invalid. He should never have needed a
doctor, but he was seldom out of their hands. Finally, they contrived,
by a course of purging, bleeding, blistering and sweating which would
have killed any ordinary man in his prime, to remove him from the world
n the seventy-second year of his reign with all his organs still sound as
a bell but naturally a little fatigued from the constant 'refreshment'—
t is the favourite word of Daquin—which had been lavished on them
for over forty years. The royal dentists had by this time removed his
eeth and perforated his palate so that he could no longer masticate or
even taste his food. Nothing in the comedies of Molière concerning the
doctors of the period exceeds the fantastical reality as disclosed in this
professional record and in none of his attacks upon contemporary preju-
dices does he keep more strictly to the sober facts of the case."[1]

Such is the background of Molière's attack on the doctors.
Although doctors appear frequently in the plays written after 1664
and *Dom Juan* and *l'Amour médecin* both contain some very perti-
nent criticisms of the profession, it is to his last play—*le Malade
imaginaire*—that we must turn for the fullest and most searching
examination of the place of medicine in society. M. Diafoirus and
his appalling son are among the most brilliant of Molière's minor
characters. The father boasts of his son's conservatism:

"... il s'attache aveuglément aux opinions de nos anciens ... jamais
l n'a voulu comprendre ni écouter les raisons et les expériences des
prétendues découvertes de notre siècle, touchant la circulation du sang
et autres opinions de la même farine."

In the course of his incredibly gauche proposal of marriage to
Argan's daughter, the son invites the company

"... à venir voir l'un de ces jours, pour vous divertir, la dissection
d'une femme sur quoi je dois raisonner."

These comments are deadly, but in this play the focus shifts
from the doctors to the patient. The play is, indeed, a remarkable
illustration of the way in which Molière not only used, but also
transmuted his personal experience in his work. It is, as Palmer

[1] *op. cit.*, pp. 350–1. (I am indebted to this writer's chapter on "The Impious
n Medicine" for most of the facts in this account of seventeenth-century
medicine.)

points out, the story of the death of Molière; and the way in which he puts himself into the play as the imaginary invalid is a singular example of the courage of a great writer. The play bears a marked resemblance to *Tartuffe*. In the earlier play he had studied the effects of extreme credulity in religion; in his last play he studies the same phenomenon in medicine. Argan's cult of ill-health and his faith in medical charlatans is similar to Orgon's cult of a debased religiosity and his naïve trust in the religious charlatan, and it has the same corrosive effect on his personality. When he explains his reasons for wishing to marry his daughter to the young Diafoirus by saying

"Ma raison est que, me voyant infirme et malade, comme je suis, je veux me faire un gendre et des alliés médecins, afin de m'appuyer de bons secours contre ma maladie, d'avoir dans ma famille les sources de remèdes qui me sont nécessaires, et d'être à même des consultations et des ordonnances"

—we see at once that he is living in a world of fantasy, that his supposed illness insulates him as effectively from the world of common experience as Orgon's religion or Harpagon's avarice.

The heart of the play, however, is the scene between Argan and his brother:

BÉRALDE:
J'entends, mon frère, que je ne vois point d'homme qui soit moins malade que vous, et que je ne demanderais point une meilleure constitution que la vôtre. Une grande marque que vous vous portez bien, et que vous avez un corps parfaitement bien composé, c'est qu'avec tous les soins que vous avez pris, vous n'avez pu parvenir encore à gâter la bonté de votre tempérament, et que vous n'êtes point crevé de toutes les médecines qu'on vous a fait prendre . .

ARGAN:
. . . Que faire donc, quand on est malade?

BÉRALDE:
Rien, mon frère.

ARGAN:
Rien?

BÉRALDE:
Rien. Il ne faut que demeurer en repos. La nature, d'elle-même quand nous la laissons faire, se tire doucement du désordre où elle est tombée. C'est notre inquiétude, c'est notre impatience qui gâte

tout, et presque tous les hommes meurent de leurs remèdes, et non pas de leurs maladies.

ARGAN:

Mais il faut demeurer d'accord, mon frère, qu'on peut aider cette nature par de certaines choses.

BÉRALDE:

Mon Dieu! mon frère, ce sont pures idées, dont nous aimons à nous repaître; et, de tout temps, il s'est glissé parmi les hommes de belles imaginations, que nous venons à croire, parce qu'elles nous flattent et qu'il serait à souhaiter qu'elles fussent véritables ... lorsqu'il [le médecin] vous parle de rectifier le sang, de tempérer les entrailles et le cerveau, de dégonfler la rate, de raccommoder la poitrine, de réparer le foie, de fortifier le cœur, de rétablir et conserver la chaleur naturelle, et d'avoir des secrets pour étendre la vie à de longues années; il vous dit justement le roman de la médecine.

This sounds like Molière's usual methods applied to medicine, or rather to what he calls *le roman de la médecine*; and while this is true, we perceive that he strikes a fresh note in this scene. Béralde is Molière's spokesman as surely as Cléante in *Tartuffe*; but it must be remembered that though Molière was never tempted to indulge in the extravagances of Orgon or to join the *dévots*, he was a very sick man when he wrote *le Malade imaginaire*. It seems to me that the scene between Béralde and Argan is not the usual exchange between the author and his victim, but a dialogue of the artist with himself. For Molière is both Béralde and Argan. Béralde stands for the normal, healthy impulses in Molière's own character and his zest for life; Argan is the sick Molière, is a projection of corrupt tendencies which he may have felt were present in him or of what he may have regarded as a temptation. The whole scene is a dramatic struggle between sickness and health. We see Molière turning his own weapons against himself; we see Molière in his prime ironically chiding the sick Molière, telling him that he must get a grip on himself, that he mustn't brood over his ailment, that there's precious little wrong with him, that all he needs to do is to empty his medicine bottles down the drain, send the doctors away and give nature a chance.

The projection of this personal conflict into the play gives it its special poignancy, and the climax is reached in the final exchanges between Béralde and Argan:

F

BÉRALDE:

> ... j'aurais souhaité de pouvoir un peu vous tirer de l'erreur où vous êtes, et, pour vous divertir, vous mener voir sur ce chapitre quelqu'une des comédies de Molière.

ARGAN:

> C'est un bon impertinent que votre Molière avec ses comédies, et je le trouve bien plaisant d'aller jouer d'honnêtes gens comme les médecins.

BÉRALDE:

> Ce ne sont point les médecins qu'il joue, mais le ridicule de la médecine . . .

ARGAN:

> Par la mort non de diable! si j'étais que des médecins, je me vengerais de son impertinence; et quand il sera malade, je le laisserais mourir sans secours. Il aurait beau faire et beau dire, je ne lui ordonnerais pas la moindre petite saignée, le moindre petit lavement, et je lui dirais: "Crève, crève! cela t'apprendra une autre fois à te jouer à la Faculté." . . .

BÉRALDE:

> Il sera encore plus sage que vos médecins, car il ne leur demandera point de secours.

ARGAN:

> Tant pis pour lui, s'il n'a point recours aux remèdes.

BÉRALDE:

> Il a ses raisons pour n'en point vouloir, et il soutient que cela n'est permis qu'aux gens vigoureux et robustes, et qui ont des forces de reste pour porter les remèdes avec la maladie; mais que, pour lui, il n'a justement de la force que pour porter son mal.

The sequel was a tragic one. A week after the first production of *le Malade imaginaire*, Molière was obviously ailing. Armande and his friend Baron begged him not to play that night. The reply was characteristic of the man:

"What do you expect me to do? There are fifty poor workers who have only their daily wage to live on. What will become of them if the performance does not take place? I could not forgive myself for failing to support them for a single day if it were humanly possible to do so."[1]

During the performance he became seriously ill, but he went on to the end of the play. When he left the stage he collapsed and had to be carried to his lodging. His last words to Armande and Baron

[1] Grimarest quoted by Mauriac, *Trois grands hommes devant Dieu*, Paris 1930, p. 50.

recall Béralde's: "Il n'a justement de la force que pour porter son mal":

"When my life was evenly divided between pleasure and pain, I thought myself happy; but now that I am weighed down by suffering without being able to count on a moment's comfort or relief, I see that the time has come to throw in my hand. I cannot hold out any longer against the pain which never leaves me a second's respite."[1]

A few minutes later he was dead. There was no time for "la moindre petite saignée" or "le moindre petit lavement."

3

I have made extensive use of the word *malade* in discussing the characteristics of Molière's art, but though this is his own word it needs to be used with great circumspection. I do not wish to give the impression that I regard the plays as case-books or as studies in abnormal psychology which anticipate the methods and findings of the modern novelist. The eccentricities and social abuses which he criticizes are placed in their true perspective. They are seen to be flaws in an otherwise healthy organism. For Molière believed in his age in a way that is impossible for the contemporary writer. In spite of the wealth of detail with which they described the life of their time, the great French novelists who came after Constant and Stendhal—Balzac, Flaubert and Proust—do not seem to me to be the heirs of Molière. They are much closer to Racine. Their work is in the main a study of *une maladie des sentiments* which sometimes bears a superficial resemblance to Molière's approach, but their concentration on one aspect of their characters is so complete that the *sentiment* tends to dissolve into the *maladie*. Flaubert's description of Frédéric Moreau at the end of *l'Education sentimentale* might well serve as an epigraph for them all: "La véhémence du désir, la fleur même de la sensation était perdue." This limits their value as social criticism and, indeed, as criticism of any kind. For the more we read them, the more evident it becomes that their sensibility only touches life at comparatively few points. They do not show the human being with his foibles and his passions—the character-

[1] *ibid.*, p. 46.

istics which alternately join him to and divide him from society —in relation to an existing order as Molière does. They are only interested in him in so far as he is the product of his immediate environment and his feelings are conditioned and corrupted by it. The accent should, therefore, fall on the breadth and variety of Molière's vision of man and society, on his sense of society as a coherent whole, on his fundamental sanity and on that wisdom which belongs peculiarly to the great European masters.

JEAN RACINE

"Dans Racine, je vois la passion toute pure et sans contre-poids. Ni le devoir, ni la religion, ni la politique ne balancent la passion un seul moment. De là que Racine est si vrai et si grand et si terrible."
—ANDRÉ SUARÈS : *Xénies*

I. THE SOCIAL SCENE

1

WHEN Corneille, very old, very lonely and very grand, nodded his head solemnly over a performance of *Britannicus* and complained that the author dwelt too much on the *faiblesses* of human nature, he spoke for a large body of influential people. They were shocked by the violence of Racine's tragedies and by the poet's apparent indifference to the ideal of "honour" which had had a long and successful run on the seventeenth-century stage. It was difficult for Corneille himself to be fair to the young man who was taking his place in the affections of the coming generation and who made little attempt to conceal his contempt for all that Corneille had stood for. And a man of Racine's temperament was not likely to forget or forgive Corneille's patronizing comment on his early work: "Young man," he had said, "you have no gift for the theatre."

Corneille's admirers stood loyally by him and professed to discover a new and subtle beauty in his later work, but it may be doubted whether their applause was altogether successful in reassuring him. For in his later plays the familiar voice of the old poet had become harsh and strained, and the ideals which had been a magnificent inspiration in the *Cid* and *Polyeucte* had grown a little hollow.

At bottom the problem was not a personal one; it arose from the clash between two generations rather than from the clash between two temperaments. "In spite of the success which still greeted his work," wrote Pierre Lièvre, "people began to feel that the atmosphere of the century was no longer the same."[1] It would be difficult to put the matter better or more fairly. Although Corneille and Racine lived in the same century, they belonged to different ages.

[1] *Corneille: Théâtre Complet* (Bibliothèque de la Pléiade), I, p. 12.

Corneille's work marks the end of the old age and Racine's the beginning of a new. Corneille did not see—perhaps did not wish to see—that he stood on the threshold of a new age bringing fresh problems which demanded fresh solutions.

The mistake has been a common one, and Racine's true role has not always been appreciated by his critics. The nineteenth century saw clearly that his poetry was the direct expression of the life of his time, but when Sainte-Beuve declared that this poetry was the product of "le commerce paisible de cette société où une femme écrivait *la Princesse de Clèves*," we may conclude that his reading of the age was at fault.[1] It was Sainte-Beuve and Taine who created the "tender Racine," the neat and accomplished craftsman whose poetry reflected the elegance of the Court of King Louis—an elegance which seemed a little faded to those who were accustomed to the revolutions of the nineteenth century and whose ears were too familiar with the thud of Hugo's rhetoric to appreciate the subtler Racine.

In our own time we may flatter ourselves that we have reached a truer estimate of Racine's genius. The "tender Racine" of the nineteenth-century myth has been swept away to be replaced by the "implacable Racine" whose ferocity delights our age as it shocked Racine's own. Yet the old error reappears in another form. Jean Giraudoux, who has done full justice to Racine's ferocity, tells us that there is not a sentiment in his work which is not a literary sentiment and that it contains no trace of the great movements of his time which have left their mark on the letters of Madame de Sévigné.[2]

Racine's great gifts—his honesty and integrity, his clarity and critical detachment—are so badly needed at the present time that it is worth while insisting on a neglected aspect of his genius. So far from being the laureate of Versailles, he was (whether consciously or not) the critic of an age of false stability. He exposed the corruption of the Court in *Britannicus* and more pointedly in *Athalie*; but as a rule he did not refer directly to political events. He was more concerned with "the atmosphere of the century," with the

[1] As a corrective to the genteel, anaemic society described by Sainte-Beuve and Taine, see the valuable collection of documents in Félix Gaiffe's *l'Envers du grand siècle*, Paris, 1924, *passim*.

[2] *Racine*, Eng. tr., Cambridge, 1938, p. 7.

changes that were taking place in the moral life of the people. Because the seventeenth century in France was one of the greatest centuries in European literature, it does not follow that the social order which produced this literature was sound or healthy. "Louis XIV made a mess—but there was *Phèdre*," wrote Mr. E. M. Forster.[1] In spite of its outward magnificence, the age of Louis XIV was beginning to disintegrate from within, and in order to appreciate the nature of the process we must go behind Racine's poetry and look at the conditions in which he wrote and perhaps at the man himself.

"The seventeenth century," writes an historian, "is peculiarly baffling because it appears on the surface so simple. It is simple because the *Mémoires* dealing with the upper classes are as excellent as they are numerous: it is difficult because the peasant and the tradesman of the period are elusive persons who will not stand and deliver any information about themselves."[2] We may think that though this is part of the difficulty, it is only a part. The difficulty does not lie least in the nature of the sources. Madame de Sévigné and Saint-Simon were essentially *individualists*. Their aim was not to write a history of their times. It was, in Saint-Simon's own words (which are as true of the letter-writer as of the memoir-writer), to give an account of their own lives which included "tout ce qui a un rapport particulier à moi et aussi un peu en général et superficiellement une espèce de relation des événements de ces temps, principalement des choses de la Cour."[3] They were almost exclusively concerned with personalities and events which had a strict bearing on their own lives and feelings. They have left us a picture of unsurpassed vividness of what happened to them and what interested them. We follow the trial of Fouquet with breathless interest in the *Letters* and we share Madame de Sévigné's hopes and fears; we know from the *Mémoires* exactly how Fénelon looked when he made a public retraction after the condemnation of some of his writings by the Holy See; we see every gesture and we almost catch the intonation of his voice; but it was no part of the writers' intention to indicate the precise significance or the causes of those events.

[1] "The New Disorder" in *Horizon*, IV, No. 24, December, 1941.
[2] Hugon, *Social France in the Seventeenth Century*, London, 1911, p. 7.
[3] *Mémoires* (ed. Chéruel et Régnier), I, Paris, 1889, p. 28.

Another thing that makes the seventeenth century difficult to understand is the preponderance of Versailles which was in reality a vast façade, a symbol of outward splendour that hid an interior deterioration. The stage is so crowded with Kings, Princes, Bishops and Ambassadors that we do not at first notice the absentees or grasp the meaning of the intrigues which are recounted with such wealth of detail. It is only later that we perceive the significance of the spectacle and the way in which these events fit into the complete pattern of the century. Nothing appears to matter except Madame de Sévigné's emotion on becoming a grandmother, or the mixture of vexation and amusement with which she learns that her son has contracted a disgraceful malady, or the disputes over whose turn it was to hold His Majesty's nightshirt.

It is only occasionally that the even flow in the *Letters* is disturbed by a deeper note which betrays the weariness, the sadness, of what Paul Bourget called in a different context *une civilisation vieillissante.* "Il semble qu'il n'y ait plus qu'à nous faire enterrer," she writes in a letter to Madame de La Fayette. And when she remarks in another letter: "The balls at Saint-Germain are of a deadly sadness," we seem to catch a prophetic glimpse of the courtiers, their faces weary and drawn beneath their make-up, as they revolve mechanically round the doddering monarch.[1]

Saint-Simon belongs to a later generation than Madame de Sévigné. The process of decay had become more evident when he wrote his great work, and though he, too, relies for the most part on indirect criticism, his indictment is more radical. His *Mémoires* are often biased and inaccurate; a great deal of his bitterness is that of an able man whose abilities found no outlet in a period of corruption and incompetence; but the bitterness is not merely personal. The remorselessness with which he strips away the gorgeous clothing to reveal the ugliness of his victims; the satisfaction with which he lifts the veil to show a noble lady relieving herself in church and the way in which he rakes the muck-heap in his hunt for a suitable epithet to point the contrast between the pretence

[1] *cf.*   Enfin je me dérobe à la joie importune
              De tant d'amis nouveaux que me fait la fortune;
              Je fuis de leurs respects l'inutile longueur,
              Pour chercher un ami qui me parle du cœur.
                                        (*Bérénice*, Act I. Sc. iv.)
       See, too, Funck-Brentano, *La Cour du Roi Soleil*, Paris, 1937, pp. 194–200.

and the reality, give an extraordinary feeling of the atmosphere of his times. In spite of the difference of style, his findings differ little from Racine's; and his final summing-up of the age—particularly the contrast between the confusion of the time and the order of his art—might serve as an epigraph for the tragedies.

"Since at the time of which I have written," he says, "particularly towards the end, everything was falling into a state of decadence, confusion and chaos which has grown steadily worse until the most complete and universal ignorance has extended its empire everywhere; and since these Memoirs stand for order, law, truth and fixed principles, it follows that [if given to the public] this mirror of truth would cause a general uproar."[1]

"La Cour," he wrote in another place, "fut un autre manège de la politique du despotisme." This sentence goes to the roots of the trouble. The spiritual life of France was being strangled, the old social solidarity of the people was being undermined by a ruthless despotism. The policy of Louis XIV was to make France safe for dictatorship. The nobility was deprived of its functions and replaced by a bureaucracy to prevent it from becoming a challenge to the royal omnipotence.

The ruling classes were encouraged to pursue a life of reckless extravagance because a ruined nobility and a ruined bourgeoisie would be dependent on royal favours. The Court served another purpose. It not only impressed the world with the magnificence of the reign, but it also kept the nobility dancing attendance on the King's person instead of retiring to their estates where they might have become centres of independence and disaffection. The same policy was pursued, though with less success, in religion. Louis XIV tried to establish the Gallican Church in order to make his authority over the clergy absolute. He persecuted the Jansenists (in spite of their Gallican leanings) not because they could have threatened his power, but because to the despot any independent movement seemed a potential menace.

The results of this policy are clear, but they only became clear in the cataclysm which overtook France in the next century. The structure of society was disrupted. Men were cut off from their estates; they ceased to be human beings and were transformed into artificial people who were compelled to submit to an artificial code

[1] *op. cit.*, XIX, p. 222.

F*

of manners which fettered their minds as well as their bodies. They were made to live under the royal supervision to prevent them from finding time to plot against the régime in the fastness of their châteaux, so that the Court life served much the same purpose as the cult of marching in the Third Reich. All criticism was mercilessly suppressed with scarcely a pretence of justice. The courtiers became so used to playing a game that they lost their power of criticism unless they happened to be very exceptional people. Racine and Saint-Simon were accomplished courtiers, but because they were great men they managed to distinguish between their real and their artificial selves. Saint-Simon had to wait until after his death for the publication of his life work, and Racine's championship of a dissident minority, and possibly his outspoken criticism of the condition of the peasants, brought disgrace which is said to have hastened his death.

2

On the surface the middle classes present the same homogeneous appearance as the aristocracy. Paris seems at first to be a smart Renaissance city; we hear little of the murders and crimes that went on in its streets or of the unspeakably squalid life of many of its inhabitants or their strange vices.[1] We see only the prosperous bourgeois living in their solid houses, the stuffy, richly draped rooms with their heavy furniture where they entertained their friends to vast meals with elaborate ceremony. Their only interests seem to be their business, the marriage of their children and their prospects of obtaining an appointment at Court.

The reality was very different. The relations between the aristocracy and the middle classes were close and intricate. It was the middle classes which produced most of the great imaginative writers whose work showed the direction in which society was moving. For the middle classes were far less self-contained than they appeared to be. They were, as their name suggests, a fluctuating body and we can detect three main groups. There were the patricians who tended to rise out of their class, to intermarry with the aristocracy or like the writers to move in Court circles by virtue of their calling. At the other end of the scale were the provincials

[1] V. Gaiffe, *op. cit.*, chapter IV.

who were drifting towards the peasantry and who, living dim,
ignorant and impoverished on their farms, were the constant butt
of seventeenth-century wit. In between these two extremes came
the bourgeois proper—the doctors, lawyers and merchants. They
were prosperous, respectable and pious and had for many years
been the backbone, the true moral core, of France.

Corneille and Racine were both products of the middle classes,
but they belonged to different groups. Corneille was the laureate
of the bourgeoisie whose moral integrity he had celebrated in his
greatest plays. Racine was the pure patrician and his poetry has all
the characteristics of patrician art—the characteristics that we shall
find two hundred years later in the work of the Symbolists. It is
subtle, refined, individualist, is the art of a civilization which has
reached its zenith and is leaning towards its decline.

"Your goodness in asking me to tell you about my doings," wrote
the Cardinal de Retz to his patroness, "fills me with such gratitude and
such tenderness that I cannot help giving you an account of all my
thoughts; and I experience an unbelievable pleasure in searching for them
in the depths of my mind and in submitting them to your judgment."

It is this *plaisir incroyable* that a writer experiences in analysing
his own feelings, this conviction of the immense importance of his
findings for others, which more than anything stamps an art as
patrician. The focus was shifting from the bourgeoisie to the
patrician. The writer no longer thought of himself as a member of
a closely knit community; he had become an isolated individual
whose task was not to praise but to dissect society. His was the
voice of a society which was menaced, but which was not yet fully
aware of its danger.

It is commonly assumed that the art of the seventeenth century
was the art of an *élite* in which the people had no part. It is true
that apologists of Louis XIV have little to say of the famines,
slaughter and campaigns which ravaged the country; and the
sufferings of the peasantry, the most robust and worst-treated class
in France, seem no more than a distant echo in the writings of an
elegant civilization. The truth is less simple.[1] It is a curious fact

[1] Contemporaries had a good deal to say about them. La Bruyère described
them as "animaux farouches . . . répandus par la campagne, noirs, livides et
tout brûlés du soleil, attachés à la terre qu'ils fouillent et qu'ils remuent avec
une opiniâtreté invincible," and whose sufferings "saisissent le cœur."
V. Gaiffe, chapter VII.

that Corneille is far more "class-conscious" than Racine. In his poetry the people are treated as creatures of mere instinct, are always seen *collectively*. When properly led they may be a source of strength to the existing order and when left to their own devices they may overthrow it. Corneille's *confidents* are colourless people whose only function is to act as a foil to the heroes and heroines, to make the remark that will set the machinery of the great *tirades* in motion. In Racine they possess a distinct personality. They have that simplicity which belongs peculiarly to the peasantry—a simplicity which is derived from contact with the soil. They may, like Narcisse and Œnone, corrupt their masters through their own primitive cunning or they may be corrupted by them; but usually they represent a norm of sanity in a disordered world. It is they who, in lines which have a different *timbre* from the subtle speeches of their masters, warn them when they are about to set out on some dubious enterprise to satisfy selfish desires. The contrast between the two styles can be seen in the dialogue between Bérénice and Phénice:

PHÉNICE:

> Que je le plains! Tant de fidélité,
> Madame, méritait plus de prospérité.
> Ne le plaignez-vous pas?

BÉRÉNICE:

> Cette prompte retraite
> Me laisse, je l'avoue, une douleur secrète.

PHÉNICE:

> Je l'aurais retenu.

BÉRÉNICE:

> Qui? moi? le retenir?
> J'en dois perdre plutôt jusques au souvenir.
> Tu veux donc que je flatte une ardeur insensée?

PHÉNICE:

> Titus n'a point expliqué sa pensée.
> Rome vous voit, madame, avec des yeux jaloux;
> La rigueur de ses lois m'épouvante pour vous.
> L'hymen chez les Romains n'admet qu'une Romaine.
> Rome hait tous les rois, et Bérénice est reine.

In Phénice's words we detect the accent of the old French *bonne*, and she speaks with that wisdom and directness which belong to simple people.

We can go further than this. We can say that Racine's popularity is largely due to his power of discovering a common humanity beneath the refinements of civilization, of speaking of passion as directly to the flower-seller as to the intellectual. "For," said Mauriac in a reply to some tendentious criticism,

". . . Racine had to go as far afield as Epirus and Troezene in search of his Hermione and his Phèdre to enable the shoe-stitcher or the char-woman, as well as the idle rich, to recognize themselves in these princesses whose rank spared them the necessity of any other form of occupation. It must be emphasized that if the scales are weighted in Racine, they are weighted in favour of the people. A Hermione or a Roxane are of their very nature much closer to the people than they are to the world of fashion. . . . Hermione, with her moments of respect for Pyrrhus, her sudden changes from a tone of the utmost familiarity to formulas drawn from the protocol[1], shows the extent to which the royal princess is sub-merged beneath the abandoned woman. On the other hand, the poorest worker conceals a Racinian princess. What little working girl has not murmured more than once in her life phrases which echo almost word for word some line from Racine: 'Je ne t'ai point aimé, cruel? Qu'ai-je donc fait?' "[2]

Racine is not the preserve of a small intellectual *élite*. He belongs to the French people as Shakespeare belongs to the English. When one watches the French people going about their daily occupations, when one sees the *concierges* and the old women in carpet slippers trudging along the banks of the Seine with their shopping-bags, mothers and nurses sewing and talking while their children play in the Luxembourg, the schoolgirls passing with their vivid gestures, their shrill voices coming through the autumn gardens or whispering together with a gleam—at once "tender" and "implacable"—in their eyes, one knows that these are Racine's countrymen and not Shakespeare's, that they are the raw material of Racine's heroines and his *confidentes*.

We cannot speak of Corneille with the same confidence. His characters have the timelessness of great art; they command our admiration, but we admire them from a respectful distance. They are experts in morality who sometimes remind us of a prize team playing an exhibition match or showing how easy it really is to

[1] "ses alternatives de tutoiement passionné et de formules protocolaires."
[2] *Journal*, II, pp. 117–18.

overcome the obstacles which always bring us crashing to the ground. It is an impressive performance certainly and we realize, as we watch their feats with growing discouragement, that we shall never "make the grade." Then our discouragement changes to a different feeling. For in our hearts we know that we do not really want to "make the grade." We turn, with a guilty sigh and a sense of great relief, to Racine. These princes and princesses are, after all, people like ourselves, are "our sort." They fail ingloriously at all the obstacles; they invariably yield to every temptation, and "honour" is soundly beaten every time. They are more than companions; they are accomplices whose voices insinuate themselves into our conscience asking why we worry over the obstacles, why we bother to resist instead of keeping our eye on the "prey."[1]

Of all the great French classics Racine is the most seductive as he is the most subversive. That his plays are considered fit instruction for the young while Baudelaire is banished from the academic syllabus can only be a source of amused surprise to anyone who understands his work; and that his reconciliation with Port-Royal should have been brought about through *Phèdre* is simply the best of all literary jokes.

3

French literature in the seventeenth century cannot be fully appreciated unless we know something of the religious dissensions of the time and unless full weight is given to the fact that Corneille was a pupil of the Jesuits and Racine a pupil of Port-Royal.

There were two main divisions within the Church—the Ultramontanes led by the Jesuits, and the Jansenists whose headquarters were at the Abbey of Port-Royal-des-Champs. There is no need to enter into the details of the doctrinal controversy. From a literary point of view only one difference seriously concerns us. The teaching of the Jesuits laid great stress on the importance of free-will, on the co-operation of the human will with Divine grace in the work of the Redemption. Man had fallen, but his nature was not completely ruined by the Fall, for his sin had been redeemed by the

---

[1] "Corneille nous assujettit à ses caractères et à ses idées, Racine se conforme aux nôtres . . ." (La Bruyère).

sacrifice of Christ. This was in essence a Christian optimism. It encouraged men to hope and to place confidence in their own actions. It was bound up with Ultramontanism. The Jesuits opposed all attempts to set up a local national church and to divide Christians into tiny, hostile groups. They saw the Church as a divine society which stretched beyond national frontiers, as a great hierarchy with the Pope as its earthly head. This led them to stress the basic identity of the individuals of whom this society was composed, to see man as a member of the Christian community rather than as an individual. This view encouraged corporate worship and curbed the vagaries of religious experience. It stood for authority and discipline; it was essentially a reasonable, moderate outlook.

The most important aspect of Jansenism was its view of grace and original sin. The Jansenists claimed that their teaching on original sin was derived from Augustine through Jansenius; but in practice it approximated to the Lutheran belief that man's nature had been completely ruined by the Fall and to the denial of free-will. Man was reduced to the state of a helpless individual who could not accomplish any good action without the direct intervention of grace.

Jansenism had Gallican leanings which emphasized man's isolation and minimized the normative influence of the Christian society. It was in essentials a pessimistic doctrine which placed man at the mercy of his passions and this accounts for the streak of fatalism which runs all through Racine's poetry. It was also a highly introspective religion, and whatever the intentions of Jansenist theologians, it undoubtedly exalted the importance of the individual conscience at the expense of external authority.

It can now be seen that the relation between religion and literature was a close and unusual one. The seventeenth century in France, as in England, was a period in which civilization was undergoing revolutionary changes. The old world was crumbling and a new world was emerging. There were curious cross-currents in France where, more than in England, two orders faced one another. They cannot be measured in terms of years and any attempt to do so would be misleading. All that can be said is that the century was divided by opposing but coexisting tendencies. We cannot say that the change took place in a given year; we can only say that from about 1667 onwards one of the tendencies appears to become less and the other more pronounced. One is represented by Bossuet and Corneille, the other by Pascal and Racine, for Corneille is the literary counterpart of Bossuet as Racine is of Pascal. It sometimes happens that a phase of human experience only receives its final, its consummate, expression when that phase is passing away. Thus one of the most complete defences of Catholicism was written in the century that followed the Reformation. Sainte-Beuve called Bossuet "l'âme la moins combattue qui fût au monde," and Pascal is the father of that spiritual unrest which has become so common in the modern world. His was a religion of tormented and uneasy consciences; he saw men as lonely individuals who were hopelessly lost in the universe without grace, and his work is filled with brooding about sin and doubt. The force of Corneille's criticism of Racine quoted at the beginning of this study will now be apparent. Racine's Jansenism encouraged him to dwell on man's fallen state and to represent him as incapable of resisting the impulses of his animal nature. Jansenism thus begins to assume the appearance of "modern religion," and it is not difficult to see why it fitted in well with the disintegrating forces that were at work in the latter part of the century.

II. THE MAN

It has been shown that social and religious changes in the seventeenth century had a considerable influence on literature, and before going on to a detailed study of Racine's poetry, it is necessary to ask what sort of man he was and what part heredity and early environment played in the formation of the poet.

He was born of an ardent Jansenist family at the little town of La Ferté-Milon in the Valois country about 22nd December 1639. His family belonged to the professional classes on both sides. His grandfather, Jean Racine, who had begun life as a clerk in the Salt Office, had married into the Desmoulins family. He later became a man of some note in his native town, rose to be Comptroller of the Salt Office, and was ennobled by the King.

Jean Racine had eight children by Marie Desmoulins, but only two have left any trace of themselves: the eldest, Jean Racine the younger, who was the father of the poet; and a daughter, Agnès, who entered Port-Royal as a schoolgirl at the age of twelve, never left the Abbey and became first Prioress and then Abbess. It was this daughter who, as Sœur Agnès de Sainte-Thècle, later made such desperate efforts to persuade the poet, when he was on the threshold of his career, to give up the theatre and return to the fold.

In 1639 Jean Racine the younger married Jeanne Sconin whose father was an important person at La Ferté-Milon: Royal Commissioner, Crown Attorney and President of the Salt Office. They had two children, the poet and his sister Marie who was born in 1641. The mother died at the birth of the daughter, and two years later the father, too, died at the early age of twenty-eight.

The grandparents divided the children. Racine was brought up by his grandfather and Marie Desmoulins, and his sister by the Sconins. The wordly Sconins did not mix well with the devout Desmoulins and the two children saw little of one another.

M. Masson-Forestier (a descendant of Racine's sister Marie), going a good deal further than Taine ever ventured, has argued that the district in which Racine was born and the intermarriage of the Racines and the Sconins account for most of the attributes of Racine's poetry. In the seventeenth century, he said, the wooded valley of La Ferté-Milon was a peat bog; the Ourcq, which to-day is a limpid stream, was a rapid and dangerous river. The town was surrounded by vast forests, and there was little cultivation. The townspeople were energetic, devout and somewhat gloomy; the life that they were forced to lead was narrow and inhibited.[1]

The same authority, probing into the histories of the two families, goes on to say that the Sconins were by nature violent and brutal, with Scandinavian and perhaps Frankish blood in their veins. The Racines were naturally gentle and devout, Latin by temperament and clerical.

According to M. Masson-Forestier, this explains the elegance and ferocity of Racine's plays. The theory no doubt sounds a little fanciful; but though we may discount the influence of the countryside, the intermingling of the Sconins and the Racines does to some extent illuminate the contradictions and conflicting impulses that we shall find both in Racine's character and in his poetry.

[1] *Autour d'un Racine ignoré*, Paris, 1910.

A year before Racine's birth the town of La Ferté-Milon and, adds M. François Mauriac in a characteristic sentence, perhaps "la maison où l'on s'occupait chastement à lui donner la vie,"[1] became the refuge of the Jansenists who had been driven from the Abbey of Port-Royal. Although they left La Ferté-Milon a few months after the poet's birth, they had made a lasting impression on their hosts, and Racine was brought up in an atmosphere in which the piety of *ces messieurs de Port-Royal* had already become legendary.

Racine stayed with his grandparents until, at the age of ten, he was sent to school at Beauvais, a sister house of Port-Royal. At the age of fifteen he became a pupil at Port-Royal itself. His biographers have pointed out that this fact is exceptional because as a rule Port-Royal only took children between the ages of nine and ten.

In 1656 the Abbey school was disbanded and for three years Racine was Port-Royal's solitary pupil. It would be difficult to exaggerate the influence on his character of his upbringing there during the formative years. He had, as tutors, four of the most distinguished scholars of the time—Lancelot, Nicole, Antoine Lemaître and Hamon, men who had withdrawn from the world at the height of their fame to devote themselves to the life of prayer. "Comme instruction," wrote Jules Lemaître, "c'est unique, c'est magnifique, et plus que princier. Comme enseignement religieux, c'est intense."[2]

There were, indeed, two elements in Racine's education: an immense love of the pagan classics coupled with an intense religious training, a profound love of the profane coupled with a no less profound sense of the presence of God—of the Jansenist God. Since he was the only pupil at Port-Royal, he was of necessity left a good deal to himself. His tutors spoke of him as the *petit Racine*, and he was a child in a world of grown-ups, of serious men devoting their lives to prayer and to the study of the Fathers of the Church.

"His greatest pleasure," wrote Louis Racine in his memoirs of his father, "was to bury himself in the woods in the grounds of the Abbey with a volume of Sophocles or Euripides whose work he knew almost by

[1] *la Vie de Jean Racine* (Le Roman des Grandes Existences), Paris, 1928, p. 10.

[2] *Jean Racine*, Paris, 1908, p. 9.

heart. He had an amazing memory. He happened to come upon a Greek
novel about the loves of Theagena and Charides. He was devouring it
when the sacristan, Claude Lancelot, seized the book and burnt it. He
managed to obtain another copy which met with the same fate. Then a
third, and to avoid any more trouble he learnt it by heart before taking
it to the sacristan with the words: 'You can burn this like the others'."[1]

The words "learnt by heart" must not be taken too literally.
The novel is six hundred pages long, but Racine's interest in it was
significant. The first book deals with a young man who was loved
too well by his stepmother. "Phèdre et Hippolyte sous d'autres
noms," observes Jules Lemaître.[2]

It was at Port-Royal that Racine wrote his first verses, an elegant
and somewhat frigid exercise that need not detain us here. What is
of importance is that when he left Port-Royal in October 1658
he was, as Lemaître puts it, "à la fois un adolescent très pieux et
un adolescent fou de littérature."[3] When we recall the relations
between the *bien pensants* and the men of letters in the seventeenth
century, the contrast between the atmosphere of devotion in which
Racine was brought up and the nature of his reading, the significance
is unmistakable.

In 1658 the eighteen-year-old Racine went to the Collège
d'Harcourt in Paris to do a year's philosophy. It is thought that
he lived in furnished rooms near Sainte-Geneviève. He had already
become firm friends with his cousin, the Abbé Le Vasseur, and with
the poet, La Fontaine.

A year later he was installed at the Hôtel de Luynes, Quai des
Grands Augustins, the house of his uncle, Nicolas Vitart, the
Intendant of the Duc de Luynes. Nicolas Vitart had himself been
a pupil of Port-Royal, but it does not seem to have affected him
deeply. At this time he was prosperous, worldly, and his main
interests were literature—particularly *vers galants*—and the theatre.

The atmosphere of the Vitarts' house was very different from
that of Port-Royal. They were cheerful and easy-going and untouched by the sombre Jansenism of the Racines and Desmoulins.
There was plenty of company, and Racine has left a list of the
attractive girls whom he met there and of a number of men of

---

[1] "Mémoires sur la vie de Jean Racine" in *Œuvres de J. Racine* (ed. Paul
Mesnard), I, Paris, 1865, pp. 211–12.
[2] *op. cit.*, p. 2   [3] *ibid.*, p. 30.

letters and theatrical celebrities to whom the Abbé Le Vasseur introduced him.

There is no doubt that Racine enjoyed his freedom after the years spent at Port-Royal. He could see everyone, read everything without fear of interruptions from sacristans, say everything. In a letter to Le Vasseur we catch a glimpse of a Racine who was already a little different from the pious infant of Port-Royal. Commenting on these lines from a Latin poem by a doctor named Quillet:

> Nimirum crudam si ad laeta cubilia portas
> Perdicem, incoctaque agitas genitalia coena,
> Heu! tenue effundes semen . . .

he observes:

"But it matters little to me how I write to you as long as I have the pleasure of conversing with you, just as I should find it very difficult to wait for my supper to digest on the night of my wedding. I am not patient enough to observe so many formalities."

"Sentez-vous, au milieu d'un badinage assez libre," asks Jules Lemaître in an amusing commentary, "la réserve d'un bon jeune homme encore intact, et proche encore des pieux enseignements de ses maîtres?"[1] No doubt we do, but it is also clear that Racine's latent sensuality was already coming to the surface in the freedom of Paris. There is as yet no conflict between passion and morality, but there are already indications that morality will not put up much resistance when the conflict comes.

Racine's first literary success came at the age of twenty. He wrote an ode in the artificial style of the time called *la Nymphe de la Seine à la reine* to mark the occasion of the King's marriage. Vitart showed it to Chapelain and Perrault, who were impressed. Chapelain mentioned it to Colbert and "this minister sent the poet 100 *louis* on behalf of the King, and shortly afterwards granted him a State pension of 600 *livres* a year as a man of letters."

It was an encouraging beginning and it bore fruit. In 1660 Racine completed a tragedy called *Amasis* which has not survived. A year later he is engaged on another tragedy on the *Loves* of Ovid. Reports of his activities must have reached Port-Royal and we hear the first rumblings of the storm.

[1] *ibid.* p. 38.

The initiative was taken by Port-Royal. Arrangements were made with Racine's relatives at La Ferté-Milon to have him taken away from Paris. It was decided that he should pay a prolonged visit to his uncle, Canon Sconin, at Uzès in Languedoc. The uncle held out hopes of securing a *bon bénéfice* for his nephew. Racine had never showed any signs of a vocation, but he was without any means save his State pension and he may have thought that, after all, tragedies could be written as easily in Languedoc as in Paris. He set out for Uzès without demur. The journey was a considerable undertaking in those days. There were twelve travellers in the party and they rode together as far as Lyons where they spent two days visiting the city and the neighbourhood. The second stage was a two days' sail down the Rhône. After spending a night at Vienne and another at Valence, they proceeded across country by way of Avignon to Uzès, which is on the road to Nîmes.

A letter written by Racine to La Fontaine on 11th November 1661 gives some vivid and amusing impressions of the journey which bring home to us the immense difference between Paris and *la province*:

"It was at Lyons that I first discovered that I could no longer understand the language of the country or make myself understood; but heaven knows, things were much worse at Valence where I asked one of the maids for a chamber-pot and she put a bed-warmer under my bed. You can well imagine what the sequel to this unfortunate story might have been, and what happens to a sleepy man who uses a bed-warmer if he's taken short in the night. But it's worse still at Uzès. I swear I need an interpreter as much as a Muscovite would in Paris. I am just beginning to see that this queer language is mixed with Spanish and Italian; and, as I have quite a good knowledge of both those languages, I sometimes use them to understand what's said to me and to make myself understood. But even so I often get completely lost, as I did yesterday. I wanted some tin-tacks to make a few alterations in my room, so I sent my uncle's valet into town and told him to buy me two or three hundred. When he got back, he blithely handed me three boxes of matches."[1]

In the same letter we catch a glimpse of the country and its inhabitants:

"I can't help telling you something of the beauties of the country. I had heard them very well spoken of in Paris, but I assure you without

[1] Mesnard, VI, pp. 413–14.

any exaggeration that the number and quality far exceed what I had been told. There isn't a village girl or a cobbler's daughter who doesn't put the Fouillous and the Menevilles completely in the shade. If the country-side itself had more delicacy and fewer rocks, it would be a veritable paradise. All the women are dazzling and know how to make the most of themselves in the most natural way imaginable. As for their person: *Color verus, corpus solidum et succi plenum.*"

Then, recalling the purpose of his visit to Uzès, he adds:

"But hush! It was the first thing that I was warned about, so I'll say no more about it. Besides, I should be profaning the pious house of a priest like the one I am in. *Domus mea domus orationis.* That is why you must not expect me to say anything more about such things. They said to me: 'Be blind.' If I can't quite manage that, I must at least be dumb. For, as you know, I must be clerical with the clergy just as I was a wolf with you and the other wolves of your society. *Adiousias.*"[1]

He seems on the whole to have taken kindly to the life at his uncle's home:

"I spend all my time with my uncle, with St. Thomas and Virgil [he writes to Vitart on 17th January 1662]; I copy out long extracts from theological works and a certain number from poetical works. That's how I pass my time; and I must say that I am not bored, especially when I have a letter from you which keeps me company for two whole days."[2]

The study of Augustine and Aquinas did not interfere with his passionate study of the classics or with the writing of *vers galants.* It was during his stay at Uzès that he put the finishing touches on a poem called *les Bains de Vénus,* which has been lost, and began work on *les Frères ennemis,* the first of his tragedies to survive.

His life was not marked by any external incident of special interest or importance; but though he behaved with the correctness of a *jeune abbé,*[3] we can see from his letters that the real Racine was emerging from the chrysalis:

"I had a visit this afternoon which wasted all the time that I had meant to spend writing to you [he writes to the Abbé Le Vasseur on 16th May 1662]. It was a young man who lives here. He is well favoured but passionately in love. You must realize that in these parts there are no half-hearted love affairs; they are all carried to excess. The townspeople,

---

[1] Mesnard, VI, pp. 415–16.   [2] *ibid.*, VI, p. 438.
[3] "He [my uncle] makes me dress in black from top to toe" (letter to Vitart of 17th January 1662).

who are easy-going enough in other ways, commit themselves far more deeply where their *inclinations* are concerned than the people of any other country in the world."[1]

This suggests already the world of Racine's own poetry, and it would not be easy to find a better description of his characters than "toutes les passions y sont démesurées." Nor should we overlook the detachment of "fort bien fait, mais passionément amoureux" and the appearance of the sinister word *inclinations*.

He was to go a good deal further in revealing his tastes in a letter that he wrote to Vitart a fortnight later:

"I'll tell you another little story which though not important is strange enough. A young girl of Uzès, who lived quite close to us, poisoned herself yesterday by swallowing a great handful of arsenic in order to revenge herself on her father who had given her a heavy dressing-down. She had time to make her confession and did not die until a couple of hours afterwards. Everyone thought that she was pregnant and had been driven by shame to this mad course. But, when her body was opened, it was seen that never was maid more maid than she. Such is the character of these people who push their passions to the last extremity."[2]

It was the sort of story that could scarcely fail to interest the future author of *Andromaque*, though one feels that he might have found it still more attractive if the suicide had been caused by disappointed love. It is a striking revelation of the man and the writer. The cool detachment of the earlier letters has been replaced by something which looks very like cruelty. There is not, as Lemaître observes, the slightest edifying reflection. The facts are stated baldly and it is their baldness which makes them striking. "Mais on l'ouvrit toute entière, et jamais fille ne fut plus fille." Here, already, are signs of Racine's extraordinary economy and precision of language; here too is that extreme curiosity, that desire to penetrate and lay bare the final secrets whether they are psychological or physiological. Here is the skilful mingling of the two which will be a notable characteristic of *Phèdre*.

There are other letters which sound a more personal note. On 30th April 1662 he had written to the Abbé Le Vasseur:

"You know very well that a wounded heart always needs someone to whom it can go for sympathy. If I were one of that sort, I would never

---

[1] Mesnard, VI, p. 468. [2] *ibid.*, p. 473.

confide in anyone but you. But I am still free, thank goodness, and if I left this place tomorrow, my heart would still be as much my own as when I arrived. There is, however, one rather amusing little story on the subject that I must tell you. There's an attractive girl here and she has a nice figure. I had only seen her from a distance of five or six yards and had always thought her pretty. Her complexion appeared fresh and sparkling; her eyes big and dark; her throat and all the rest which is so freely displayed in these parts was as white as snow. I felt rather attracted to her, felt something not unlike an *inclination*; but I only saw her in church, for, as I have already explained, I keep pretty much to myself—rather more in fact than my cousin had advised. Well, I wanted to be sure that I hadn't made any mistake about her, so I waited until an opportunity occurred and went up and spoke to her. All this happened less than a month ago and I only wanted to see what sort of an answer I should get. I began to chat about things of no importance, but as soon as I opened my mouth I thought that I was going to dry up altogether. I saw that her face was covered with blotches as though she had just got over an illness. That made me change my ideas a bit; but I didn't stop talking and she answered me very sweetly and politely. To tell the truth, I think I must have struck one of her bad days. For she is considered very good-looking in this town and I know lots of young men who rave about her. She is also considered a good girl and one of the most cheerful hereabouts. Still, I am rather relieved at our meeting, which has put a stop to my tender feelings, because I am trying to behave rather more sensibly and not to let myself be carried away by anything that comes along. I am starting my noviciate. . . ."[1]

It is an amusing story, but there is a vein of seriousness running through it. Racine is no longer altogether the detached and ironical observer, and his concern for his natural susceptibility is genuine. There is a difference between the light-hearted banter at the beginning of the passage and "J'en avais toujours quelque idée assez tendre et assez *approchante d'une inclination*." There is a genuine feeling of relief behind "Je fus bien aise de cette rencontre, qui me servit du moins à me délivrer de quelque *commencement d'inquiétude*," which is very different from the sententious reference to his noviciate. For the unfortunate girl's blotches were a better protection than Racine's vocation.

Meanwhile, the negotiations for the *bon bénéfice* were not going well. On 30th May Racine remarked bitterly in a letter to Vitart:

[1] Mesnard, VI, pp. 457–8.

"The monks here are the greatest fools alive and, what is more, ignorant fools. They never open a book and I take care to keep out of their way completely. To tell the truth, I have developed a sort of horror for this slothful monkish life which I can scarcely hide."[1]

On 4th July he wrote to Le Vasseur:

"There is no fresh news here. My affairs don't seem to be making much progress which reduces me to despair."[2]

He added significantly:

"I am looking round for a subject for a play and should like to set to work on it, but I have too many reasons to feel moody where I am now. One needs to have one's mind free from the sort of preoccupations that fill mine at present."

In the meantime the situation over Racine's living was becoming very delicate. His uncle spoke at one time of resigning his own living in favour of his nephew:

". . . I haven't dared to broach the subject of resigning his living again [Racine writes to Vitart on 25th July], because I don't want him to think me self-seeking. Still, he must realize that I haven't come all this way for nothing; but so far I have been so docile and so frank with him that he thinks that I should be content to go on living with him as we are now without having any designs on his living, and I certainly hope that he will always have the same good opinion of me."[3]

We do not know how the problem was solved, but in the summer of 1663 Racine left Uzès on excellent terms with his uncle. As soon as he was back in Paris, he settled down to the life of a man of letters. *Les Frères ennemis* was produced in July 1664, exactly a year after his return, and *Alexandre le Grand* followed in 1665.

Racine was sometimes inclined to lament his lost career as a monk, but he had little cause to do so. His two and a half years' stay at Uzès had not been altogether in vain. A living eventually materialized and Racine found himself endowed with the income of the Priory of Sainte-Madeleine de l'Épinay in Anjou. When a change in public opinion compelled him to give up his priory in 1673, he had no difficulty in obtaining another sinecure. He became treasurer of France for the town of Moulins where he never set foot in his life.

[1] *ibid.*, p. 472.   [2] *ibid.*, p. 485.   [3] *ibid.*, p. 495.

His relations with the Church were not always so happy. Port-Royal was naturally horrified by his new vocation and it did not intend to let him go without a fight. In August 1665 his aunt, Sœur Agnès, wrote to tell him how deeply grieved she was by the news that he had "plunged more deeply than before into the society of those persons who are abominable in the sight of all who, in however feeble a degree, are truly pious; they are people against whom the church door is closed."[1]

A more formidable attack came from a different quarter. "A poet," wrote Nicole, the celebrated Jansenist theologian, "is a public poisoner and a writer for the stage should be considered as guilty of the murder of innumerable souls." The tears of Sœur Agnès could be ignored, but not the redoubtable Nicole. His attack drew a devastating retort from Racine.

"And so [he wrote] the man who writes a novel or a comedy is a Public Poisoner? And the man who writes the *Provincial Letters* is a Saint! Sir, I pray you, tell me what difference you see between the two of them. M. Pascal—no less than any of us—was a writer of comedies. What takes place, after all, in a comedy? You put on the stage a sly fellow of a servant, or a miserly old cit, or an extravagant marquis. It is certain that M. Pascal aimed higher than this. He chose his *dramatis personæ* in the convents and at the Sorbonne. And sometimes he put on the stage this order of monks and sometimes that, but all of them were Jesuits. How many different parts he made them play! Sometimes he shows us an affable Jesuit, and sometimes a bad Jesuit and always a ridiculous Jesuit. Admit then, sir, that since your comedies and ours are so surprisingly alike, ours cannot be entirely criminal."

This was something that could not be forgiven. The *Lettres provinciales* were among the sacred books of Port-Royal, and Racine's reply caused a rupture which lasted for nearly twelve years.

The Langres portrait of Racine is an extremely revealing piece of work. We can see at a glance that this elegant young man, with the full-bottomed wig falling over his shoulders, is a courtier to his finger-tips. It does not need any great acumen to perceive that the face, with its sensitive, highly strung expression, is the face of an artist. The portrait can tell us a good deal more besides. The sitter,

[1] Mesnard, VI, p. 510.

one feels, is proud and disdainful, and the tiny moustache seems to emphasize the superciliousness of his general expression. It is a handsome face certainly, the face of a remarkably sensual man, but the sensuality is not tempered by the kindliness and good nature which make the Molière of the Mignard portrait a genial figure. There is a hard, determined look in the eyes which gives the face its suggestion of cruelty. The man behaved exactly as anyone who has studied his portrait intently would expect. He was interested in one thing and one thing only—his career. He was determined to be a success at all costs. He was completely merciless in his treatment of his enemies and sacrificed his friends ruthlessly if they seemed likely for a moment to stand in his way.

One need have no sympathy with Jansenism to feel that Racine's treatment of Port-Royal is difficult to defend on human grounds, though it is easy to see that the new threat to his career from his pious friends must have driven the haughty, irritable dramatist into a frenzy of exasperation. His treatment of Molière is less excusable and far more shocking. It was Molière who brought him to the stage when the royal tragedians had been hesitating for months over the production of his first play. It was Molière, too, who produced *Alexandre le Grand* at the Palais Royal in December 1665. No trouble or expense was spared to make the production a success. Molière himself did not act, probably as a concession to Racine who admired Montfleury and could not therefore admire Molière as a tragic actor. Madeleine Béjart was also omitted from the cast to make way for Marquise du Parc—the most beautiful and the least intelligent of Molière's actresses—because Racine was already passionately in love with her.

The première was something of an occasion; but though Monsieur, Madame, the great Condé and the Princess Palatine were present, the play was not the success that Racine had hoped. He jumped to the conclusion that this was due to faulty production and, without a word of warning to Molière, he arranged for a fresh production to be staged by a rival company at the Hôtel de Bourgogne. On 18th December, exactly a fortnight after the original production, the play was performed simultaneously at both theatres. The comment of La Grange, Molière's manager, is a model of restraint. "The troupe," he wrote in his Register, "was surprised to discover that the same tragedy was being played at the Théâtre de l'Hôtel de Bourgogne. As the new arrangement had been made with the connivance of M. Racine, the company did not feel bound to pay him his share as author, since he had used them so ill as to give his play to another theatre."

"Trahison fameuse qui rompt à jamais une amitié," observes M. Pierre Brisson.[1] Racine, however, seems to have taken the breach with Molière as lightly as the breach with Port-Royal. But though he did not mind sacrificing his friend to his career, he had no intention of losing his mistress, and it was not long before she was induced to follow him to the Hôtel de Bourgogne. *Andromaque*, the first of his major works, with the fascinating Mlle du Parc in the chief part, was produced in 1667 and *les Plaideurs*, a witty attack on lawyers, a year later. But the year 1668 ended tragically. Marquise du Parc died in mysterious circumstances. It was whispered that her death was caused by an abortion and that Racine was the father of the child, though this was probably only malicious gossip of the kind that accused Molière of marrying his own illegitimate daughter.

Racine took the blow hardly, but he did not allow it to affect his work as a writer. *Britannicus*, one of his three greatest plays, was produced in 1669 and *Bérénice*, with his new mistress, Mlle de Champmeslé, in the name part, followed the next year. *Bajazet* was produced in 1672, *Mithridate* in 1673, *Iphigénie* in 1674 and *Phèdre* in 1677.

III. THE WORLD OF TRAGEDY

1. The Moral Obstacle Race

We have seen something of the situation in which Racine's poetry was written and we know something of the man who wrote it. When we turn to the poetry, it is possible to discover evidence

---

[1] *Les deux visages de Racine*, Paris, 1944, p. 20.

This may be an over-statement. It is said that Molière later defended *les Plaideurs* against the ill-judgment of the town and that Racine once snubbed a detractor of the *Misanthrope* by retorting that it was impossible for Molière to write a bad play. But Racine's conduct was too much even for the good-natured Molière, and their relations seem to have been no more than "polite" for the rest of their lives.

not only of a searching criticism of contemporary France, but also of a highly personal outlook in almost every line.

When we compare some characteristic lines from Corneille and Racine, we begin to understand the changes that were taking place in French civilization. When, for example, we compare Corneille's

> Contre mon propre honneur mon amour s'intéresse

with Racine's

> Je n'ai pour lui parler consulté que mon cœur

we see that in the first line there is a conflict between a principle and a feeling, a struggle to fit the experience of the individual into the framework of the community life. The speaker contemplates the situation with a certain detachment; he is able to stand back and examine his love, to weigh the two values—the claims of society and personal interest—calmly and objectively. In Racine's line *honneur* has not simply disappeared; it has been carefully eliminated. The clear-cut lines of *amour* are transformed into something more complex. The word *cœur* stands for the shadowy world of the unconscious, that region of tangled desires which Racine explored with such marvellous insight and which becomes the centre round which all things revolve. This is made clearer by a second comparison. When a character in Corneille's *Sertorius* remarks

> Il est doux de revoir les murs de la patrie

we are in a clearly defined territory—a country governed by its proper laws and its moral code. There is a perfect correspondence between the emotion and its object, and the line expresses the sentiment of the *honnête homme* for his fatherland. But when Néron's mother exclaims:

> Ai-je mis dans sa main le timon de l'État
> Pour le conduire au gré du peuple et du sénat?
> Ah! que de la patrie il soit, s'il veut, le père;
> Mais qu'il songe un peu plus qu'Agrippine est sa mère

the scene is altered. The individual becomes the centre of the picture. Law and morality are swept away. *Patrie* is set against the vast disorder of Agrippine's own emotions and becomes a plaything to be exploited in the selfish interests of the ruler. These lines reveal a fundamentally different attitude towards the life of the community. Corneille's hero has a definite place in the community; and the recognition of its moral code determines his personal feelings and imposes a discipline which constitutes a positive value. Racine's characters have no place in the social order; they are outsiders who have lost their bearings as completely as Frédéric Moreau or any other nineteenth-century hero. It is one of the paradoxes of despotism that the attempt to impose complete uniformity on the common life defeats its own end, encourages a revolutionary individualism, and promotes a subterranean hostility between the individual and the artificial group which it tries to set up in place of the natural community of the people.

This change is a subtle one and is clearly seen in the way in which the two poets handle words. When Corneille uses a word like *légitime* or *gloire*, it has a fixed, unchanging meaning. Actions are right or wrong, good or bad; there is no middle course. The Cornelian hero always knows what line of conduct he must adopt in any given circumstances; the well-tried tests never let him down. Racine's use of words reveals a far wider range of experience; words have no fixed meaning, but are constantly acquiring fresh overtones; and though he appears to employ the same vocabulary as Corneille, he succeeds in presenting a situation which is diametrically opposed to that in Corneille's plays. Racine sets his personal stamp on words as surely as any other great poet. It would be possible, for example, to write an essay on the different meanings that the word *loi* has for him, and in the course of this study we shall see that the development in the meaning of the word corresponds to a development in Racine's experience as a whole. There is a marked contrast between Corneille's *devoir* and Racine's *loi*. *Devoir* implies an obligation, but it is not a mere abstraction; there is a wealth of living human feeling behind it and its power lies precisely in the fact that the obligation is freely accepted by the Cornelian hero in virtue of his place in the community. It is a sign that he recognizes a valid relationship with the community and with his fellow-men as members of it. *Loi* also implies an obligation, but save in Racine's later plays, the emphasis falls on the repressive nature of the obligation. There is nothing human and living about *loi*. It is a dry, legal abstraction imposed by force from without.

and so far from being recognized, the one desire of Racine's characters is to circumvent it.

Another example is their use of the word *honneur*. When Corneille speaks of *honneur*, he means the attitude of heroic virtue which enables the hero to dominate the life of instinct and accomplish actions which order the whole of his being instead of destroying it by placing him at the mercy of conflicting desires. Now when Œnone persuades Phèdre to pretend to Thésée that it was Hippolyte who tried to seduce her instead of her trying to seduce him by saying:

> . . . pour sauver notre *honneur* combattu,
> Il faut immoler tout, et même la *vertu*

it is evident that *honneur* means primarily "keeping up appearances." The implications of this change are far-reaching. *Honneur* has ceased to be a reality and become an attitude to be maintained—an attitude to which the positive value implied by *vertu* is unhesitatingly sacrificed. Conduct itself, therefore, becomes a series of postures which no longer correspond to any moral feeling; it follows from this that there is a complete divorce between the public and private life of the individual which leads to thoroughgoing moral anarchy. "When," wrote Taine, "Hippolyte speaks of the forest where his youth was spent, we must understand the avenues of Versailles."[1] Those critics who are still disposed to think of Racine as the laureate of Versailles might consider the significance of "palaces" in his poetry. When he describes his characters wandering alone and without any sense of direction in the vast empty palaces:

> Errante et sans dessein, je cours dans ce palais
> . . . errant dans le palais sans suite et sans escorte

—does he not point the contrast between the disorder of the individual life and an order of society which had ceased to be a true order and degenerated into mere formalism? The word "palace" has a curious ambiguity in his poetry. Palaces and temples —using the words in a wide sense—played a large part in his personal life. He had been brought up in the sheltered seclusion of the Abbey of Port-Royal, but the freedom of the Court turned out to be an illusion too. The "palaces" are, therefore, at once a symbol

[1] *Nouveaux essais de critique et d'histoire*, 3 ième éd., Paris, 1880, p. 188.

of refuge and prison; and though it is to the "temple" that he will return (in the person of a converted and repentant Abner) in his last play, it will only be at the close of a long struggle and in a spirit of profound disillusionment. In the secular plays the "palace" is the sign of the rootless existence of the individual, and it is not surprising that it sometimes assumes the aspect of a prison where the individual is kept by the "Sovereign." Thus we read in *Bajazet*:

> Songez-vous que je tiens les portes du palais,
> Que je puis vous l'ouvrir, ou fermer pour jamais,
> Que j'ai sur votre vie un empire suprême,
> Que vous ne respirez qu'autant que je vous aime?

It is not suggested that Racine's world is a world in which there are no moral values. On the contrary, they are often perceived by his characters with the same clarity as Corneille's; but instead of conforming to them, their one desire is to impugn their validity or to evade their obligations. This explains why the plays abound in words like *artifice* and *stratagème*. In a remarkable passage Andromaque explains to her *confidente* that she is going to marry Pyrrhus in order to save her son's life:

> Pyrrhus en m'épousant s'en déclare l'appui.
> Il suffit: je veux bien m'en reposer sur lui.
> Je sais quel est Pyrrhus. Violent, mais sincère,
> Céphise, il fera plus qu'il n'a promis de faire.
> Sur le courroux des Grecs je m'en repose encor:
> Leur haine va donner un père au fils d'Hector.
> Je vais donc, puisqu'il faut que je me sacrifie,
> Assurer à Pyrrhus le reste de ma vie;
> Je vais, en recevant sa foi sur les autels,
> L'engager à mon fils par des nœuds immortels.
> Mais aussitôt ma main, à moi seule funeste,
> D'une infidèle vie abrégera le reste,
> Et, sauvant ma vertu, rendra ce que je doi
> A Pyrrhus, à mon fils, à mon époux, à moi.
> Voilà de mon amour l'innocent stratagème;
> Voilà ce qu'un époux m'a commandé lui-même.

Andromaque knows very well that her plan is an evasion of the promise given "at the altars"; but she also knows that in spite of his shortcomings, Pyrrhus will carry out his part of the bargain scrupulously. She counts on his "sincerity," on his doing "more than he promised," and tries to excuse her own action by describing it as "un *innocent* stratagème." The word *innocent* is skilfully used to confuse the real issue, and to conceal the profound immorality of her action, by pretending that she is acquitting herself of her obligations to Pyrrhus, her husband and her son.

The desire of Racine's characters to evade their obligations is also symbolized by the back door escape from the palace. In *Andromaque* Oreste has been sent as ambassador by the Greeks to hasten the marriage of Pyrrhus and Hermione. Instead, he proposes to carry off Hermione and leave by a secret door:

> Je sais de ce palais tous les détours obscurs:
> Vous voyez que la mer en vient battre les murs;
> Et cette nuit, sans peine, une secrète voie
> Jusqu'en votre vaisseau conduira votre proie.

The criticism implied is a destructive criticism; the only standards of conduct are the prescriptions of the Court, but they are hollow and unreal. The individual cheerfully throws over this remnant of morality and discipline in the pursuit of his "prey," in response to the promptings of his "heart." Yet these "secret ways" and "innocent stratagems" do not solve any problems; they merely create fresh ones. They lead the characters to a boat tossing on the stormy seas—the stormy seas of passion—which significantly "beat against the palace walls."

2. L'Amour

"We simply regard love as a passion of the same nature as all the other human passions, that is to say, its effect is to derange our reason and its aim to provide pleasure. The Germans, on the other hand, regard love as something sacred and religious, as an emanation of the divinity itself, as the fulfilment of man's destiny on earth, as a mysterious and all-powerful link between two souls which only exist for one another. According to the first of these views, love is common to man and beast; according to the second, it is common to man and God."

—BENJAMIN CONSTANT: *Réflexions sur le théâtre allemand*

"The English, whatever they were in the Elizabethan era, are not an amorous race. Love with them is more sentimental than passionate.

G

They are of course sufficiently sexual to reproduce their species, but they cannot control the instinctive feeling that the sexual act is disgusting. They are more inclined to look upon love as affection or benevolence than as passion. They regard with approval its sublimations which dons describe in scholarly books, and with repulsion or with ridicule its frank expression. English is the only modern language in which it has been found necessary to borrow from the Latin a word with a depreciatory meaning, the word uxorious, for a man's devoted affection for his wife. That love should absorb a man has seemed to them unworthy. In France a man who has ruined himself for women is usually regarded with sympathy and admiration; there is a feeling that it was worth while; and the man who has done it feels a certain pride in the fact; in England he would be thought and will think of himself as a damned fool. That is why *Antony and Cleopatra* has always been the least popular of Shakespeare's greater plays. Audiences have felt that it was contemptible to throw away an empire for a woman's sake. Indeed if it were not founded on an accepted legend they would be unanimous in asserting that such a thing was incredible."[1]

—SOMERSET MAUGHAM: *The Summing Up*, pp. 142–3

i

Corneille would no doubt have been deeply distressed had he known that one day the *faiblesses* which shocked him in *Britannicus* would be given statutory recognition as the *crime passionnel*, that multitudes would flock to the Comédie Française to salute Racine as its first great laureate, and rise to their feet with claps and cheers when the great passages were declaimed on the stage.

The French preoccupation with love has sometimes appeared to foreigners to be an amiable but eccentric trait. It reminds us of the illustrations in those old-fashioned editions of Maupassant's stories, showing a demure young lady in a long black dress with an innocent-looking muff and a wicked-looking veil who is plunged suddenly, hopelessly, into a fatal passion by a chance encounter in a shop or a discreet squeeze in the bus, and who suffers all the agonies of disappointed love until the story ends with shots in a taxi and a grim paragraph in the *Ami du Peuple*.

---

[1] The fact that Titus sacrifices Bérénice to an empire is probably the reason why English critics are inclined to rate *Bérénice* more highly than most French critics.

In English, expressions like "love at first sight" or "a broken heart" are not taken altogether seriously. It is thought unreasonable and unseemly to allow one's life to be ruined by such things, and love is reduced to the unlovely terminology of the Divorce Court: "Intimacy took place." In France it is far otherwise. There is a wealth of human experience behind the simple phrases: *une inclination aveugle*—sudden, blind, helpless passion; *chagrin d'amour*—the overwhelming despair of the person who has loved and lost; the passion of *une femme au déclin de l'âge*—the terrifying, destructive love of the woman on the threshold of middle age, and its counterpart in men—the *démon de midi* which plays such havoc with human happiness.[1]

In no other country has love been studied with such passionate interest. The study has not been confined to the scholarly disquisitions of dons or even to the works of poets and novelists. The greatest French moralists have written of it with the same care and seriousness as of the other great human problems, and with far more enthusiasm. The nature and growth of sexual passion, the various kinds and degrees of love, the difference between love and friendship, love and gallantry, love and ambition, have been carefully analysed and diligently classified and the findings enshrined in a number of imperishable maxims. The works of Descartes, La Rochefoucauld and Pascal, La Bruyère and a host of lesser writers are a mine of *practical* wisdom on this absorbing subject. The soothing tone of the moralist banishes a dull *malaise* by telling you exactly what you feel, and the philosopher explains why you feel as you do. You disregard their "tips" at your peril. If you mistake a momentary *froideur* for *indifférence*, you will probably miss your chance and be condemned to lifelong unhappiness. On the other

[1] No one who has lived in France can suppose that this is an exaggeration or can doubt that for the French *l'amour* is the most absorbing, the most exciting, thing in life. I well remember the sense of hushed expectancy which descended on the company when a visitor to the family in which I was living entered with the remark: "Madame X a quitté son mari." "Tiens, Madame X. Je ne l'aurais jamais cru." "Mais si, Thérèse, tu sais . . ." The record of this family in love was by no means unremarkable. I recall one *coup de foudre* and three serious cases of *chagrin d'amour*. Two of the victims languished silently, but the third almost came to an untimely end. A sixteen-year-old girl, who had fallen wildly in love with an Indian student, threw herself from a third-story window in a fury of despair, turned a complete somersault in mid-air and landed, miraculously, on her feet on the soft earth underneath and escaped with a severe shaking.

hand, if you mistake a passing *inclination* for a *grande passion* you will certainly end up in the Divorce Court.

"Il est difficile de définir l'amour," said La Rochefoucauld: "ce qu'on en peut dire est que, dans l'âme, c'est une passion de régner; dans les esprits, c'est une sympathie; et dans les corps, ce n'est qu'une envie cachée et délicate de posséder ce que l'on aime après beaucoup de mystères."

The same astringent, slightly acid note is perceptible in his other maxims:

"Si on juge de l'amour par la plupart de ses effets, il ressemble plus à la haine qu'à l'amitié."
"Il y a des gens qui n'auraient jamais été amoureux s'ils n'avaient jamais entendu parler de l'amour."

La Bruyère is a more genial and sometimes a more penetrating guide:

"L'amour naît brusquement, sans autre réflexion, par tempérament ou par faiblesse: un trait de beauté nous fixe, nous détermine . . ."

He is a master of the phrase that echoes in the memory long after one has closed the book, distilling its essence slowly like lavender which perfumes a whole wardrobe:

"C'est faiblesse que d'aimer; c'est souvent une autre faiblesse que de guérir."
"L'amour commence par l'amour; et l'on ne saurait passer de la plus forte amitié qu'à un amour faible."
"L'amour qui naît subitement est le plus long à guérir."

These maxims are not a cure for love—the moralists all agree that it is incurable—their aim is to enable the *malade* to probe and understand his *maladie*.

The most striking thing about the great French moralists is the continuity of their work. The maxims are not isolated discoveries made by solitary individuals experimenting in their own laboratories. They not only have behind them layers and layers of civilization; they are a product of the collective experience of the race, so that we detect the voice of civilization itself in the single maxim. It is interesting to watch the evolution of this collective experience, to see the different writers stretching their hands out to one another across the ages, to listen to the new voice taking up the old theme and adding something to it.

"L'amitié peut subsister entre des gens de différents sexes, exempte même de toute grossièreté," said La Bruyère . . . "Cette liaison n'est ni passion ni amitié pure: elle fait classe à part."

It was left for a later writer to find the perfect definition of this friendship—*l'amitié amoureuse*.

When La Rochefoucauld urbanely remarks:

"On a bien de la peine à rompre quand on ne s'aime plus"

the voice that answers him is the anguished voice of Benjamin Constant:

". . . telle est la bizarrerie de notre cœur misérable, que nous quittons avec un déchirement horrible ceux près de qui nous demeurions sans plaisir."

And when he observes in still another maxim:

"La jalousie naît toujours avec l'amour; mais elle ne meurt pas toujours avec lui"

it is the figure of the seedy, asthmatic Proust that he conjures up, brooding darkly in his cork-lined room over the infidelities of the dead Albertine.

Stendhal distinguishes four kinds of love: *l'amour-passion*, *l'amour-goût*, *l'amour-physique*, *l'amour de vanité*. But it was Jules Lemaître who coined the perfect word for the first of the four in his study of Racine—*l'amour-maladie*.

ii

It is for these reasons that the French interest in love seems to me to be one of the signs of the intense psychological realism of a great people. It is with love that the greatest French poet of the seventeenth century is concerned from one end of his secular plays to the other. Although there is much that is undeniably original in his study of sexual passion and some dangerous secrets are given away, Racine has his roots deep in the past, and his conception of love is largely derived from a much older tradition. He reveals impulses which lay buried—and buried for good reason—in the unconscious memory of the race. In his fascinating book, *l'Amour et l'Occident*,[1] M. Denis de Rougemont has shown that Racine can only be fully appreciated when we know something of the "myth" which received its classic formulation in the twelfth-century *Roman de Tristan* and has pervaded European literature ever since. It is worth giving a brief account of his findings before going on to study the texts of the plays.

"My Lords, will it please you to hear a fine tale of love and death?"

The opening sentence of Bédier's *Roman de Tristan et Iseut*[2] provides us with the first clue to the myth—the connection between love and death. It will be recalled that Tristan went on a mission to Ireland to find a bride for his uncle, King Mark of Cornwall. Tristan slays the dragon and is given the King of Ireland's daughter, Iseut la Blonde, as a reward. He announces that he does not intend to marry Iseut himself, but proposes to take her to England to be the wife of his uncle. The pair set out for Tintagel. During the sea voyage, Iseut's maid accidentally gives Tristan and her mistress the "love potion" which Iseut's aunt had prepared for King Mark and his bride. Tristan and Iseut are overcome by a violent and fatal passion for one another which they proceed to satisfy at once. Nevertheless, Tristan decides to keep his promise, but though he hands Iseut over to his uncle, they do not cease to be lovers. The rest of the legend is taken up with their adventures: their three years' wandering in the forest, their repentance and Iseut's return to King Mark, Tristan's exile and his marriage to Iseut aux Blanches Mains in France, which remains *un mariage blanc*. Finally, when Tristan lies dying in France, he persuades his brother-in-law to fetch Iseut la Blonde from England for a last meeting. His wife overhears their plan to put up a white sail on the ship if Iseut is with him and a black one if she is not. The boat comes in sight. In a fit of jealousy Tristan's wife tells him that the sail is black. Tristan collapses and dies. Iseut la Blonde arrives, kisses the dead Tristan, lies down beside him and dies too.

[1] Paris, 1939. See especially Books I–IV. (An abridged edition of this book has been published in English under the title of *Passion and Society*. My references are to the French edition and the renderings are my own.)

[2] *Le Roman de Tristan et Iseut*, traduit et restauré par Joseph Bédier, Paris, 1900.

"As long as one is free to stick to the facts and to express them openly and directly," writes M. de Rougemont, "there can be no myth. On the contrary, the myth makes its appearance when it would be either dangerous or impossible to admit openly certain facts about religion, society and emotional relationships which we are anxious to preserve or which we could not allow to be destroyed. For example, we have no need of myths to express scientific truths . . . *But we do need a myth to express the obscure and inadmissible fact that passion is linked with death.*"[1]

M. de Rougemont goes on to analyse certain symbols which recur in all the early versions of the Tristan legend. The two most important are the *philtre* (the "love potion") and the "obstacle." When Tristan announces that he is taking Iseut back to England to marry his uncle she is a little piqued, not because she is in love with him but because it is customary for the hero who slays the dragon to marry the King's daughter himself. She also has a grudge against him because it was he who three years earlier had slain her own uncle, Morholt the Giant, who had terrorized the Kingdom of Cornwall. When they drink the love potion, we are told:

"Non, ce n'était pas du vin: c'était la passion, c'était l'âpre joie et l'angoisse sans fin, et la mort."[2]

The legend makes it clear that the love of Tristan and Iseut is a "sin," but it is also made clear in their meeting with the hermit that they are under a spell, that they cannot help themselves. The hermit says:

> Amors par force vos demeine!
> Combien durra vostre folie?
> Trop avez mené ceste vie.

When they are urged to repent and separate, they excuse themselves by saying that they are not in love with one another:

> Q'el m'aime, c'est par la poison
> Ge ne me pus de lié partir,
> N'ele de moi . . .

Thus Tristan, and Iseut supports him:

> Sire, por Dieu omnipotent,
> Il ne m'aime pas, ne je lui,
> Fors par un herbé dont je bui
> Et il en but: ce fu pechiez.

[1] p. 8 (italics in the text). [2] Bédier, *op. cit.*, p. 75.

The symbol of the "obstacle" is not less interesting. Tristan might have refused to hand Iseut over to Mark and they could have gone away together and married. Instead, he hands her over; she marries Mark, and her passion for Tristan leads to adultery. When Tristan is exiled, he marries Iseut aux Blanches Mains whom he does not love and thus of his own free will creates another "obstacle."

M. de Rougemont adopts the psycho-analytical explanation of these symbols, and he seems to me to prove his case up to the hilt. The "love potion" is an "alibi." "C'est ce qui permet aux malheureux amants de dire: 'Vous voyez que je n'y suis pour rien, vous voyez que c'est plus fort que moi.' "[1] It stands for the irresistible nature of sexual passion which excuses every excess, every breach of divine or human law because it deprives the lovers of free-will and they cease to be answerable for their own actions. They are right in protesting that they are not in love with one another: they are in love with love. The hidden motive of their love—the motive that society for its own safety cannot admit—is the death-wish. The object of desire is not another human being, but death. It follows from this that love is regarded as being essentially anti-social and disruptive. It is also of its nature unhappy or, as M. de Rougemont puts it, it is *l'amour réciproque malheureux.*

"Happiness in love has no history [he continues] ... Without the husband, there would be nothing left for the two lovers to do but to marry. Now one simply cannot imagine Tristan marrying Iseut. She is the sort of woman that one doesn't marry. For if one did, one would stop loving her because she would no longer be the woman that in fact she is. Mrs. Tristan—just imagine it!"[2]

And of course we can't imagine anything so prosaic as "Mrs. Tristan"! They would not love one another unless there were an obstacle which threatened to separate them and maintain their unhappiness. The obstacle is, therefore, an irritant, a stimulant that prevents their love from dying or the effects of the love potion from wearing off.[3] That the principal obstacle should be marriage underlines the essentially anti-social nature of passion and the myth becomes a symbol of a subterranean attack on society and its

---

[1] *l'Amour et l'Occident*, p. 39.   [2] *ibid.*, pp. 2, 35.

[3] In some versions of the legend the effects of the love potion last only for three years; but though Tristan and Iseut repent at the end of that time and she returns to Mark, they soon start all over again!

institutions. The other obstacle—Tristan's marriage—has a twofold
significance. It is intended to stimulate the first Iseut's desire for
him, but the fact that the marriage is not consummated also makes
it a symbol of suicide and another manifestation of the death-wish.

There is a further point which is not perhaps sufficiently brought
out in M. de Rougemont's analysis. Although the love of Tristan
and Iseut is clearly seen to be "sinful," the anonymous authors of
the legend do everything possible to work up their audience's
sympathy for the lovers. Their love may be sinful, but that does
not prevent divine protection and miraculous intervention from
saving them at moments of great danger, such as Tristan's leap
from the chapel or Iseut's trial by ordeal, when she succeeds by a
trick. The barons, who repeatedly warn the King of the love between his wife and nephew and who evidently stand for society
trying to safeguard its institutions, are invariably described as *barons
félons*; and the King's retainers who act as spies and informers against
the lovers all come to a violent end at the hands of Tristan or his
friends. I think that this must be ascribed to the influence of the code
of chivalry. Love and marriage were always regarded as incompatible, and passionate love meant adultery. The barons thus become the symbols of the "bourgeois respectability" of a later day,
and are the enemy. The lesson is obvious. Love may be sinful, unhappy and anti-social, but it is also sacrosanct, and though the lovers
are doomed from the first this does not prevent them from enjoying
special favours until the moment of their doom.

M. de Rougemont goes on to trace the fortunes of the "myth" in
French life and literature from the twelfth century down to our
own times. He discusses its revival in the seventeenth century, its
"profanation" in the eighteenth and nineteenth centuries and its
final degradation in the twentieth century, when he argues that in
the popular film it is a potent factor in the modern attack on marriage.

It is, however, the seventeenth century that interests us here.
Corneille's work is well described as *le mythe combattu* and Racine's
as *le mythe déchaîné* and finally as *le mythe puni*. For the potency of
the "myth" in Racine's plays is unmistakable. In almost every play
we are confronted, in varying forms, with the "love potion" and
the "obstacle." There is an obvious parallel between the mission of
Tristan and the mission of Oreste in *Andromaque*. Tristan has been
sent to find a wife for the King, falls in love with her himself and

G*

seduces her. Oreste arrives in Epirus as the Ambassador of Greece on a special mission to see that Pyrrhus keeps his promise to marry Hermione. Instead, he murders Pyrrhus and attempts to carry off Hermione. In other plays the obstacle is a "law" which separates the lovers, or a "vow" which binds one of them to a third party, or even a blood-relationship which would make their love "incestuous."[1] In *Britannicus* the lovers are separated by the claims of the Emperor, in *Bérénice* by the "claims of State," in *Mithridate* by the rivalry of father and son, and in *Iphigénie* by the need to propitiate the gods by a sacrifice. It is, however, *Phèdre* that provides the perfect illustration of M. de Rougemont's thesis. The "obstacle" is twofold: it is "incest" which stands between Phèdre and Hippolyte, and the "law" imposed by Thésée which separates Hippolyte and Aricie. The "love potion" is disguised as Venus and its origins are plain in the celebrated lines:

> Ce n'est plus une ardeur dans mes veines cachée;
> C'est Vénus toute entière à sa proie attachée.

For in blaming Venus for her guilty passion, Phèdre uses precisely the same argument as Tristan and Iseut when they visit the hermit. It is this that enables her to plead: "Vous voyez que je n'y suis pour rien, vous voyez que c'est plus fort que moi."

The passion that Racine's characters feel for one another is clearly of the same nature as the passion of Tristan and Iseut. Their habit of describing lovers and mistresses as their "prey" is evidently the reappearance of the "death-wish." Their love is heavy with doom and we know from the first that death is the only outcome. Racine's originality, as we shall see, lies largely in his concentration on the "paroxysm" and in the light that he throws on the state of mind of his characters when the crisis is reached.

iii

Although there is undoubtedly an element of complicity in Racine's study of sexual passion, his approach to the problem was a serious one and he did not indulge, as hostile critics have alleged, in the analysis of violent passion merely for its own sake.

---

[1] Compare the incident in the legend where King Mark finds the lovers asleep in a cabin in the forest fully dressed and with Tristan's sword between them. The King removes the sword and places his own there in its place, so that it becomes a symbol of the "law" which the lovers have transgressed.

In making sexual passion the mainspring of human action, he anticipated some of the more revolutionary findings of contemporary psychologists. It did not narrow the scope of his work; it enabled him to make one of the most searching examinations of human nature in French literature; and as I have already suggested, it was precisely his interest in love that helped him to break down the barriers between the different classes and to concentrate on emotions which are common to human nature as a whole without distinction of class or creed.

There is a passage in *Bajazet* which provides a good illustration of the sombre power of Racine's study of man and also serves to remind us that he lived in the same century as John Donne. Atalide is proposing to surrender her lover to Roxane and to commit suicide:

> Roxane s'estimait assez récompensée,
> Et j'aurais en mourant cette douce pensée
> Que, vous ayant moi-même imposé cette loi,
> Je vous ai vers Roxane envoyé plein de moi;
> Qu'emportant chez les morts toute votre tendresse,
> Ce n'est point un amant en vous que je lui laisse.

We must not misunderstand the word *tendresse*—"that terrible little word," as a French critic once called it. It is not the same as love; it is the capacity for love, a capacity which is transformed from potency to act as soon as a suitable object presents itself.[1] In Racine's poetry love is always what Corneille called *une inclination aveugle*, a blind urge for possession which not only prefers the death of the beloved to allowing him to fall into the clutches of a rival, but which sees consummation not in union with, but in the pursuit and destruction of its "prey." The tragic dilemma lies in the fact that lacking *tendresse*, man is deprived of something vital without which he ceases to be man and becomes an impotent shell. With it he is inexorably dedicated to destruction and death.

In a passage which I set at the head of this chapter, the great Benjamin Constant declared that the effect of love is to *égarer notre raison* and its aim to *procurer des jouissances*. Racine is almost exclusively concerned with its effect, and the *jouissances* invariably elude his characters. The word *égarer* was carefully chosen by Constant and it was a favourite word of Racine's, a word that goes a

[1] *cf.* "*L'amour* où je voulais amener sa *tendresse*" (*Britannicus*).

long way towards illuminating the central experience of his poetry.
The rhythm of passion is also the rhythm of the plays and it always
follows the same course. The movement is indeed almost physiological, and it is well illustrated by Néron's speech in *Britannicus*,
Act II. Sc. ii:

> Excité d'un désir curieux,
> Cette nuit je l'ai vue arriver en ces lieux,
> Triste, levant au ciel ses yeux mouillés de larmes,
> Qui brillaient au travers des flambeaux et des armes;
> Belle, sans ornements, dans le simple appareil
> D'une beauté qu'on vient d'arracher au sommeil.
> Que veux-tu? Je ne sais si cette négligence,
> Les ombres, les flambeaux, les cris et le silence,
> Et le farouche aspect de ses fiers ravisseurs,
> Relevaient de ses yeux les timides douceurs.
> Quoi qu'il en soit, ravi d'une si belle vue,
> J'ai voulu lui parler, et ma voix s'est perdue:
> Immobile, saisi d'un long étonnement,
> Je l'ai laissé passer dans son appartement.
> J'ai passé dans le mien. C'est là que, solitaire,
> De son image en vain j'ai voulu me distraire:
> Trop présente à mes yeux je croyais lui parler;
> J'aimais jusqu'à ses pleurs que je faisais couler.
> Quelquefois, mais trop tard, je lui demandais grâce;
> J'employais les soupirs, et même la menace.
> Voilà comme, occupé de mon nouvel amour,
> Mes yeux, sans se fermer, ont attendu le jour . . .
> Soit que son cœur, jaloux d'une austère fierté,
> Enviât à nos yeux sa naissante beauté,
> Fidèle à sa douleur, et dans l'ombre enfermée,
> Elle se dérobait même à sa renommée;
> Et c'est cette vertu, si nouvelle à la cour,
> Dont la persévérance irrite mon amour.
> Quoi, Narcisse! tandis qu'il n'est point de Romaine
> Que mon amour n'honore et ne rende plus vaine,
> Qui, dès qu'à ses regards elle ose se fier,
> Sur le cœur de César ne les vienne essayer,
> Seule dans son palais la modeste Junie
> Regarde leurs honneurs comme une ignominie,
> Fuit, et ne daigne pas peut-être s'informer
> Si César est aimable, ou bien s'il sait aimer?
> Dis-moi, Britannicus l'aime-t-il?

Racine's critics have pointed out that Néron is only seen in this play on the threshold of his career of crime and that he is far milder than the monster of history. Now it was no part of Racine's purpose to tone down Néron's character out of respect for contemporary susceptibilities or to present posterity with an exact picture of the historical Nero. His Néron is the blasé representative of an ageing civilization and a vehicle for Racine's criticism of the ruling class. The passage is an admirable example of the beauty and subtlety of his poetry. It can be seen that the language is psychological. Racine does not describe the physical appearance of people or things for its own sake; he only does so in order to reveal the state of mind of an observer. His descriptions of things are therefore general, and his descriptions of feelings concrete and particular. We do not see Junie herself; we only see her through Néron's eyes. He himself does not see her as an individual; his attention is concentrated on his own feelings and Junie is merely the "prey" who will provide him with fresh sensations. His interest is selective and limited to those features which appeal directly to his sexual desires or, as he puts it, "irrite mon amour." Only general terms are used to describe her such as "yeux mouillés de larmes," "belle, sans ornements," "timides douceurs" and "naissante beauté."

Néron's own feelings, however, are complex. The "désir curieux" contains an element of refined corruption, but it also suggests the devious, winding course of his desires. The absence of all ornament is a symbol of simplicity and purity which are distinguished from the tricks and disingenuousness of the ladies of the Court. The flickering torches reflect the stirrings of Néron's feelings and may recall the décor of the Court orgies. The "arms" and the "soldiers" emphasize the softness and helplessness of the victim and are also a sign of Néron's power over her. This power is purely physical and the victim remains remote and inaccessible, which only serves to titillate Néron's jaded senses. His corruption is underlined by his sudden shyness; but there is no real volition behind "J'ai voulu lui parler"; the shyness is a perverse archness and is contrasted with the genuine timidity of Junie.

The success of the passage depends to a large extent on the way in which the movement of feeling is woven into the movement of the procession of soldiers with their captive. It determines the tempo and it gives the passage its internal coherence. The procession passes with great rapidity, and the rapidity—the shift and change of exciting, stimulating feelings blending with the measured tread of the guards—reflects the rapid growth of Néron's "interest." But as Junie disappears from view with her captors, whose *farouche* vitality makes Néron even more conscious of his need for stimulation, there is a sudden slowing down of the tempo.

> Immobile, saisi d'un long étonnement

provides the speaker with a *soulagement*, a vicarious satisfaction. He goes into his own room where the solitude increases the effect of his impressions and he indulges in a form of *delectatio morosa*. The solitude is invaded by sexual fantasies which torment him. He tries to brush them aside, but they return with renewed force. The tempo quickens as momentary satisfaction changes to the irritation of exasperated desires. The *austère fierté* and the *vertu* are both attractive and irritating; attractive because they offer a fresh, inviolate "prey"; irritating because they represent a formidable obstacle in the way of satisfaction—a moral obstacle.

Néron is not restrained by moral scruples of his own, but by a code which is recognized by the intended victim and which he himself does not recognize. This turns the chase into a moral obstacle race. In nearly all the plays, Racine's principal characters start at a point *inside* the moral code of society, but they are driven by their own furious passions *outside* society altogether. This is Néron's journey, and, in the other plays, by the time they have reached the state of paroxysm the characters are in the same position. Néron's starting-point is the *désir curieux* which leads him to the moral barriers represented by *austère fierté* and *vertu*. He knows that he cannot break them down and will have to circumvent them by the removal of Britannicus. The line

> Dis-moi, Britannicus l'aime-t-il?

is the point at which he has arrived. He is now ready to commit murder, is indeed a potential murderer. For these stories always end with murder or suicide or both, and the characters never have any difficulty in finding people to tell them that the moral code not only does not matter, but does not exist once the heart is engaged.

> Mais l'amour ne suit point ces lois imaginaires

cries Roxane, and she speaks for all Racine's heroines. Passion is the reality, "law" but the shadow. Passion sweeps aside law, reason and morality as it hurries humanity down the dizzy slope to destruction.

The conviction that passion is absolutely irresistible is common to all the characters, and it appears to be a matter for rejoicing or lamentation according to their personal outlook. Roxane proclaims the fact triumphantly in a line of immense vitality:

> Viens m'engager ta foi: le temps fera le reste.

But some of Racine's finest lines express a different view—a tragic sense that it is too late, that all the supports have been removed:

> Il n'est plus temps. Il sait mes ardeurs insensées.
> De l'austère pudeur les bornes sont passées.

> Je me suis engagé trop avant.
> Je vois que la raison cède à la violence.

There is nothing genteel, nothing bloodless, about these feelings. Racine is at some pains to emphasize the physical side of love. In the great speech in Act IV, Sc. ii of *Britannicus* Agrippine remarks:

> une loi moins sévère
> Mit Claude dans mon *lit*, et Rome à mes genoux.

The bed sticks out in Racine's poetry. It is the ultimate goal towards which all these frenzied lovers strive; and neither the silken canopies nor the coroneted sheets can hide the violence of the drama that will be enacted there, or its appalling consequences:

> Ses gardes, son palais, son *lit*, m'étaient soumis,
> Je lui laissai sans fruit consumer sa tendresse.

Thus Agrippine, and she, too, speaks for all Racine's heroines. One of the most striking figures in the plays is the predatory female who for all her air of modesty and virtue pursues the reluctant male and sucks out his vitality.

Although the conflict, in which "law" is swept away or conveniently relaxed in order to smooth the heroine's path to an incestuous couch, springs from a profound hostility between the individual and society, it is not until we reach *Phèdre* and *Athalie* that the issue becomes a specifically moral one. The characters in the final plays are in a sense destroyed by their own guilty

consciences, but those in the earlier plays are the victims of a
catastrophe of a different nature. When, for example, Oreste
declares:

> Je pensai que la guerre et la gloire
> De soins plus importants rempliraient ma mémoire;
> Que, mes sens reprenant leur première vigueur,
> L'amour achèverait de sortir de mon cœur,

it is clear that he is not concerned with the relative values of *gloire*
and *amour*. Sexual passion is not regarded as wrong in itself, as
it is in *Phèdre*, or as the occasion of wrongful actions; it is seen to
be something very like a physical disturbance, a disease which
corrodes and undermines the native health and "vigour" of the
human organism.

In a comment on the line:

> Leur haine ne fera qu'irriter sa tendresse,

Jacques Rivière pointed out that it formulates the basic principle
of Racine's psychology. There is no conflict between principle and
feeling or between reason and emotion, but the naked friction of
one set of feelings on another which ends by destroying both.

"There is nothing in his mind," said Rivière of Oreste, "which,
properly speaking, acts as a dam against the wave of love except a contrary
feeling which you can call anger, resentment, hate or what you like,
but which at bottom is of the same nature and the same stuff as the
passion against which it is pitted."[1]

Once the paroxysm has begun, nothing can stop it. The essence
of the process is not that the characters are completely at the mercy
of their passions and that reason is impotent; it is rather that they
recognize paroxysm as their habitual state and resent any intervention of reason. When Oreste is reminded of the reason for his
presence in Epirus, he cries impatiently

> Je suis las d'écouter la raison.

When he himself proceeds to give reasons for not killing Pyrrhus,
Hermione retorts savagely:

> Ah! c'en est trop, Seigneur!
> Tant de raisonnements offensent ma colère.

[1] *Moralisme et littérature*, p. 28.

The appeal to "reason" provokes an immediate and violent reaction, not merely because it frustrates personal desires, but because it stands for a way of life which is fundamentally antipathetic to the inhabitants of Racine's world. Why this is so is explained in a remarkable utterance of Pyrrhus:

> Oui, mes vœux ont trop loin poussé leur *violence*
> Pour ne plus s'arrêter que dans l'indifférence.
> Songez-y bien: il faut désormais que mon cœur,
> S'il n'aime avec *transport*, haïsse avec *fureur*.
> Je n'épargnerai rien dans ma juste colère:
> Le fils me répondra des mépris de la mère . . .

The words "Il faut désormais que mon cœur . . ." betray a profound psychological need on the part of the speaker to live at a certain pitch of intensity, to maintain the paroxysm which is native to him. He is faced with three alternatives: "love," "hate," "indifference." Now "indifference" is ruled out precisely because it is a *neutral* state. It leaves no room for the "transports" of love or the "fury" of hatred and would lower the pitch of intensity in a manner that is inconceivable to Racine's characters, would bring them back to a norm of sanity which would be as distasteful as it would be precarious. Although "indifference" may seem to be of "the same nature and the same stuff" as love and hatred, Racine's characters instinctively perceive that it is the product of "reason," and reason is felt to be the enemy of life and spontaneity. For moderation in any form is impossible and abhorrent; the suggestion that they should even listen to reason is felt to be an intolerable affront which at once raises the paroxysm to its maximum intensity. There is no mistaking the place where the emphasis falls in a line that I have already quoted:

> Tant de raisonnements *offensent* ma colère.

When Hermione is finally thrown over by Pyrrhus, she says of him:

> Ah! je l'ai trop aimé pour ne le point haïr.

There is no middle course. They love or hate with the whole force of their being. Hatred is its own justification, and it seems natural in such a world to describe the wrath which proposes to visit the refusal of the mother on the head of an infant son as a *juste colère*.

In another place Oreste remarks:

> Détestant ses rigueurs, rabaissant ses attraits,
> Je défiais ses yeux de me troubler jamais.
> Voilà comme je crus étouffer ma tendresse.
> En ce calme trompeur j'arrivai dans la Grèce ...

"Calm" is always unnatural and deceptive, is never more than a pause between the paroxysms, an uneasy truce between the combatants. For *tendresse* lasts as long as life; it cannot be "stifled"; it is either gratified or it turns into hatred, and the transports of love and the fury of hatred both lead to the same doom.

So they live, tragic or triumphant, in a perpetual state of oscillation between two extremes, never knowing from one moment to the next at which pole they will find themselves.

> S'il ne meurt aujourd'hui, je puis l'aimer demain

says Hermione of her feelings for Pyrrhus. And when she herself is described as

> Toujours prête à partir, et demeurant toujours,

the line suggests very well the restless movement of the whole play and of all Racine's work.

Much has been written of Racine's "elegance," of his "politeness" and of his fondness for the *formules protocolaires*, but their purpose has not always been appreciated. When Bajazet makes difficulties over accepting Roxane's offer of marriage, she replies in a tone of the utmost correctness:

> Je vous entends, Seigneur; je vois mon imprudence,
> Je vois que rien n'échappe à votre prévoyance.
> Vous avez pressenti jusqu'au moindre danger
> Où mon amour trop prompt vous allait engager.

The studied politeness and the biting contempt with which she contrasts his *prévoyance* (which is a product of "reason") and her own *imprudence*, her own *amour trop prompt*, shows that she is making an immense effort to control her feelings which are clearly on the verge of eruption. Her very restraint heightens the dramatic intensity of the scene and we can imagine the spectators beginning to feel warm under their collars, wriggling happily in their seats and whispering to one another: "Tu vois. Elle va éclater."

Twenty lines later it happens. The *Seigneur* and the whole protocol go by the board, and Roxane denounces Bajazet with a savage proletarian invective:

> Ne m'importune plus de tes raisons forcées.
> Je vois combien tes vœux sont loin de mes pensées;
> Je ne te presse plus, ingrat, d'y consentir.
> Rentre dans le néant dont je t'ai fait sortir . . .
>
> Mais je m'assure encore aux bontés de ton frère:
> Il m'aime, tu le sais; et malgré sa colère,
> Dans ton perfide sang je puis tout expier,
> Et ta mort suffira pour me justifier.
> N'en doute point, j'y cours, et dès ce moment même.

"Ça y est. La voilà partie," whisper the spectators; but almost at once there is another change of tone—a change this time to a warm familiarity, to a tone of supplication:

> Bajazet, écoutez, je sens que je vous aime:
> Vous vous perdez. Gardez de me laisser sortir.
> Le chemin est encore ouvert au repentir.
> Ne désespérez point une amante en furie.
> S'il m'échappait un mot, c'est fait de votre vie.

What is interesting in these lines is Roxane's consciousness that she is suspended between "love" and "hatred," and her attempt to persuade her disdainful lover to prevent her from swinging to the other pole which will lead to death and disaster. Bajazet's clumsy reference to his brother's love for Roxane:

> Peut-être que ma mort . . .
> Vous rendra dans son cœur votre première place,

drives her back at once to the *tutoiement passionné*:

> Dans son cœur? Ah! crois-tu, quand il le voudrait bien,
> Que si je perds l'espoir de régner dans le tien,
> D'une si douce erreur si longtemps possédée,
> Je puisse désormais souffrir une autre idée,
> Ni que je vive enfin, si je ne vis pour toi?
> Je te donne, cruel, des armes contre moi,
> Sans doute, et je devrais retenir ma faiblesse.
> Tu vas en triompher. Oui, je te le confesse,

J'affectais à tes yeux une fausse fierté.
De toi dépend ma joie et ma félicité.
De ma sanglante mort ta mort sera suivie.
Quel fruit de tant de soins que j'ai pris pour ta vie!

We can see now that Racine's elegance is a surface elegance which does nothing to mitigate the violence of the tumult which goes on beneath. His aim is to probe feelings which are properly speaking anterior to all civilization and which a supreme degree of civilization covers but cannot extinguish.[1] His polished elegance is a method of penetrating the defences of his sophisticated audience—that complicated system of inhibitions which is the product of centuries of civilization—and of evoking the response that he wants. There can be little doubt that it was his skill in revealing the primitive man beneath the civilized man which disconcerted his contemporaries and provoked the bitter attacks on his work by conservative critics. For the creation of Roxane reminded them uncomfortably of the exploits of an Anne de Gonzague or a Madame Murat, reminded them too pointedly of what lay only just beneath the surface of their splendid society. It was the triumph of Racine's art not simply to lay bare these feelings, but to give them a social reference, to show that they were bound to be in a state of constant eruption in a civilization which in some respects had become a façade. It was the tragedy of a people who were deprived of an order that could provide a proper outlet for their immense vitality; a force which was of necessity turned inward against itself to become a source of waste and destruction.

"A scene in Corneille," wrote Giraudoux, "is an official rendez-vous where one comes to discuss in hopes of a settlement. In Racine, it is the explanation which closes for the time a series of negotiations between wild beasts"; and a few pages later he speaks of Racine's characters confronting one another "on a footing of awful

---

[1] Racine's characters are conscious not only of the opposition between "love" and "reason," but of the fact that love is *anterior* to reason. In the quotation from *Britannicus* which follows, *amour* and *raison* really mean "passion" and "civilization." (The third line should be compared with Oreste's declaration on p. 176 above.)

NÉRON:
> Si jeune encor, se connaît-il lui-même?
> D'un regard enchanteur connaît-il le poison?

NARCISSE:
> Seigneur, l'amour toujours n'attend pas la raison.

equality, of physical and moral nudity."[1] The morality of Racine's
world is the morality of the jungle, but the violence is intensified
and not diminished by the characters' exceptional powers of
insight, their extremely sensitive consciousness of their most
intimate feelings which belonged to a people of whom the poet
constantly uses the word *sensible*. This insight can be seen in the
lines:

> Déjà même je crois entendre la réponse
> Qu'en secret contre moi votre haine prononce,

where the movement of feeling is seized before it becomes articulate.

When exceptional insight into human feelings exists without a
true social order, it can only work destructively. Racine's use of
the words *menacé* and *atteint* is no less revealing than his fondness
for the word *sensible*. His characters are only too conscious that
their inner stability is threatened, and *atteint* shows how successful
their enemies are in destroying it. For they use their gifts to torture
themselves and each other. They possess like their creator a
remarkable streak of cruelty, and their clairvoyance makes them
immensely vulnerable for one another. It enables them to perceive,
without possibility of error, the weakness of their opponents, to
track life to its source, to strike and kill with deadly accuracy. Their
desire to annihilate and their complete absence of pity are apparent
in some lines from *Andromaque* in which Hermione recalls Pyrrhus'
exploits in the Trojan war:

> Du vieux père d'Hector la valeur abattue
> Aux pieds de sa famille expirante à sa vue,
> Tandis que dans son sein votre bras enfoncé
> *Cherche un reste de sang que l'âge avait glacé.*

After planning the assassination of Pyrrhus, Hermione sends her
confidente to Oreste with this message:

> Va le trouver: dis-lui qu'il apprenne à l'ingrat
> Qu'on l'immole à ma haine, et non pas à l'État.
> Chère Cléone, cours. Ma vengeance est perdue
> S'il ignore en mourant que c'est moi qui le tue.

The words *désordre* and *inutile* also recur all through the plays,
and they reveal more clearly than anything the nature of the

[1] *op. cit.*, pp. 24, 27.

tragedy—the sense of helpless confusion in a world that offers the individual no help, no constructive principle for the ordering of his life. *Honneur* and *gloire* had lost their meaning; all that remained was an enemy to torture and destroy.

> Je crains de me connaître, en l'état où je suis,

cries one. Of another we are told:

> Il peut, Seigneur, il peut, dans ce *désordre* extrême
> Épouser ce qu'il hait, et punir ce qu'il aime.

In *Iphigénie* it is said:

> Il fallut s'arrêter, et la rame *inutile*
> Fatigua vainement une mer immobile.

The *inutile* suggests the hopelessness of the struggle, and the *fatigua* underlines the fact that the effort, instead of strengthening and purifying character as it does in Corneille, has the reverse effect and produces a state of exhaustion which undermines character. There is only one answer:

> Puisqu'après tant d'efforts ma résistance est vaine,
> Je me livre en aveugle au destin qui m'entraîne.

In this world passion is destiny. It is at once the source of life and of death. "Songez," said Roxane to her lover, "Songez"

> Que vous ne respirez qu'autant que je vous aime.

No one is in any doubt about the outcome, which is accepted not merely with resignation but with satisfaction:

> Je trouvais du plaisir à me perdre pour elle.

In making sexual passion the supreme value in a world of dissolving values, the last refuge of the man who has lost faith in all else, Racine anticipates the writers of a later age. He also anticipates them in revealing that man deliberately attaches himself to the principle of death and destruction, that it is indeed the death-wish which is the deepest and most secret thing in passion.

3. The Pattern of the Plays

I have never felt convinced by the view that Corneille's work
represents a steady process of development from the early comedies
to the final tragedies, but it is a claim which can be made with some
confidence in the case of Racine. His poetry, indeed, is only fully
intelligible when it is seen as a whole, as a logical progression from
the early imitations of Corneille to *Phèdre* and *Athalie*.

His first play, *les Frères ennemis*, is a mechanical affair of little
intrinsic value which need not detain us; but the second, *Alexandre
le Grand*, cannot be altogether disregarded. It was in some ways an
interesting experiment. It was written as a tribute to the King whom
the poet presents in the guise of a Cornelian hero. Its interest lies
in the way in which Racine's personal sensibility peeps out from
behind phrases lifted bodily from Corneille. When Alexandre
declares:

> . . . au seul nom d'un roi jusqu'alors *invincible*,
> A de nouveaux exploits mon cœur devint *sensible*,

we feel at once that there is something wrong, that there is a contrast
between the heroic vocabulary and the lack of a corresponding drive
in the texture of the verse. *Invincible* is a borrowing from Corneille,
but "mon cœur devint *sensible*" bears Racine's own stamp. The
invincibility of the Cornelian hero might arouse the admiration of
an opponent, but it would never provoke the reaction attributed
to Alexandre in these lines, and the confusion runs all through the
play. Alexandre's use of the heroic vocabulary is false and embarrassing; he has none of the "toughness" of the Cornelian hero and he
is also without the sensitiveness of Racine's characters. He is
nothing more than a ventriloquist's doll mouthing the big words
in his thin, piping voice.

Andromaque is the first of the great masterpieces. It occupies the
same place in Racine's work as the *Cid* in Corneille's, and it possesses the same peculiar beauty. But in spite of its beauty, an
occasional roughness in the texture, which disappears in the later
plays, and a certain note of harshness make it difficult of access
when read for the first time. I have already drawn heavily on this
play because it is the perfect illustration of some of Racine's special

interests, but I cannot leave it without some further comments. One of the most striking things about it is the range of tone and mood displayed in the character of Hermione—the soft, caressing

> Le croirai-je, Seigneur, qu'un reste de tendresse
> Vous fasse ici chercher une triste princesse?

the perfidious

> Enfin, qui vous a dit que malgré mon devoir
> Je n'ai pas quelquefois souhaité de vous voir?

the haughty

> Seigneur, je le vois bien, votre âme prévenue
> Répand sur mes discours le venin qui la tue . . .

the indignant surprise of

> Qui vous l'a dit, Seigneur, qu'il me méprise?

the coarse brutality of

> Et tout ingrat qu'il est, il me sera plus doux
> De mourir avec lui que de vivre avec vous,

and what Mauriac calls the *tutoiement passionné* of

> Je ne t'ai point aimé, cruel? Qu'ai-je donc fait?

"C'est une certaine candeur violente de créature encore intacte," wrote Jules Lemaître of Hermione. Although Andromaque gives her name to the play, it is Hermione and Oreste who occupy the centre of the stage. For the play is a consummate study of youthful passion.[1] Racine chose a moment which comes once and once only in a life, and his study has the finality of great art.

The play is important for another reason. It illustrates Racine's approach to a Cornelian situation, and a comparison with the *Cid* helps us to understand in what sense Racine's impact produced a change of direction in French drama. There is an obvious conflict between Oreste's personal interests and the claims of State or, to use the Cornelian formula, between "love" and "honour." The startling innovation is not that "honour" is completely routed, but

[1] But compare: "Je parle d'Hermione comme d'une femme et non comme d'une jeune fille ce qui est contraire aux données de la pièce, mais conforme à son esprit. Le rôle n'est virginal à aucun moment." (Brisson, *op. cit.*, p. 37.)

that Oreste appears to be unaware that its claims even exist. He admits that he never had the slightest intention of carrying out his mission, but undertook it purely in the hope that it would give him a last opportunity of making a conquest of Hermione and of carrying her off. The violent conflict which eventually destroys him is not provoked by the irreconcilable claims of "love" and "honour," but by his failure to win Hermione. As the Ambassador of Greece, he hesitates, quite understandably, before making up his mind to assassinate the sovereign to whom he is accredited; but when it is done, it is not remorse for his crime that drives him mad. It is the realization that his elaborate "stratagems," which have culminated in murder, have been in vain and that Hermione is irrevocably lost to him.[1]

Although Britannicus gives his name to Racine's next tragedy, it is not primarily a study of youthful passion or even of youthful despotism. The young lovers do not occupy the centre of the stage; they are mainly interesting in that they are the pretext for Néron's crime. *Britannicus* is a more complex play than *Andromaque*. It is the first play in which Racine deals directly with political problems, and there are some lines in Act IV which show that he already understands very clearly the nature of dictatorship. Narcisse is advising his master against a policy of clemency:

> Mais, Seigneur, les Romains ne vous sont pas connus.
> Non, non, dans leurs discours ils sont plus retenus.
> Tant de précaution affaiblit votre règne:
> Ils croiront, en effet, mériter qu'on les craigne.
> Au joug depuis longtemps ils se sont façonnés.
> Ils adorent la main qui les tient enchaînés.

Britannicus points the way to *Athalie*, but the study of despotism is much more limited in scope than it is in Racine's last play. The despot only uses his absolute powers in an attempt to rid himself of one wife and to secure another. His crime is essentially a *crime d'amour*, but Racine's treatment of the connection between love and politics breaks fresh ground in his work. Néron's personal vanity is outraged by Junie's refusal, but he also feels that her refusal is an affront to his position as emperor:

---

[1] His apology to Hermione, when announcing the murder of Pyrrhus, for not being able to find a place to stab him himself, is a characteristic touch.

> Du sang dont vous sortez rappelez la mémoire;
> Et ne préférez point, à la solide gloire
> Des honneurs dont César prétend vous revêtir,
> La gloire d'un refus, sujet au repentir.

The *solide gloire* which Néron dangles vainly before Junie's eyes is something much less estimable than Cornelian glory, but it shows the extent to which "love" and "ambition" are interrelated in the "police state." In *Britannicus* love is sought not merely for its own sake, but as a means to an end. Its exploitation is seen to be one of the most effective ways of obtaining political power and the brazen Agrippine admits it frankly:

> Je souhaitai son lit, dans la seule pensée
> De vous laisser au trône où je serais placée.

The royal bed is the symbol of political domination. The banishment or escape of one of the partners from the bed is the sign of a change in the political "line-up":

> Je vois de votre cœur Octavie effacée,
> Prête à sortir du lit où je l'avais placée.

In *Bajazet* Roxane uses her dictatorial powers to try to force her "brother-in-law" to marry her, but it is not a political play in the same sense as *Britannicus*. Racine said in his Preface that it was based on an incident which took place in Turkey in 1638 and that he had heard the story from the Comte de Cézy who was French Ambassador to the Ottoman Empire at the time. No one has succeeded in tracing a copy of the account which Racine purported to have read, and some of his editors have suggested that the story is a *supercherie*. It may well be that Racine invented it in order to forestall criticism of the content of the play. There is no doubt that it was the setting of the seraglio which fired his imagination, and in the creation of Roxane he went a good deal further in his study of violent passion than in any of the preceding plays. *Bajazet* is interesting for another reason. It is strikingly like *Phèdre* with the religious *motif* omitted. In essentials it is the same story—the story of a woman whose "guilty" passion destroys "innocent" lovers.

The innocent couple whose happiness is threatened by the

claims of State but who eventually escape destruction is the theme
of both *Mithridate* and *Iphigénie*. Neither of these plays is among
Racine's supreme achievements, but *Mithridate* is a new departure.
Xipharès says of his father's love for Monine:

> En ce malheur je tremblai pour ses jours;
> Je redoutai du roi les cruelles amours.
> Tu sais combien de fois ses jalouses tendresses
> Ont pris soin d'assurer la mort de ses maîtresses.

The *cruelles amours* and the *jalouses tendresses* show the direction
in which Racine was moving. Mithridate, as Racine presents him,
is a comparatively harmless and rather pathetic figure; but we
have the impression that his creator was itching to give his audience
a powerful study of sadism and was only prevented from doing so
by the *bienséances*. The weakness of the play lies mainly in the
contrast between Mithridate's reputation and the poor, jealous
old man who actually appears on the stage.

These, then, are the lines along which Racine's work was developing, but it remains to point out a further change which took place
after *Andromaque* and which goes deeper than any of those I have
already mentioned. *Andromaque* is a consummate study of youthful
passion certainly, but it is a play which could only have been
written at a particular moment in a poet's development. In the
plays which followed, the focus shifts from youth to middle age.
Racine's greatest plays are not studies of innocence; they are
studies of crises in the lives of middle-aged women who are certainly
not *intactes*. As his genius ripened, characters like Agrippine,
Roxane, Phèdre and Athalie and, to a lesser extent, the middle-
aged warrior in *Mithridate* who returns home after his armies
have been defeated and his country laid waste by a "useless campaign," became the symbols of a spiritual crisis through which
society was passing. When played by a distinguished actress, the
great *tirades*—Agrippine's encounter with Néron in *Britannicus*
Act IV. Sc. ii, Phèdre's confession of her jealousy and Athalie's
dream—have an impressiveness which is unique in the European
theatre.[1]

[1] Racine's genius was in many ways a feminine one and this is apparent in
the immense superiority of his female characters. Oreste is the only one of his
men who can be compared with the greatest of his women.

4. *Bérénice*

Bérénice, like *Andromaque*, has a special place in the Racinian canon, and a few words must be said about it before passing on to a detailed discussion of *Phèdre* and *Athalie*. The play was in the nature of a "command performance." Louis XIV's sister-in-law, the charming and tragic Henriette d'Angleterre, suggested to Corneille and Racine that they should write plays on the love of Titus and Bérénice. The two poets set to work each unaware that the suggestion had been made to the other. Their plays were both produced in the autumn of 1670 and the competition led to a signal defeat for the ageing Corneille. It is probable that Henriette would have regretted her mischievous suggestion had she been there to see the result. But she was not. She had died during the previous summer either of a gastric ulcer or of appendicitis.

It is said that Henriette herself provided Racine with the material as well as the subject of his play, that Titus and Bérénice are none other than Louis XIV and Henriette. "She only meant the King to love her as a sister-in-law," wrote Madame de La Fayette in her *Histoire de Madame Henriette d'Angleterre*,[1] "but I fancy that he loved her differently. And she, I think, believed that she merely returned his fraternal affection; yet, perhaps, she gave him something more. At all events, since they were both infinitely lovable and both of an amorous disposition, since they met day after day in a continual round of pleasure and festivity, there were onlookers who thought that they possessed for one another the attraction and charm which precede a *grande passion*."

In spite of its success on the seventeenth-century stage, *Bérénice* has not worn well. It was felt in the next century by Vauvenargues to be inferior to Racine's finest work. This view was shared by Sainte-Beuve—we remember his *mot* about the "charmante et mélodieuse faiblesse"—and is held among living French critics by M. Pierre Brisson. It is curious that Lemaître, whose book did so much to dispose of the "tender Racine," should have declared that *Bérénice* is "the most Racinian of the plays because it is the most tender."[2] It seems to me on the contrary to be the least success-

[1] *Mémoires de Madame de La Fayette*, publiés avec préface, notes et tables par Eugène Asse, Paris, 1890, p. 36.

[2] *op. cit.*, p. 204.

ful of the mature tragedies precisely because Racine was obliged
to handle a theme which was eminently unsuited to his genius. It
is the only one of his plays in which "honour" triumphs over
"love," and his palpable disbelief in the values invoked drove him
to strange lengths in order to impose on others convictions which
he himself did not hold. It is this that makes the verse seem hollow
and inflated. At bottom it is a curious *tour de force*. Racine hovers
on the verge of a highly refined and very personal sentimentality,
and only his extreme virtuosity prevents him from succumbing to
it.

"It is not necessary to have blood and corpses in a tragedy," he
wrote in his Preface; "it is sufficient if the action is great, if the
characters are heroic, the passions aroused, and if the whole play
makes us feel that majestic sadness which is the pleasure proper
to tragedy."

We may suspect that heroism and *tristesse majestueuse* are
incompatible and that it was the attempt to combine them which
makes the verse of the play so instructive. Titus is no hero; he is
a prig who dwells voluptuously on his own weaknesses which he
manages both to excuse and to boast about:

> Tu ne l'ignores pas: toujours la renommée
> Avec le même éclat n'a pas semé mon nom.
> Ma jeunesse, nourrie à la cour de Néron,
> S'égarait, cher Paulin, par l'exemple abusée,
> Et suivait du plaisir la pente trop aisée.

It is not surprising after this to find that *honneur* and *gloire* are
invoked with great frequency. When Titus declares:

> Bérénice a longtemps balancé la victoire;
> Et si je penche enfin du côté de ma *gloire*,
> Crois qu'il m'en a coûté, pour vaincre tant d'amour,
> Des combats dont mon cœur saignera plus d'un jour,

or

> Forcez votre amour à se taire;
> Et d'un œil que la *gloire* et la raison éclaire
> Contemplez mon devoir dans toute sa rigueur.
> Vous-même contre vous fortifiez mon cœur:
> Aidez-moi, s'il se peut, à vaincre sa faiblesse,
> A retenir des pleurs qui m'échappent sans cesse,

or

> Plaignez ma *grandeur* importune.
> Maître de l'univers, je règle sa fortune;
> Je puis faire les rois, je puis les déposer:
> Cependant de mon cœur je ne puis disposer

—we feel that though he is giving up Bérénice in obedience to the claims of State, he is not concerned with the common good or even with the sufferings of Bérénice; he is completely taken up with his own feelings. All these passages begin with a reference to *gloire* or *grandeur*, which are *public* virtues, but they all lead back to his *private* feelings, to his "bleeding heart" or the "tears" which are shed with such abundance throughout the play.[1] The same morbid concern for his own feelings is apparent in the references in other places to his *cruel sacrifice* and his *cruelle constance*. The word *gloire* has no moral content; it simply means reputation or what people will think of him if he prefers love to an empire. There is something repellent about this selfish and self-centred preoccupation with his reputation which makes him oblivious to everyone's sufferings but his own. The rhetorical tone in which *gloire* is invoked betrays a note of falseness which runs all through the play and which we may feel sure was no part of the poet's intention. The weaknesses of Racine's hero point to an element of uncertainty in the poet's mind and this is brought home by the way in which the verse, after a few flourishes, simply peters out. Thus in the line

> Des combats dont mon cœur saignera plus d'un jour

the *saignera* is evidently an attempt to heighten feelings which are in danger of flagging.

These weaknesses become still more pronounced in Bérénice's

> Ah! Seigneur, songez-vous en vous-même
> Combien ce mot cruel est affreux quand on aime?
> Dans un mois, dans un an, comment souffrirons-nous,
> Seigneur, que tant de mers me séparent de vous?

[1] *cf.* "The whole play is inundated with tears. Bérénice weeps; Antiochus weeps; Arsace and Phénice weep because they see them weeping. As for Titus he doesn't weep, he streams. . . . It is a veritable deluge. There is not a dry eye in the play. There is not a handkerchief, not a carpet, not a scene, not a couplet, not even a sigh which isn't drenched in tears." (Brisson, *op. cit.* pp. 73, 76.)

Que le jour recommence et que le jour finisse
Sans que jamais Titus puisse voir Bérénice,
Sans que de tout le jour je puisse voir Titus?

This passage is an example of the hollow, inflated verse of which
have spoken. There is an obvious attempt on the part of the speaker
o create a "big scene" and every resource is used to heighten the
ffect, from the over-statement of

Combien ce mot *cruel* est *affreux* quand on aime . . .

o the emphasis on time and space, and the sentimental reflections
n the sun rising and the sun setting.

As the play progresses, the impression becomes stronger that
ne characters are not characters at all, but dummies who declaim
ne arbitrary sentiments which the poet puts into their mouths. In
lace of a detached analysis of emotion, they look at themselves
om without. Their one concern is the effect of their high-flown
ntiments on the audience; they do not consider the intrinsic
ghtness or wrongness of their actions and feelings, but only what
eople will think if they choose some other course, or how much
eople will be impressed by their *cruel sacrifice*. It is on a note of
nug self-satisfaction that the play ends, when Bérénice urges the
nfortunate Antiochus (who at least is honest about his feelings)
take a leaf out of her book:

Sur Titus et sur moi réglez votre conduite:
Je l'aime, je le fuis; Titus m'aime, il me quitte.
Portez loin de mes yeux vos soupirs et vos fers.
Adieu, servons tous trois d'exemple à l'univers
De l'amour la plus tendre et la plus malheureuse
Dont il puisse garder l'histoire douleureuse.

There is something disconcerting about the complacency of a
oman who can hold her own conduct up as a model not merely to
few friends but to the "universe," and who is so convinced of
e importance to history of her own emotions.

IV. *PHÈDRE*

"L'entraînement de notre misérable nature humaine n'a jamais été plus mis à nu." Sainte-Beuve's shrewd comment on *Phèdre* explains very well the change that was taking place in Racine's approach to contemporary problems. In his earlier plays he had revealed himself as the critic of an age of false stability. He had recorded the disintegration of a society whose spiritual life was threatened by a ruthless despotism; he had probed the maladies of the individual soul, had exposed the brittleness of honour and morality in the conflict with sexual passion; but his own attitude had remained one of detachment. He had not troubled about a constructive solution of the problems that he had handled and was undisturbed by the indifference to moral sanctions displayed by his own characters. *Phèdre* belongs to a transitional period in his life. It reveals a deepening of experience; it is richer and more complex than any of its predecessors and the sustained magnificence of the poetry is not surpassed even in *Athalie*. Jules Lemaître called it the first stage in his conversion, and it does show a concern for moral values which is new in Racine's poetry. It is shot through and through with the doctrines of predestination and original sin. Destiny broods darkly over the play and the *motifs* of *race* and *sang* are constantly recurring. Phèdre and Hippolyte are the children of parents who were themselves the victims of guilty passion, and Jansenist theology is enlisted to show the hopelessness of the struggle against heredity and fate without the intervention of grace.

Racine uses the design which had become familiar in his other plays—the triangle in which A pursues B who is desperately in love with C. His contemporaries found it difficult to understand why he had so far departed from tradition as to give Hippolyte a lover, and his frivolous reply that it was to prevent Hippolyte from being suspected of what were discreetly known as "Italian tastes" could scarcely satisfy them. This innovation enabled Racine not only to contrast two forms of love, but also to throw fresh light on the tragic nature of sexual passion. He emphasizes the difference between "innocent" and "guilty" love, and the Christian view of sin and temptation is apparent in the lines:

Grâces au ciel, mes mains ne sont point criminelles.
Plût aux dieux que mon cœur fût innocent comme elles!

Le jour n'est pas plus pur que le fond de mon cœur.
Et l'on veut qu'Hippolyte, épris d'un feu profane ...

It is still more strongly marked in Phèdre's

Ne pense pas qu'au moment que je t'aime,
Innocente à mes yeux je m'approuve moi-même,
Ni que du fol amour qui trouble ma raison
Ma lâche complaisance ait nourri le poison,

which suggests already that Phèdre's guilty conscience plays its part in her downfall. It is noticeable, however, that though sin and temptation are among the principal *motifs* of the play, Phèdre's knowledge that her love is sinful does not increase her powers of resistance; the knowledge that this is so and the sense that she is heading for disaster are part of her temptation.

Racine had become so obsessed by the Jansenist sense of the inherent sinfulness of sexual love that even Hippolyte's love for Aricie is described as *un fol amour*, as an aberration of his *sens égarés*. It leads to disaster as surely as Phèdre's incestuous passion, but to assume that he is destroyed merely because he abandons the role assigned to him by tradition is to underrate the subtlety of Racine's interpretation. The view underlying the play is that once a "limit" has been passed, once weakness or wickedness has entered into the human heart, it can never be cast out again and nothing can stop its ravages. This is felt strongly by Phèdre and Hippolyte, who both realize too late that the limit has been passed:

Il n'est plus temps. Il sait mes ardeurs insensées.
De l'austère pudeur *les bornes sont passées*.

Quiconque a pu franchir *les bornes légitimes*,
Peut violer enfin les droits les plus sacrés.

This applies to the "innocent" as well as to the "guilty." Hippolyte is described more than once as *l'insensible Hippolyte*, and it is precisely his "insensibility" which provides the best protection against the consequences of the furious passions which are unleashed among those who surround him. The stoic ideal, however, is a negative one and Hippolyte is fully conscious of its inadequacy.

H

As soon as his father is reported to be dead, he moves away from it towards something more positive and more human. His feelings for Aricie lead to a relaxation of his father's prohibition against her marrying and when he tells her:

> La Grèce me reproche une mère étrangère.
> Mais, si pour concurrent je n'avais que mon frère,
> Madame, j'ai sur lui de véritables *droits*
> Que je saurais sauver du caprice des *lois*

—there is a distinction between *droits* and *lois*, between natural human "rights" and inhuman "laws." The distinction is a vital one and it is apparent in all Racine's work. In his earlier plays he had exposed the hollowness of an order which had ceased to be a true order and had degenerated into mere "legalism," into the external observance of empty formulas. In *Phèdre* the criticism becomes more searching. The dilemma lies in the fact that though "laws" are incapable of providing a constructive solution of the problems which confronted Racine's contemporaries, they were the only barrier against anarchy. Once a "law," however capricious, was set aside, the way was open to confusion and disorder. This is brought home by the tragic accents of Phèdre's declaration:

> Moi, régner! Moi, ranger un État sous ma *loi*,
> Quand ma faible raison ne règne plus sur moi,
> Lorsque j'ai de mes sens abandonné l'empire,
> Quand sous un joug honteux à peine je respire . . .

The choice lies between legalism and disaster, between an "insensibility," which excludes natural "rights," and a "shameful yoke." In a tragic world the person who desires no more than his natural rights follows the road to destruction. Thésée forbade Aricie to marry because she came of contaminated "blood." Hippolyte's relaxation of his father's prohibition is tantamount to an infringement of "law" which at once involves him in the intrigues that are going on in his entourage. The maxim, as always in Racine, is that there is not and indeed cannot be a middle course which offers security and honour.

One of the most interesting things about the imagery of this play is the symbolism of light and darkness. M. Denis de Rougemont speaks of the opposition between "la Norme du Jour et la

Passion de la Nuit," between the normal feelings of the "daylight"
world and the dark passions which are unleashed "in the night."[1]
In the minds of Phèdre and Hippolyte, "daylight" is associated
with "innocence" and "night" with "guilt." This explains Phèdre's
desperate longing to regain her lost "innocence" and Hippolyte's
battle to protect his "innocence" by an assumed "insensibility."
In the speeches of both characters we are aware at times of an
immense effort—a moral effort—to escape from *la nuit infernale*,
to prevent it from swallowing up the "innocent" everyday life.
When Phèdre discovers that Hippolyte is in love with Aricie, she
cries:

> Tous les *jours* se levaient *clairs* et sereins pour eux.
> Et moi, triste rebut de la nature entière,
> Je me cachais au *jour*, je fuyais la *lumière*.
> La mort est le seul dieu que j'osais implorer,

which shows that she has abandoned all hope, is resigned to
"night" and "death." "Je voulais," she declares in another place

> Je voulais en mourant prendre soin de ma gloire,
> Et dérober au *jour* une flamme si *noire*.

Flamme is normally a symbol of light, a guide in darkness. When
used to describe love it is also a symbol of life, but in making
flamme noire, a fresh significance is given to it. Light is turned
into darkness, life itself into death. There is a great deal in the play
about Thésée's exploits in the pagan hell where he has gone to
help a friend to carry off Pluto's spouse. It seems at first as though
these references are a concession to legend, are mere classical
ornament; but when we look at the texts we find that they have
a different significance and are closely connected with Racine's
interest in darkness. There may be a contrast between the pagan
hell from which a man might escape, and the real hell of spiritual
and emotional torment from which there is no escape. But there is
something more besides. Ismène tells Aricie that Thésée

> a vu le Cocyte et les rivages *sombres*,
> Et s'est montré vivant aux infernales *ombres*.

And Aricie replies:

[1] *op. cit.*, p. 13.

> Croirai-je qu'un mortel, avant sa dernière heure
> Peut pénétrer des morts la *profonde* demeure?

Thésée himself refers to the exploit in similar terms:

> Moi-même, il m'enferma dans des cavernes *sombres*,
> Lieux *profonds* et voisins de l'empire des *ombres*.

The word *ombres* is one of the focal words of the play because it is at once a symbol of "imprisonment" and "refuge." When, for example, Phèdre cries:

> Dieux! que ne suis-je assise à *l'ombre des forêts*!

the cool, leafy green of the forests offers a prospect of escape from her trouble; but though it brings a moment of release from the torments of passion, it is an illusion. It is the struggle of the trapped animal to escape, but there is no escape from the *interior* torment which pursues the victim into the shady refuge:

> Dans *le fond des forêts* votre image me suit;
> La *lumière* du jour, les *ombres* de la nuit,
> Tout retrace à mes yeux les charmes que j'évite,
> Tout vous livre à l'envi le rebelle Hippolyte.

It may well have been of these lines that Taine was thinking when he remarked that when Hippolyte speaks of the forests where his youth was spent, we must substitute the avenues of Versailles. It is a strange assumption which scarcely contributes to a true interpretation of the play. In Racine's lifetime a large part of France was covered by real forests and one of them actually extended to the outskirts of La Ferté-Milon. France was not a vast Versailles, a country of trim gardens and shady walks. It was a country in which a few towns were surrounded by belts of forest, a country in which a high degree of civilization was surrounded by the darkness of the uncivilized provinces. Now this corresponds exactly to the view of human nature that we find in Racine's plays. Human nature was highly reasonable and well-balanced up to a point, but men were becoming increasingly aware of the psychological hinterland, the hidden motives which played a decisive part in human actions. The philosophers, the moralists and the dramatists made common cause in the attempt to penetrate into this psychological jungle. No one was more clearly aware than Racine of what to-day is

called the unconscious, and his aim was to probe the obscure
regions of the mind which are constantly suggested by the phrases
l'empire des ombres, *le fond des forêts*, and others which are equally
significant.

The ambiguity which surrounds "forests" heightens the tragic
urgency of the poetry and is characteristic of the whole play. All
the chief characters are the victims of two conflicting impulses—
the impulse to conceal their true motives from themselves, to force
them into the subconscious and seal them off by using the phrases
le fond des forêts or *l'empire des ombres*, and the impulse to bring
them out into the open by confession. The subtlety and insight
with which Racine exposes this tangle of conflicting feelings has
never been surpassed in French literature.

The first of these impulses is illustrated by Aricie's declaration
of her love for Hippolyte:

> Non que, par les yeux seuls lâchement enchantée,
> J'aime en lui sa beauté, sa grâce tant vantée,
> Présents dont la nature a voulu l'honorer,
> Qu'il méprise lui-même, et qu'il semble ignorer.
> J'aime, je prise en lui de plus nobles richesses,
> Les vertus de son père, et non point les faiblesses.
> J'aime, je l'avoûrai, cet orgueil généreux
> Qui jamais n'a fléchi sous le joug amoureux.
> Phèdre en vain s'honorait des soupirs de Thésée:
> Pour moi, je suis plus fière, et fuis la gloire aisée
> D'arracher un hommage à mille autres offert,
> Et d'entrer dans un cœur de toutes parts ouvert.
> Mais de faire fléchir un courage inflexible,
> De porter la douleur dans une âme insensible,
> D'enchaîner un captif de ses fers étonné,
> Contre un joug qui lui plaît vainement mutiné:
> C'est là ce que je veux, et c'est là ce qui m'irrite.
> Hercule à désarmer coûtait moins qu'Hippolyte,
> Et vaincu plus souvent, et plus tôt surmonté,
> Préparait moins de gloire aux yeux qui l'ont dompté.

The impress of Jansenism is clearly visible in these lines. Aricie's
declaration that she is not attracted by Hippolyte's physical beauty
is perfectly sincere; she does not know that an unconscious fear of
physical love is making her hide her real feelings. There is a certain

satisfaction in the reference to his beauty which is already suspect, and Aricie's true feelings become abundantly clear as the passage develops. The minx peeps out from behind the solemn puritan. She is the familiar figure of the predatory female pursuing the reluctant male.

> Il oppose à l'amour un cœur inaccessible:
> Cherchons pour l'attaquer quelque endroit plus sensible,

cries Phèdre, and Aricie's sentiments are no different. She is spurred on by the love of the hunt, by the desire of making a conquest of someone who is reputed to be insensible to feminine charms. *Gloire* is something very different from the Cornelian glory; in its present context it means no more than success in the chase—the satisfaction of outdistancing one's "rival." Aricie does not think of the pursuit in terms of a goal or of "domestic happiness" any more than the equally demure Atalide in *Bajazet*; she thinks of it in terms of "romance." It is not merely possession that she desires; she wants to dominate Hippolyte, to make him feel the *douleur* of love, to captivate a warrior with "chains" so that all resistance becomes vain. It is characteristic of these "hunts" that they always end in the destruction of the unhappy male. The female is bent on domination and subjection, and the innocent-looking word *fléchi* has a sinister inflection. We cannot shut our eyes to it. This passage is an episode in the sex-war, the eternal rivalry of Man and Woman.

As Racine's genius ripened, he became a pastmaster of the art of revealing the true feelings of his characters which were concealed beneath the elaborate psychological subterfuges constructed by them, and this highly personal form of ambiguity became a persistent feature of his style.

The "innocent" lovers try to hide their feelings, but the "guilty" lover feels impelled to confide in someone. The role of Phèdre seems at first to be one long confession, but in reality there are three distinct confessions and all of them serve different purposes. The confession to Œnone is made partly to rid herself of a crushing sense of guilt and partly to obtain practical assistance in her attempts to win Hippolyte. The confession to Hippolyte himself is intended to break down his resistance. Only the final confession to Thésée is disinterested, is a belated attempt to expiate a wrong.

The nature of the conflict between the need to confess and the desire to conceal can be seen in the symbolical utterance which precedes the great speech in Act I. Sc. iii:

> Que ces vains ornements, que ces voiles me pèsent!
> Quelle importune main, en formant tous ces nœuds,
> A pris soin sur mon front d'assembler mes cheveux?
> Tout m'afflige et me nuit, et conspire à me nuire.

The constraint suggested by *nœuds* is so intense that the confession brings with it a sense of *physical* deliverance:

> Mon mal vient de plus loin. A peine au fils d'Egée
> Sous les lois de l'hymen je m'étais engagée,
> Mon repos, mon bonheur, semblait être affermi,
> Athènes me montra mon superbe ennemi.
> Je le vis, je rougis, je pâlis à sa vue;
> Un trouble s'éleva dans mon âme éperdue;
> Mes yeux ne voyaient plus, je ne pouvais parler,
> Je sentis tout mon corps et transir et brûler.
> Je reconnus Vénus, et ses feux redoutables,
> D'un sang qu'elle poursuit tourments inévitables.
> Par des vœux assidus je crus les détourner:
> Je lui bâtis un temple, et pris soin de l'orner;
> De victimes moi-même à toute heure entourée,
> Je cherchais dans leurs flancs ma raison égarée,
> D'un incurable amour remèdes impuissants!

The abrupt statement with which the speech opens has a curiously steadying effect. It gathers up the diffused emotions of the whole scene and fixes them on a single point: the definition of Phèdre's *mal*. We feel her groping dimly in the subterranean depths of her mind. The word *mal*—the realization that she is a sick woman—is a talisman which sets complicated mental processes in movement and the guilty secret seems to burst out of her.

The poet presents a picture of ordinary, everyday married life which is shattered by a guilty passion. The alexandrines, with the verb pushed to the end of the second line, express perfectly the moral effort made by Phèdre to submit to the marriage "law," and they also reinforce the apparent stability of her happiness. It must be remembered that she is *une femme au déclin de l'âge*; her love for her young and handsome stepson offers a last chance of romantic happiness. *Superbe*, with its suggestion of "glamour" and "romance," is pitted against the humdrum, domestic associations of *engagée* and *affermi* which offer, or once offered, spiritual security. The sudden change of tense—*Athènes me montra*—gives an extraordinary sensation of the "enemy" being hurtled into the attack on conventional married life. The immediate surface reactions, the rapid changes of colour, are carefully noted; the physiological reactions are the prelude to a profound psychological disturbance. There is an inward movement (admirably expressed by *trouble* with its suggestion of limpid water clouding over) and Racine begins to probe the deeper levels. The happiness, which seemed solid and well founded, crumbles at once and the clear-cut lines of *affermi* dissolve into the paroxysm suggested by one of Racine's favourite words—*éperdue*. The psychological disturbance is so violent that it provokes a fresh physical reaction indicated by *brûler* and *transir*. The simple, homely words—*trouble, rougis, brûler, transir*—express Phèdre's state of mind and the complicated interplay of the physiological and the psychological elements with an almost terrifying clarity. It is a sign of Racine's art that *brûler* and *transir*, which are normally associated with the contrary extremes of heat and cold, are here combined to convey the absolute mental and emotional paralysis which overtakes Phèdre.

The analysis has now been pushed to the utmost possible limit —to the point at which it is no longer possible to differentiate between the various sensations—and the result is a form of psychological black-out. It is remarkable how the masterly compression of Racine's verse and the rapidity with which the changes of feeling follow one another contribute to the sense of complete spiritual and moral collapse that we get from the passage as a whole. This impression is heightened by the return to lucidity in l. 9, and Phèdre's realization that she is doomed. The introduction of Venus is not a piece of classical decoration, but an example of the way in which Racine adapts the classics. Venus is not something external to man as she was for the Greeks, but a projection of his own passion which by this means becomes invested with super-human, with irresistible force.[1] Once Venus appears the issue is

---

[1] This explains the tragic irony in the latter part of the speech. Phèdre tells Œnone that in order to escape from Hippolyte, she demanded his banishment:

Je pressai son exil, et mes cris éternels
L'arrachèrent du sein et des bras paternels.

virtually decided. She is contrasted with the humdrum married life, and by a skilful shifting of the emphasis the *feux redoutables* are flung against *bonheur . . . affermi*. It is significant that she attaches herself to the "blood" which is the seat of the primeval passions that Racine uncovers. The reference to the sacrifice is a stroke of irony. Phèdre is engaged in a superstitious game, but is herself the real "victim." The feverish, futile slaughter of the animals indicates her growing desperation. *Entourée* contains a sinister hint that she is being engulfed by passion, by "blood"; *raison* dissolves into *égarée* which refers back to *éperdue*, intensifying the sickening sense of dissolution that we experience in listening to the lines. The whole is clinched by the despairing *remèdes impuissants*.

"All that she is, all that she says, thinks and does only half belongs to her," writes M. Pierre Brisson of the role of Œnone. "Her mind is the invisible emanation of those dark impulses in Phèdre's nature which Phèdre herself is least capable of perceiving."[1]

I think that we can go further than this. Œnone is a symbol rather than an independent person. She is personification of part of Phèdre's mind, a projection of her worse self, always counselling actions which can only lead to disaster, always revealing Phèdre's motives to herself in a way that increases her *trouble*.

> Je t'ai tout avoué; je ne m'en repens pas,

says Phèdre at the end of this speech. But the "confession," far from bringing relief, has precisely the reverse effect. For, writes M. Brisson, "she succumbs to the most corrupting of all sins: the sin of knowledge."[2]

This passage seems to me to be a complete answer to the usual criticisms of Racine's style. It is part of his greatness that the apparent limitations of his medium became one of the main sources of his

---

The remedy failed, and another reference to Venus tells us why it failed:

> Ce n'est plus une ardeur dans mes veines cachée:
> C'est Vénus toute entière à sa proie attachée.

Physical exile could not possibly relieve a *mal* which is essentially an interior one, which belongs to "blood" and entrails, and the disproportion between the evil and the remedy simply intensifies the paroxysm.

[1] *op cit.*, p. 165.   [2] *ibid.*, p. 152.

H*

strength. The alexandrine was not for him, as one feels that it sometimes was for Corneille, a constraint; it was a positive discipline which made possible an extremely *ordered* presentation of emotion. The nineteenth-century view that the great monologues were carefully rehearsed speeches which failed to carry conviction seems to me to be untenable. They are not frigid recitals of old emotions; it is in the retelling that feelings come to life and assume their proper place in the pattern of the plays as psychological events. All the great monologues turn out on examination to be definitions of particular states of mind. In the present case it is the definition of Phèdre's *mal*, and we notice that the passage moves with a mathematical precision from one point to another, as the *mal* is analysed into its component parts. *Éperdue* and *égarée* are stages on the way which follow one another logically. When we look at the passage as a whole—it is forty-eight lines long altogether —we find that Phèdre's state of mind has undergone a change and that just as there are stages within the passage, so the passage itself represents a complete stage in the unfolding of the play.

I have used the word "analysis" to describe the process, but it may be doubted whether the term is altogether exact. There is a sharp distinction between the method of the great imaginative writers of the seventeenth century—it applies in the main to Madame de La Fayette as well as to Racine—and the method of the modern novelist. The characters of Constant and Stendhal consciously and deliberately take their minds to pieces, and in more recent authors the analysis is sometimes pushed to the point at which emotion is destroyed. In Racine there is properly speaking no such thing as analysis. The plays record, to be sure, a process of progressive and destructive self-knowledge, yet it is the result not of carefully calculated analysis, but of intuition, of a sudden insight into their own feelings, of repressed feelings becoming conscious and causing the collapse of personality.

The passage also illustrates the peculiar virtues of Racine's language. The conventional vocabulary has sometimes appeared to English readers to be colourless and inexpressive; but Racine's style is not only perfectly adequate to his experience, it is an instrument of extraordinary delicacy in revealing emotional states. His method is entirely different from that of English poets. English poetry is remarkable for the richness and variety of its imagery and

for its accumulation of sense-perceptions. In Racine's poetry there
are comparatively few images and no accumulation; there is often
simply bare *statement*. He owes nearly everything to the *precision*
with which his language renders the obscurest sensations and to
his exquisite sensibility. The simple, conventional words seem
somehow to penetrate into the furthest layers of the mind, to catch
and fix emotion at the moment of its formation.

I think that we may add that Racine's genius is also the genius
of the French language. In English and still more in German
literature—particularly in the *weltschmerz* of the Romantics—there
almost always remains an unanalysed residue in the feelings
presented which makes a whole poem or a whole play vague and
misty. In the great French masters there is no mist and no blur.
It is because they realized the limitations of language that they have
achieved an extraordinary degree of clarity and depth in the presentation of emotional states. It is, perhaps, for this reason that the
Romantic Movement in France has seemed to many good critics
to have been a betrayal of the French tradition.

From this we can turn to the famous *déclaration* in Act II. Sc. v:

> Oui, Prince, je languis, je brûle pour Thésée.
> Je l'aime, non point tel que l'ont vu les enfers,
> Volage adorateur de mille objets divers
> Qui va du dieu des morts déshonorer la couche;
> Mais fidèle, mais fier, et même un peu farouche,
> Charmant, jeune, traînant tous les cœurs après soi,
> Tel qu'on dépeint nos dieux, ou tel que je vous voi.
> Il avait votre port, vos yeux, votre langage,
> Cette noble pudeur colorait son visage,
> Lorsque de notre Crète il traversa les flots,
> Digne sujet des vœux des filles de Minos.
> Que faisiez-vous alors? Pourquoi sans Hippolyte
> Des héros de la Grèce assembla-t-il l'élite? . . .
> Par vous aurait péri le monstre de la Crète,
> Malgré tous les détours de sa vaste retraite.
> Pour en développer l'embarras incertain,
> Ma sœur du fil fatal eût armé votre main.
> Mais non, dans ce dessein je l'aurais devancée:
> L'amour m'en eût d'abord inspiré la pensée.
> C'est moi, Prince, c'est moi dont l'utile secours
> Vous eût du Labyrinthe enseigné les détours.

> Que de soins m'eût coûtés cette tête charmante!
> Un fil n'eût point assez rassuré votre amante.
> Compagne du péril qu'il vous fallait chercher,
> Moi-même devant vous j'aurais voulu marcher;
> Et Phèdre, au Labyrinthe avec vous descendue,
> Se serait avec vous retrouvée, ou perdue.

One's first impression is that Phèdre has deliberately abandoned any further attempt to conceal the nature of her feelings for Hippolyte and that the ambiguity of her speech is a trick to make him listen to her. There is nothing here of the minx's satisfaction over catching a man who is reputed to be indifferent to all women. Her attitude is that of an experienced woman who is determined to find her way to the bed of a young man who has never known woman; and for this reason she dwells, a little enviously perhaps, on his *noble pudeur*. Her feelings are frankly sexual and there is a rapt ecstatic note in her description of his physical beauty, in the soft, caressing

> Charmant, jeune, traînant tous les cœurs après soi,

or in the weary sigh that one detects in

> Que de soins m'eût coûtés cette tête charmante!

While there is no doubt that Phèdre does wish to seduce Hippolyte, these impressions are only partly correct. The speech is far more than an impassioned declaration of love, and Phèdre's tactics are far from being carefully and deliberately calculated. In reality, the confession is torn from her in spite of herself and it is this that gives it its peculiar intensity. The more we study the passage, the more conscious we become that Phèdre is speaking in a trance in which she betrays her innermost feelings. She is aware of what she is doing, but is powerless to stop herself.[1]

The Labyrinth of the Minotaur is evoked because it is the perfect expression of Phèdre's feelings. It is a far more complex image than the "palaces" of the earlier plays and its *détours* have a deeper significance. The Labyrinth is at once objective and subjective. Phèdre would like to see Hippolyte trapped by the Minotaur—trapped and helpless—so that she can rescue him and win his love.

---

[1] *cf.*   Que dis-je? Cet aveu que je te viens de faire,
                   Cet aveu si honteux, le crois-tu volontaire?

It is a romantic dream, but it is also an astonishing piece of psychological realism. We are all familiar with the extravagances of the psycho-analytical critics, but this seems to me to be one of the very few instances in great literature where the Freudian symbols offer a complete explanation of the unconscious motives of the poet and his characters. There is no need to dwell on the meaning of the "descent," the guiding "thread" or the more obvious significance of the Labyrinth itself, beyond remarking that the whole passage is an allegory of the sexual act, an allegory which is driven home by the extraordinary urgency of

> C'est moi, Prince, c'est moi dont l'utile secours
> Vous eût du Labyrinthe enseigné les détours,

where the focus of the picture suddenly becomes sharp and the general erotic associations at the beginning of the passage crystallize, concentrating attention on a particular relationship between two individuals.

It is precisely in the use of symbols that Phèdre's state of mind resembles a trance or dream. The Labyrinth is the labyrinth of our hidden desires, a region beyond the range of normal human intercourse and therefore outside conventional tabus. It is the labyrinth in which Phèdre herself is a prisoner, but it offers a prospect of gratifying illicit desires. She is anxious to see Hippolyte trapped in the same prison; she wants to make him fall in love with her or possibly to show him that, without knowing it, he is already in love with her. The obstacle is not only his "insensibility"; it is also his relationship with her which is a tabu that can only be evaded in the Labyrinth, in the place which is "beyond good and evil."[1] Phèdre sees that their problem is a common one which can only be solved in partnership, and her excitement is, perhaps, heightened by the thought that it is a partnership of guilt. It is only by working together that they can overcome their difficulties and find their way out of the Labyrinth which is also paradoxically the only place where desire can be satisfied. They are joined by a bond which must bring either ecstatic happiness or complete destruction:

[1] The Labyrinth also seems to me to be a symbol of the poet's own unconscious desire to escape from convention, from the constraint of the "palaces" of earlier plays, just as Abner's return to the Temple in *Athalie* is a symbol of Racine's return to the life of convention and respectability.

> Et Phèdre, au Labyrinthe *avec vous* descendue,
> Se serait *avec vous* retrouvée, ou perdue.

This extraordinary fantasy provides Phèdre with a vicarious satisfaction, but the ultimate goal eludes her. The *perdue* marks the passing of the trance and the return to the actual world with its shattering sense of disillusionment, which is underlined by Hippolyte's shocked but prosaic

> Dieux! qu'est-ce que j'entends? Madame, oubliez-vous
> Que Thésée est mon père, et qu'il est votre époux?

and by the exchange which follows:

PHÈDRE:

> Et sur quoi jugez-vous que j'en perds la mémoire,
> Prince? Aurais-je perdu tout soin de ma gloire?

HIPPOLYTE:

> Madame, pardonnez. J'avoue, en rougissant,
> Que j'accusais à tort un discours innocent.
> Ma honte ne peut plus soutenir votre vue,
> Et je vais . . .

PHÈDRE:

>   Ah! cruel, tu m'as trop entendue.
> Je t'en ai dit assez pour te tirer d'erreur.
> Hé bien! connais donc Phèdre et toute sa fureur.
> J'aime. Ne pense pas qu'au moment que je t'aime,
> Innocente à mes yeux je m'approuve moi-même,
> Ni que du fol amour qui trouble ma raison
> Ma lâche complaisance ait nourri le poison.
> Objet infortuné des vengeances célestes,
> Je m'abhorre encor plus que tu ne me détestes.
> Les dieux m'en sont témoins, ces dieux qui dans mon flanc
> Ont allumé le feu fatal à tout mon sang,
> Ces dieux qui se sont fait une gloire cruelle
> De séduire le cœur d'une faible mortelle.

The effectiveness of the scene as a whole lies in the contrast between these two speeches. The line

> Ah! cruel, tu m'as trop entendue,

with its immensely effective switch from the *formules protocolaires* back to the *tutoiement passionné*, seems to me to be one of those

miracles which only Racine could have accomplished. There is a
whole civilization behind its singular richness. Hippolyte was
certainly intended to "understand" Phèdre's indirect advances, but
he was no less certainly intended to accept or reject them in accord-
ance with the seventeenth-century code which governed such
matters. His blunt retort crashes through all the reticences. The
secret is out and the game of refined pretence is useless. The real
disaster, however, is the psychological effect of Hippolyte's blunt-
ness. He has given a name to "un amour qui n'ose pas dire son
nom," and in doing so he has destroyed Phèdre's powers of resistance. It is this that provokes the bitter reproach of "Tu m'as *trop*
entendue." He tries, to be sure, to repair his *gaucherie*, but the
damage is done. Phèdre herself can no longer bear the thought that
he might after all not have "understood"; she is driven to intervene
in spite of herself, and it is this that makes the brief exchange between
the two great speeches one of the most dramatic moments in the
play.

Although there is no lowering of the tension, it is clear that
Phèdre is speaking on a different plane. The world of erotic
fantasy with its Labyrinth has disappeared. She looks at her love
with the eyes of an ordinary moral citizen and condemns the
rapture of a moment ago as a "fol amour qui trouble ma raison."
The references to *raison, innocente* and *lâche complaisance* imply a
belief in a clearly defined moral order, but—this is the tragedy—it
can no longer do anything to enable Phèdre to dominate her
emotions.

"Her mind," writes M. Brisson with his usual acumen, "judges and
betrays her at the same time, *inflames her passion at the very moment at
which it appears to be fighting against it.* Through a reversal of the normal
process, which is of profound significance, it is the mind of Phèdre which
contaminates the flesh. No figure of the universal theatre gives away such
dangerous secrets as hers, none comes closer to the eternal abyss."[1]

In all Racine's plays, reason is powerless to resist the swirls of
passion. Phèdre's attempt to shift the blame for her downfall on
to the gods is the purest Jansenist doctrine and it shows the weaknesses of that line as a guide to living. At the same time, it does
nothing to mitigate its votaries' sense of guilt. The honesty and

[1] *op. cit.*, pp. 153–4 (italics mine).

lucidity with which Phèdre faces the implications of her conduct and her recognition of the code which she has outraged are characteristic of seventeenth-century literature.

The movement of the play is essentially a destructive movement. The human personality is shattered by its own passions and the play closes with its total dislocation. The false report of Thésée's death raises Phèdre's hopes for a moment; in spite of her rebuff by Hippolyte, she is led on by the thought that her love is no longer illicit and may be satisfied. The violence of passion is increased by the simultaneous discovery that Thésée is living and that Hippolyte is in love with Aricie. The terrible clarity with which these discoveries are registered in Phèdre's mind throw a good deal of light on the tragic process. When she says

> Mon époux est vivant, et moi je brûle encore!

the activity implied by *brûler* is felt to be *morally* wrong and *physically* destructive. It puts an immense strain on the human personality which rapidly disintegrates. The violence of the "fire," which eats up life, is contrasted with the decorous domestic feelings which should be felt by a wife of Phèdre's age for her husband and which alone are compatible with "living." The exasperation and frustration of unrequited passion have seldom been more powerfully expressed than in the line:

> Hippolyte est sensible, et ne sent rien pour moi!

It is a wonderful example of Racine's gift of condensation. The fondness of the seventeenth century for the word *sensible* was, as we know, characteristic of a society which was acutely conscious of its most intimate feelings. Racine's sense of language enabled him to set his stamp on the word and enrich its meaning. For Phèdre becomes so acutely *sensible* that the disappointment of her hopes of physical satisfaction makes the sense of bodily frustration unbearable. Her brooding over the intimate details of the satisfaction enjoyed by other people plunges her into a fresh orgy of sexual fantasy:

> Ah! douleur non encore éprouvée!
> A quel nouveau tourment je me suis réservée!
> Tout ce que j'ai souffert, mes craintes, mes transports,
> La fureur de mes feux, l'horreur de mes remords,

Et d'un refus cruel l'insupportable injure,
N'était qu'un faible essai du tourment que j'endure.
Ils s'aiment! Par quel charme ont-ils trompé mes yeux?
Comment se sont-ils vus? Depuis quand? Dans quels lieux?
Tu le savais. Pourquoi me laissais-tu séduire?
De leur furtive ardeur ne pouvais-tu m'instruire?
Les a-t-on vu souvent se parler, se chercher?
Dans le fond des forêts allaient-ils se cacher?
Hélas! ils se voyaient avec pleine licence.
Le ciel de leurs soupirs approuvait l'innocence;
Ils suivaient sans remords leur penchant amoureux;
Tous les jours se levaient clairs et sereins pour eux.
Et moi, triste rebut de la nature entière,
Je me cachais au jour, je fuyais la lumière.
La mort est le seul dieu que j'osais implorer.

The poignancy of this passage lies in the sense of frustration and waste.[1] The activity signified by *craintes*, *fureur* and *horreur* has been in vain; the reward has gone to another. The situation has undergone a change since the reflections on the Labyrinth in Act II, and this passage only yields its full flavour when it is seen in relation to the earlier one. The first passage derives its power from its sense of hot, guilty intimacy; the second from an agonizing sense of exclusion from intimacy which is heightened by the knowledge of other people's enjoyment of it. Hippolyte and Aricie are united in a real forest (as distinct from the fanciful Labyrinth) and are beyond Phèdre's reach. The darkness of the forest prevents her from seeing them, and their actions can only be the subject of unhealthy imaginings. One of the most curious things about the passage is the use of the words *innocence*, *licence* and *penchant*. The idea of love has become for Phèdre inseparable from the idea of sin. The ardour of Hippolyte and Aricie is therefore *furtive*, and though the logical sense of *licence* is innocent, there is clearly a suggestion—perhaps an unconscious suggestion—of moral licence. Nor can we have any doubts about the implications of *se chercher*. It is a reflection on Phèdre's state of mind that though she associates love with sin, she is particularly fascinated by the lovers who (she implies) are innocent in the sense that this is "the first time" and who provide a "thrill" to the jaded senses of the ageing Amazon.

[1] *cf.*   J'ai langui, j'ai séché dans les feux, dans les larmes.

The words *licence* and *penchant* are deliberately ambiguous. They suggest freedom, but it is a freedom for others; it brings Phèdre a vicarious satisfaction and at the same time intensifies her sense of personal inhibition. The line

> Ils suivaient sans remords leur penchant amoureux

reveals the subtle temptation, which is always present to the minds of Racine's heroines, to throw off all restraint—to throw off the veneer of civilization and give full rein to instincts that are by no means civilized. The word *remords* is of particular interest. It stands for the moral barrier which ought to have arrested Phèdre's downward course; but it is no barrier for the innocent lovers who are free to follow the incline which is fatal to Phèdre. Instead of arresting her downfall, "remorse" has merely poisoned her pleasure and incensed her against the others. The most painful thing in the passage is Phèdre's sense of *physical* separation, and the short, staccato questions:

> Comment se sont-ils vus? Depuis quand? Dans quels lieux?

convey very well the vibration of nerves which have reached an intolerable degree of sensitiveness. The feeling of physical separation is heightened and complicated by her consciousness of *moral* ostracism. The last six lines refer back to the lines in an earlier passage in which she reproaches the gods:

> Ces dieux qui se sont fait une gloire cruelle
> De séduire le cœur d'une faible mortelle.

For the same gods, who have turned her into a moral outcast, look down benevolently on the loves of Hippolyte and Aricie. There is an immense despair behind

> Tous les jours se levaient clairs et sereins pour eux.
> Et moi, triste rebut de la nature entière,
> Je me cachais au jour, je fuyais la lumière.
> La mort est le seul dieu que j'osais implorer.

Phèdre looks longingly at the darkening skies in the vain hope that the miracle will take place, that grace will intervene to save her; but there are no miracles in this world. When she describes herself as "triste rebut de la nature entière," moral and physical exclusion is implied which brings a sudden numbing sense of the annihilation

of all feeling, the dissolution of all moral values. There is a genuine
nostalgia in Phèdre's reference to the "innocence" which is denied
her and in her reference to the symbols of grace—*clairs*, *sereins*,
jour, *lumière*—but the absence of any supernatural aid drives her
to her final crime. We can now perceive more clearly the force of
a remark of M. Brisson's which I have already quoted: "Her
mind judges and betrays her at the same time, inflames her passion
at the very moment at which it appears to be fighting against it."
For Phèdre's attempts to control her emotions simply exasperate
her feelings and in this way contribute largely to the destruction
of her moral scruples. The paroxysm does not reach its full intensity
until the next *tirade* and it is, significantly, Œnone who provokes
the final crisis.

ŒNONE:
>   Quel fruit recevront-ils de leurs vaines amours?
>   Ils ne se verront plus.

PHÈDRE:
>   Ils s'aimeront toujours!
>   Au moment que je parle, ah! mortelle pensée!
>   Ils bravent la fureur d'une amante insensée.
>   Malgré ce même exil qui va les écarter,
>   Ils font mille serments de ne se point quitter.
>   Non, je ne puis souffrir un bonheur qui m'outrage,
>   Œnone. Prends pitié de ma jalouse rage.
>   Il faut perdre Aricie. Il faut de mon époux
>   Contre un sang odieux réveiller le courroux.
>   Qu'il ne se borne pas à des peines légères:
>   Le crime de la sœur passe celui des frères.
>   Dans mes jaloux transports je le veux implorer.
>   Que fais-je? Où ma raison se va-t-elle égarer?
>   Moi, jalouse! Et Thésée est celui que j'implore!
>   Mon époux est vivant, et moi je brûle encore!
>   Pour qui? Quel est le cœur où prétendent mes vœux?
>   Chaque mot sur mon front fait dresser mes cheveux.
>   Mes crimes désormais ont comblé la mesure.
>   Je respire à la fois l'inceste et l'imposture.
>   Mes homicides mains, promptes à me venger,
>   Dans ce sang innocent brûlent de se plonger.

The focal word is *insensée*. For Phèdre has now lost all control
over herself; but it does not affect her lucidity. In the middle of

her *égarement* she realizes with horror what she is doing, but she cannot help herself. "Moi, jalouse!" she cries with a horrified astonishment, but there is at the same time a moral resignation in

> Mes crimes désormais ont comblé la mesure.

When, at the close of the scene, she turns on Œnone and denounces her evil advice, it is in reality her own worse self that she is denouncing:

> Puisse le juste ciel dignement te payer;
> Et puisse ton supplice à jamais effrayer
> Tous ceux qui, comme toi, par de lâches adresses,
> Des princes malheureux nourrissent les faiblesses,
> Les poussent au penchant où leur cœur est enclin,
> Et leur osent du crime aplanir le chemin;
> Déstestables flatteurs, présent le plus funeste
> Que puisse faire aux rois la colère céleste!

The moral is obvious. The activity of the senses—the *sens égarés*—does not lead for Phèdre, as it should, to life and companionship, but to exile and death. "Fuyons," she cries,

> Fuyons dans la nuit infernale.

The "clear" and "serene" skies grow dark. Phèdre recoils from "life" and turns to face "death." She is resigned to the final crime, but she is also resigned to the doom which must follow it, to *la nuit infernale*.

With the confession of her jealousy, the evolution of Phèdre's character is virtually complete. Although the brief confession to Thésée is in a sense an expiation, its main function is to round off the play:

> Déjà jusqu'à mon cœur le venin parvenu
> Dans ce cœur expirant jette un froid inconnu;
> Déjà je ne vois plus qu'à travers un nuage
> Et le ciel, et l'époux que ma présence outrage;
> Et la mort, à mes yeux dérobant la clarté,
> Rend au jour, qu'ils souillaient, toute sa pureté.

In these lines physical extinction, with its deliberate emphasis on the heart as the seat of the passions, is seen to be the consummation of the interior disintegration of Phèdre's personality. The removal of the corrupt element is supposed to lead to the restoration of a sane order. The skies appear to clear; purity seems once more to be supreme. That, at least, is what happens in theory, and there is little doubt that Racine intended to give this impression. The play, however, has a deeper significance, a significance that Racine may well have had unconscious reasons for wishing to conceal. Shortly before Phèdre makes her first appearance, Théramène describes her as

Une femme mourante, et qui cherche à mourir.

In nearly all Racine's plays, passion leads logically to death; but in *Phèdre* the connection between passion and death is much closer and much more complex. The connection is underlined by the incest *motif*. *Phèdre* appears to be the only play in which the theme of incest is introduced, but it would be more accurate to say that it is the only play in which it is *openly* introduced. For, as Jean Giraudoux once suggested, the passions in all Racine's plays are surrounded by an atmosphere of incest. He also made another interesting suggestion. He suggested that in Racine passion is always *contagious*, and the point is worth developing. In the other plays the principal character suffers from a fatal passion which infects those who surround him or her, so that each of them develops the same passion for a third person. Oreste infects Hermione who becomes infatuated with Pyrrhus who in turn is infatuated with Andromaque. Roxane infects Bajazet who falls in love with Atalide. Phèdre infects the "insensible" Hippolyte who becomes desperately in love with Aricie.

This leads to another point. The connection between the poet and his characters in *Phèdre* is closer than in any of the other plays with the possible exception of *Athalie*. Phèdre and Hippolyte are both portraits not of the artist, but of certain sides of the artist's character. Phèdre stands for the guilty Racine of the past, the Racine who seduced Mlle du Parc and later Mlle de Champmeslé, the actress who created the part of Phèdre; Hippolyte stands for the new Racine, the pure young man that he would like to have been. This seems to me to be the true explanation of Phèdre's desperate concern with "purity" and the concentration on light and darkness of which I have already spoken. "It is her nature, which is in love with innocence," writes M. Blanchot, "that carries her irresistibly towards the Amazon's son, towards the man who is intact, the Thésée without a blemish for whose impossible resurrection she hopes in vain."[1] The solution is, indeed, impossible, unthinkable. Phèdre, we remember, is

> Une femme mourante, *et qui cherche à mourir*.

It may well be, as M. de Rougemont suggests,[2] that Racine set out to punish his own guilty passion in this play, but the curse which Phèdre persuades Thésée to lay on Hippolyte is the outward sign of the internal ravages of her love for him. For the play is nothing less than a *suicide pact*. The Past infects the Present and, in a sense, the Future; the old Racine infects the new, dragging him inexorably down into the abyss. "Phèdre," says M. Blanchot, "can only achieve consummation in the abyss. She demands ruin. Hers is a nature on which nothing can be built. Her kingdom is annihilation. . . . She may withdraw into the shadows in order to give back to the day its light, but the day that she leaves behind her is an empty shattered day."[3] When we consider *Phèdre* from this angle, we have less difficulty in understanding the twelve years' silence. The doom hanging over the kingdom, of which I spoke in my opening chapter, has fallen. Human society is obliterated and only the eternal values remain intact. There is nothing left except to rebuild the human kingdom from the start with fresh material.

Phèdre is therefore not Racine's last word on contemporary problems. In spite of the part played by religion, he was primarily

---

[1] *op. cit.*, p. 87.

[2] "Under cover of his 'classical subject,' Racine contrives to punish himself twice over in *Phèdre*. In the first place, he punishes himself by making the 'obstacle' an incestuous passion, that is to say, an obstacle that one no longer even has the right to want to overcome. Public opinion, to which Racine is very sensitive, is always on Tristan's side against King Mark, is always on the side of the seducer against the husband whom he deceives; but it is never on the side of incestuous lovers. In the second place, Racine punishes himself by introducing other people between Phèdre and her passion and by refusing to allow it to be reciprocated by Hippolyte. Now *Phèdre* was written for Champmeslé who played the part of the queen. Hippolyte is none other than Racine as he would like to be—insensible to mortal charms. . . . By confusing Phèdre with the woman he loves, he takes his revenge on the object of his passion and, at the same time, he proves to himself that this passion must be condemned *without appeal*." (*op. cit.*, pp. 193–4. Italics in the text.)

[3] *ibid.*, pp. 88, 89.

concerned with the fate of the individual and made little attempt to see the individual in relation to society as a whole. The order which is "restored" is a metaphysical order and is defined in terms of "the great abstractions." This is partly for the reasons given above and partly for other reasons. For though there is much in this play about "innocence" and "purity," Racine's negatives are far more convincing than his positive values. One feels that there is something timid and shrinking about the "virtue" which prompts Aricie to ask coyly whether Hippolyte's intentions are "honourable" before deciding to run away with him, and Hippolyte himself to reply sententiously:

> Arrachez-vous d'un lieu funeste et profané,
> Où la vertu respire un air empoisonné.

For a detailed application of these principles to the religious and political situation of Racine's day, we have to wait for *Athalie*, his last and in some respects his greatest play.

V. *ATHALIE* AND THE DICTATORS

1

The twelve years' silence that followed the production of *Phèdre* is one of the most curious and intriguing of all literary problems. The critic is confronted with the spectacle of a great poet, who was at the height of his powers, deliberately turning his back on the art which had made him famous and refusing not merely to write, but to take any further interest in literature. The decision was the outcome of a personal crisis; and since the crisis had a decisive influence on *Athalie*, no account of Racine's final period is satisfactory without some discussion of the events which led to it.

Phèdre was produced at the beginning of February 1677, and was a complete failure. The failure was not due to any flaw in that incomparable poem or to mere caprice on the part of the public. It was skilfully engineered by Racine's enemies. It is doubtful whether any other French writer of the same eminence has aroused more antipathy than Racine. He had been the constant victim of professional jealousy and malicious intrigue, but this time matters were carried to unprecedented lengths. As soon as it became known that he was at work on *Phèdre*, the Duchesse de Bouillon commissioned a wretched hack named Pradon to write a play on the same theme and both plays were produced simultaneously. Similar tactics had been employed with *Iphigénie*, but this time nothing was left to chance. The Duchess bought up most of the seats for the first six nights at both theatres, and while Pradon's work was played to a house filled to capacity with her minions dutifully applauding the feeblest lines, Racine's was played before empty benches.

This prank is said to have cost the Duchess 15,000 *livres*. It was not, perhaps, an exorbitant price to pay for the destruction of the greatest French poet of the century, and its success was complete. Racine was haughty and irritable and bitterly resented any criticism of his work. He had had a good deal to put up with, but in the past he had generally outmatched his enemies. The Prefaces to the tragedies contain biting comments on the folly and ignorance of critics. Their miserable, halting epigrams provoked devastating retorts which were sometimes out of all proportion to the offence and in which we detect a savage pleasure in the infliction of pain.

The collapse of *Phèdre* was followed by the usual bitter exchange of epigrams, but the poet's heart does not seem to have been in the battle. This time he capitulated. He turned his back on his enemies, proceeded to compose his differences with Port-Royal and his mind turned once more to the possibility of the priesthood. He talked indeed of becoming a Carthusian, but allowed himself to be dissuaded from this extreme course by his confessor who counselled marriage. The elegant courtier, who had been the lover of two of the most celebrated actresses of the day, chose what must seem a strange companion. "L'amour ni l'intérêt n'eurent part de ce choix," wrote Louis Racine of his father's marriage to Catherine de Romanet.[1] His wife was a staid, middle-class lady; she was plain and devout, proved an excellent wife and mother, but had little sensibility for the arts. It is generally believed that she never read her husband's works, either from lack of interest or on account of religious scruples. The marriage was celebrated on 1st June 1677,

[1] Mesnard, I, p. 268.

less than four months after the disaster, and for the next twelve years Racine divided his time between his duties as *père de famille* and recording the victories of Louis XIV in his capacity as official historian.

These facts have been variously interpreted by writers of widely differing views. Some have attributed the silence to religious scruples, others to disgust with the literary coteries, and others still to the fact that for the time being Racine had nothing more to say. It is probable that all these interpretations contain a measure of truth, but none of them alone can provide an explanation of all the facts. The reasons for the decision must be sought in an unusual *combination* of circumstances. I think that it can be said that the brutality of the attack on *Phèdre* provided the shock which was needed to set in motion certain latent psychological factors which might otherwise have remained inactive.

It must be remembered that at the time of his marriage Racine was in his thirty-eighth year. It is an age at which surprising things can happen. Men who have led disorderly lives sometimes feel the need of stability or of committing themselves *irrevocably* to a particular course of action; and this need often assumes the choice between two extreme courses leading in opposite directions. It thus happens that some men—particularly men of letters approaching their fortieth year—who have been indifferent Christians or unbelievers all their lives suddenly undergo a violent conversion, while others make a final break with religion. Some who have led irreproachable domestic lives fall a victim to the *démon de midi*, while others still, who like Racine have been profligates, become the model husbands of plain women. It is also the age at which men who have led stormy, quarrelsome lives suddenly yearn for peace and quietness and simply give in.

"La piété fut en lui le fruit de l'agenouillement," said M. Mauriac of Racine's conversion.[1] No one to-day doubts the sincerity of Racine's beliefs, but conversion does not exclude the human element. The way is often prepared by factors which seem to have little to do with religion, and conversion is nearly always coloured by the milieu of the convert. When he looked back on his secular plays, Racine may well have wondered where his work was leading him, whether there was not after all something in Nicole's descrip-

[1] *La Vie de Jean Racine*, p. 156.

tion of playwrights as "public poisoners"; and it is not surprising
that he should have turned in his perplexity and his search for
security to the religion of his youth. He was no doubt influenced
by other considerations as well. He had been brought up in an
atmosphere of the most rigid puritanism, but his was an exception-
ally sensual nature which had been indulged to the full since the
break with Port-Royal. In spite of his preoccupation with "sin"
and "temptation" in *Phèdre*, that play is not the simple drama of
good and evil which Racine contrived to suggest in his Preface.
There is an unmistakable element of complicity in the magnificent
study of sexual mania, a boldness in the exploration of erotic
fantasy which points to a deep-seated conflict in the poet's mind.
Racine had hovered between God and Eros, and perhaps the weariness of the old *roué* and the ugly circumstances of the death of Mlle
du Parc played their part in his final choice. It must never be
forgotten that he was a man of violent extremes. His Jansenist
upbringing had left an indelible impress on his personality and a
complete break with religion was impossible. It was only natural
that the imperious claims of Port-Royal should have reasserted
themselves at a time when his career as a dramatist seemed to be
foundering, and that his conversion should have taken the form of
a return to the strict Jansenism of his childhood. There was nothing
in Catholic teaching to prevent him from continuing his work as
a poet, but in the Jansenist interpretation of that teaching there was
a great deal.

His conversion produced a change of direction; his outlook
became positive instead of negative. Although there does not seem
at first to be any evidence in his plays to support the view that
he had nothing more to say, it is difficult to believe that the
new outlook and his growing sense of responsibility for his
writings could have been reconciled with the production of more
plays in the manner of *Phèdre*, or that the change could have
been accomplished without some break in his work. A writer
who has passed through a crisis of this sort clearly needs time to
settle down before he can translate his new approach to contemporary problems into poetry. The distance that Racine travelled can
only be appreciated after a close comparison between *Phèdre* and
Athalie. In spite of Lemaître's description of *Phedre* as "the first
stage in Racine's conversion," *Athalie* is not a development of

tendencies which are present in *Phèdre*; it is a new departure in
his work. Those critics who have lamented the effects of his conversion and the loss of the masterpieces which might otherwise
have been written between *Phèdre* and *Athalie* were, perhaps, short-
sighted. It is certain that without the conversion there would have
been no *Athalie*, and no one who has studied the play attentively will
feel that the twelve years' silence was altogether a waste of time.

Whether Racine would have turned his conversion to such good
account without some form of outside stimulus may be doubted.
Fortunately the stimulus was provided in a way that could scarcely
remain without effect. In 1689 he was invited by Madame de Maintenon to devote his leisure moments to writing "some sort of moral or
historical poem from which love was to be completely banished."
It did not matter, she said, whether the poem conformed to the
rules or not provided that it "helped her with her plans for amusing
the young ladies of Saint-Cyr while at the same time improving
their minds."[1]

Racine carried out his instructions to the letter. I have sometimes felt tempted to describe *Esther* as "slight," but the term is
not exact. It is not of the same calibre as the great tragedies, but
it is clearly the work of a master whose powers were in no way
diminished and who has done exactly what he set out to do. The
brutality of the Bible story is discreetly toned down and the play has
a freshness—one might almost call it a fragrance—which is unique
in Racine's poetry. It is not a religious play in the same sense as
Athalie; it does not possess the richness and complexity of that
work; but it expresses the awakening of the *jeunes filles* to the
realities of the life about them. The combination of freshness and
gravity that one feels in the lines:

> Jeunes et tendres fleurs par le sort agitées
> Sous un ciel étranger comme moi transplantées,

[1] Love was apparently not one of the subjects in which the young ladies
needed instruction. "For," wrote Madame de La Fayette, "anyone who thinks
that the three hundred girls who stay there until they are twenty and who have
a court filled with people whose passions are awakened on their very door-
step, particularly when the King's authority does not make itself felt; anyone,
I repeat, who thinks that girls and young men can be so close to one another
without jumping over the walls is scarcely reasonable." (*op. cit.*, p. 213.)

The anonymous author of a pamphlet published in Holland was more
explicit, describing Saint-Cyr as "little better than a seraglio which an aged
sultana was preparing for a new Ahasuerus."

gives the play its special charm. It is the only one of Racine's plays which deserves the misused epithet "tender."

Racine was himself responsible for the production of the play. He rehearsed the young ladies of Saint-Cyr with the same care with which years before he had rehearsed Marquise du Parc and Mlle de Champmeslé. *Esther* was performed before the King and his Court with such success that Madame de Maintenon repeated her invitation. Racine could never resist success and the new invitation was accepted with alacrity. He devoted the whole of his great powers to *Athalie*, but the result was very different from its predecessor. The play was performed on three occasions only, during January and February 1691, in Madame de Maintenon's room without music or décors, and when it was printed it attracted little attention. It is said that Madame de Maintenon considered it unsuitable for Saint-Cyr and this point of view is certainly understandable. She may also have been prompted by other considerations, by the attack on absolute monarchy in Act IV. Sc. ii, and by the author's open sympathy with the Jansenist cause. Her reasons are not, perhaps, of great importance. For Racine success was success, and failure was failure. Once more he turned his back on the theatre and this time there was no recall. He devoted himself more assiduously than ever to his duties as *père de famille*, as the King's historian and as the agent of Port-Royal at the Court.

Mauriac speaks in one of his essays of the disproportion which exists between Racine and his work. "When we say that we are fond of Racine," he writes, "we mean that we are fond of Racine's tragedies. We know very little of the man who wrote them and that is a sign of his pre-eminence. For when posterity remembers a lot about the private lives of great writers, it often forgets about their most important books."[1] I think that we must add that what we do know we do not like. There is nothing very sympathetic about the young Racine angling for his *bon bénéfice*, quarrelling with Port-Royal and ruthlessly sacrificing his friends to his determination to be a success at all costs. But there is something peculiarly repellent about the middle-aged Racine, the Jansenist spy, the fond parent weeping copiously when one of his daughters took the veil, or the prig who, learning that his former mistress lay dying, could write to his son: "The day before yesterday I heard from M. Rost

[1] *Journal*, III, pp. 203–4.

RACINE
From a lithograph after a portrait by Santerre

that the Chamellay (*sic*) was at death's door. He appeared to be greatly distressed, but there is another thing which is much more distressing and which did not seem to worry him at all—I mean the obstinacy with which this unhappy woman refuses to renounce the stage."[1]

2

Incest naturally seems to most of us to be a more amusing subject for a play than the factions between Biblical tribes, and the present writer is probably not alone in coming to *Athalie* only after reading and re-reading nearly all Racine's other plays. Yet it would be a pity to allow one's distaste for a play with "a religious subject" and a discouraging sub-title—"Tragédie tirée de l'Écriture sainte" —to prevent one from studying a work which has a peculiar relevance for our own time. Racine's last play is not simply a searching criticism of the religious and political situation in France at the close of the seventeenth century; it is an attempt to state his problem in terms of religion and to find a solution.

The subject of the play is the struggle between a religious order based on *loi*—a word that assumes an intense positive significance in *Athalie*—and a pagan order based on force and bolstered up by ignoble superstition. The high lights are the extraordinary study of the personality of the "dictator" and her immediate entourage, and the frontal attack on absolute monarchy in Act IV. Although the play ends with the "liberation" of the people from despotism and the restoration of "law," the poet himself seems to have per-ceived clearly that it was no more than a temporary and precarious restoration. *Athalie* is a religious play in the fullest sense of the term; it is not like *Polyeucte* a great play which happened to have a religious subject. Yet we cannot help feeling that it is the quality not of the poet's *faith*, but of his *doubt*, which makes it so arresting. Racine does not offer us a social panacea or a facile solution. In his last play he looks wistfully back to the time when, as he imagined, a sane order was an established fact. He believes that this order has been preserved in a fragmentary state by one section of the community, and he considers the means of extending it to

1 Mesnard, VII, pp. 243–4. (Letter of 16th May 1698.)

the rest of society. He comes to the conclusion that the only guarantee of "law" lies in the union of Throne and Altar, but it is apparent all through the play that he had very little confidence either in bringing about this union or in its effectiveness if it were achieved. For this reason his order remains potential; it is never actually realized in the life of the community *as a whole* as it is in Corneille's greatest plays.

Athalie has long been regarded as a *pièce à clef*. When it was published, one of Racine's allies, the Père Quesnel, remarked with satisfaction that it contained portraits "où l'on n'a pas besoin de dire à qui ils ressemblent." Attempts have been made by French critics to discover the "key," but this sort of detective work is likely to prove unprofitable and misleading. *Athalie* is not, as Sainte-Beuve alleged, "a simple and powerful story"; still less is it a gallery of contemporary portraits or a "philosophical play" in which ghostly characters debate abstract problems. The characters are poetic creations, are the vehicles of a poetic criticism of the contemporary situation which is pre-eminently concrete and particular. Racine may well have had Bossuet in mind when he drew his portrait of Joad, but Joad's importance has nothing to do with his resemblance to Bossuet or to the Old Testament model. It lies solely in the fact that he represents a particular element in the pattern of the play.

One of the most interesting characters in the play is Athalie's general. Abner, whom the High Priest calls "l'un des soutiens de ce tremblant État," occupies an intermediate position between the two warring orders. He tries to combine fidelity to the true religion with loyalty to the person whom he believes, until the last Act, to be his lawful sovereign. It is not, perhaps, unduly fanciful to see him as the representative of Racine's own point of view, to see in his struggle a reflection of the difficulties experienced by Racine in trying to work out the relation of the individual to the social order. It is into his mouth that the great opening speech is placed.

> Oui, je viens dans son temple adorer l'Éternel.
> Je viens, selon l'usage antique et solennel,
> Célébrer avec vous la fameuse journée
> Où sur le mont Sina la loi nous fut donnée.
> Que les temps sont changés! Sitôt que de ce jour
> La trompette sacrée annonçait le retour,

Du temple, orné partout de festons magnifiques,
Le peuple saint en foule inondait les portiques;
Et tous, devant l'autel avec ordre introduits,
De leurs champs dans leurs mains portant les nouveaux fruits,
Au Dieu de l'univers consacraient ces prémices.
Les prêtres ne pouvaient suffire aux sacrifices.
L'audace d'une femme, arrêtant ce concours,
En des jours ténébreux a changé ces beaux jours.
D'adorateurs zélés à peine un petit nombre
Ose des premiers temps nous retracer quelque ombre.
Le reste pour son Dieu montre un oubli fatal,
Ou même, s'empressant aux autels de Baal,
Se fait initier à ses honteux mystères,
Et blasphème le nom qu'ont invoqué leurs pères.
Je tremble qu'Athalie, à ne vous rien cacher,
Vous-même de l'autel vous faisant arracher,
N'achève enfin sur vous ses vengeances funestes,
Et d'un respect forcé ne dépouille les restes.

I think it will be agreed that this opening speech is an impressive example of the grand manner. We are carried along by the sweep of the verse, the rich, open vowel-sounds, the trumpets and the pageantry. We cannot help being impressed by the certainty with which the great positive values are apprehended, the physical sense of them crowding in and enveloping us. The accent falls on four words: *Éternel, solennel, loi, ordre.* They may seem at first to be abstractions, but the *festons magnifiques*, the *foule qui inondait les portiques* and the *nouveaux fruits* transform them into the concrete embodiment of a vividly apprehended way of life. "The chief or rather the only character in *Athalie*," said Sainte-Beuve, "is God." It is a highly plausible view. We seem to feel all through the play a presence which is mysteriously shaping the destinies of the characters until it becomes something almost tangible, and the *Éternel-solennel* recurs like a theme in music. The poet evokes a stable order, a world in which "law" is supreme and its claims paramount. It is "law" which brings Abner to the Temple on the feast day; its significance is reinforced by the traditional associations of *antique*, and the offering of the firstfruits stresses its connection with the life of the common people living on the soil. It is the recognition of "law" which creates "order" and guarantees the calm and peaceful life. The point is emphasized by the homely picture of the priests shepherding the faithful into the Temple in an "orderly fashion."

All this is true, but the more we consider it, the more evident it becomes that the tragic force of the passage lies in the contrast between the order which has been lost, or which the poet believes to have been lost, and the present chaos; between the imagined splendour of the past and the very real distress and division of the present. A shadow falls across the scene transforming the *beaux jours* into *jours ténébreux*. The harsh, rending sounds of *audace* and *arracher* slash across the tranquil picture of the past which quivers and disintegrates. *Ombre* becomes the focal word. The rhyme points the contrast with *nombre*, and the reference back to *trompettes*, *annonçait* and *inondait* changes the splendour of the past into the insubstantial shapes of a dream.

For Racine the present is the reality and the past no more than a tantalizing dream. When he compares the crowds who once flocked to the Temple with the scattered wavering remnant of the faithful who remained, he was almost certainly thinking of the persecution of Port-Royal in his own time, and this accounts for the intensely personal feeling behind the lines. When he wrote *Athalie*, he was openly identified with the Jansenist cause and he must have been aware of the parallel between the *peuple saint* in his play and the Jansenist community. He felt that the task of preserving the true faith and restoring "law" belonged to Jansenism. In the play the Temple is the last stronghold of religion in a pagan world is the place from which the saviour (Joas) will emerge. This was the role that Racine hoped that Port-Royal would play, but it is already apparent that the solution is not a very promising one. There was nothing in the past history of Jansenism which was comparable to the past of the *peuple saint*, and this emphasizes Racine's own scepticism. He must have realized that the movement had no past and no future and that there was not the slightest prospect of its producing a "saviour." It is a striking fact that in this, the opening speech which sets the tone of the rest of the play it is the note of doubt which predominates. Abner is Racine's spokesman, and Abner is a doubter. His words remind us irresistibly of Auguste's great speech in *Cinna*.[1] For here, as surely as in *Cinna* there are two voices—the voice of the orthodox believer reaffirm

[1] See pp. 36–7 above.

ng his faith in God and the divine order, and the voice of the doubter
who, in spite of his faith, does not believe for a moment that his
prayer will be answered. All through the speech we overhear the
dialogue between scepticism and belief going on in a muttered
undertone inside the elegant periods. Sainte-Beuve's theory that
God is the only character in *Athalie* fits in very well with his view
of the play, but this view is open to serious criticism. It is not the
presence of God that we feel so much as the presence of a god who
is a cross between the jealous tribal god of the Old Testament and
the remote god of the Jansenists. For the reality of Jansenism is
not the presence of God, but the tormented and uneasy conscience
of the individual as he stumbles blindly through the doomed world.

We have already seen that "temples" and "palaces" had played
an important part in Racine's life and in his poetry. In his last play
he elaborates and develops the image. The Temple of the Jews and
the palace of Athalie stand for the two orders that face one another;
they are the symbols of religion and secularism, of the Church
and the world. There can be little doubt that Abner's return to the
Temple symbolizes the return of the prodigal but repentant Racine
to the bosom of Port-Royal. When Abner remarks nervously:

> J'attendais que, le temple en cendre consumé,
> De tant de flots de sang non encore assouvie,
> Elle [Athalie] vînt m'affranchir d'une importune vie . . .

he seems to reflect Racine's well-founded fear that Port-Royal
would one day be destroyed by the royal power.[1] Racine also seems
to identify himself to some extent with Joas whose childhood in
the Temple strongly resembled his own. He is exposed to the same
temptations. Athalie tries to entice him into making what Racine
may have felt to have been his own mistake:

> Venez dans mon palais, vous y verrez ma gloire.

The secular "glory" of her palace is contrasted, in a magnificent
line, with the sanctity of the Temple:

> Lieu terrible où de Dieu la majesté repose.

Sainte-Beuve's description of *Athalie* as "a simple and powerful
story" seems to me to have been based on an incomplete analysis of

---

[1] The Abbey was closed by royal decree in 1705 and destroyed in 1710.

I

the religious elements in the play. They are not simple, but complex. There is the hard "official" religion—the religion of the orthodox—which is represented by the High Priest, and the uneasy "personal" religion which breaks through in the speeches of Abner and still more in the choruses.

The nostalgic note which is discernible in the opening speech becomes more pronounced as the play proceeds. In the lines:

> O divine, ô charmante loi!
> O justice, ô bonté suprême!
> Que de raisons, quelle douceur extrême
> D'engager à ce Dieu son amour et sa foi!

the hard, precise connotations of *loi*, *justice* and *raison* dissolve into the fragile, exotic beauty of *charmante* and *douceur*; and the action of *engager* becomes submerged in a voluptuous, mystical ecstasy. In the description of David praising God, the process is the same:

> Au lieu des cantiques *charmants*
> Où David t'exprimait ses *saints ravissements*,
> Et bénissait son Dieu, son seigneur, et son père,
> Sion, chère Sion, que dis-tu quand tu vois
> Louer le dieu de l'impie étrangère,
> Et blasphémer le nom qu'ont adoré tes rois?

The warrior-king is obscured by the mystic king lost in his *saints ravissements*.

The pronouncements of the High Priest are in a different style. His is a militant religion. He chides Abner and the Jews for their weakness and want of faith and glories in a God of vengeance:

> Faut-il, Abner, faut-il vous rappeler le cours
> Des prodiges fameux accomplis en nos jours?
> Des tyrans d'Israël les célèbres disgrâces,
> Et Dieu trouvé fidèle en toutes ses menaces;
> L'impie Achab détruit, et de son sang trempé
> Le champ que par le meurtre il avait usurpé;
> Près de ce champ fatal Jézabel immolée,
> Sous les pieds des chevaux cette reine foulée,
> De son sang inhumain les chiens désaltérés,
> Et de son corps hideux les membres déchirés . . .

The High Priest represents the tough, practical element in the "party" whose sinister methods are more apparent to us than they were to Racine. He does, indeed, go into a trance at one moment in the play, but his principal work is to bring about the destruction of his enemies by turning their own weapons of violence and cunning against them, by inciting the faithful to carry the struggle into the pagan stronghold

> . . . réveillant la foi dans les cœurs endormie,
> Jusque dans son palais cherchons notre ennemie.

In this work, he assures them, they will have God's help:

> Dieu sur ses ennemis répandra sa terreur.
> Dans l'infidèle sang baignez-vous sans horreur.[1]

The practical element is visible in the staccato order that he gives to his assistants:

> Qu'à l'instant hors du temple elle soit emmenée;
> Et que la sainteté n'en soit plus profanée,

and perhaps in the short, brutal announcement of one of his lieutenants:

> Mathan est égorgé.

The skill with which Racine wove these diverse strands into the texture of his play gives it its subtle and varied beauty and its tragic urgency. The quality of the play also helps us to appreciate the complexity of the problem which confronted the poet. The High Priest and Abner are both concerned in their different ways with the restoration of "law" in the world. The High Priest stands not only for officialdom, but also for the institutional element in religion which is the necessary corollary to the personal element of the choruses. Racine may not have cared much for what Joad stood for, but he saw clearly that his peculiar and somewhat repellent gifts were necessary if the goal was to be reached, and he may well have regretted that Port-Royal did not possess a champion of this calibre to stand up to the royal persecution. It is significant that the High Priest is always regarded as a means to an end. With the

---

[1] Stendhal declared, characteristically, that the play was "souverainement immorale en ce qu'elle autorise le prêtre à se soulever contre l'autorité et à massacrer les magistrats." (V. Martino, *Stendhal*, Paris, 1934, p. 48.)

crowning of Joas and the death of Athalie, his work as a "resistance leader" is done and he becomes at once a figure of less importance. We may conclude that in the new order which was supposed to emerge from the existing state of anarchy he would have been a minor functionary, a sort of ecclesiastical policeman who would have kept an eye on the machinery. For the new order was to be centred not merely in the somewhat dubious figure of the Priest-King, but in that perpetual hope—the "new generation," the child of tender years whom Racine, unable to deceive himself, describes sadly as

> Triste reste de nos rois,
> Chère et dernière fleur d'une tige si belle,
> Hélas! sous le couteau d'une mère cruelle
> Te verron-nous tomber une seconde fois?

"The subject of the play is Joas who is recognized as king and enthroned," wrote Racine in the Preface to *Athalie*, "and strictly speaking I should have called it *Joas*. But as most people have only heard it spoken of as *Athalie*, I did not see any point in publishing it under a different title; and besides, Athalie plays a very important part in it and it is her death that brings the play to a close."

We may wonder whether Racine altogether believed what he said in his Preface. He was inclined to use the Prefaces to tell the public what it ought to think about the plays. He may have considered it politic to emphasize the religious aspect of *Athalie* as he had emphasized the moral aspect of *Phèdre* in the Preface to that play. Racine's religion was remarkable for its intense preoccupation with sin, and he did not allow his search for a constructive solution of the problem to diminish his passionate interest in evil in the forces that were undermining the religious order. In *Athalie* as in the other plays, one of his principal interests is the disintegration of the personality of his "heroine." Athalie herself clearly belongs to the tragic sisterhood of the other plays. There is a world of difference between the simple Biblical character who is struck down by the servants of an avenging God, and the complex "modern woman" who is studied with such marvellous psychological insight.

Athalie is presented as a ruthless, inhuman monster who has usurped the throne of the rightful king and who did not stop a murder in order to achieve her aims. She has broken with the historic faith and slaughtered its priests. For, like all despots, she has found religion the most serious obstacle to the rule of force, and superstition the most potent ally. She has carried all before her, and at the opening of the play she is faced only with a remnant of the faithful who, led by the High Priest, is openly hostile to the usurper. She prepares to "liquidate" this remnant by the usual methods, but—to the surprise of friends and enemies alike—she hesitates. Her methods of violence have failed to create an *interior* unity and her own personality cannot resist the destructive forces that she herself has unleashed. From the beginning of the play she is seen under two different aspects. Josabet describes her on the day of the attempted murder of Joas:

> Un poignard à la main, l'implacable Athalie
> Au carnage animait ses barbares soldats.

This image, which has burnt itself into the imagination of the faithful, is suddenly replaced by a different one. In his opening speech Abner declares:

> Enfin depuis deux jours la superbe Athalie
> Dans un sombre chagrin paraît ensevelie.

Then her henchman Mathan says of her:

> Ami, depuis deux jours je ne la connais plus.
> Ce n'est plus cette reine éclairée, intrépide,
> Élevée au-dessus de son sexe timide,
> Qui d'abord accablait ses ennemis surpris,
> Et d'un instant perdu connaissait tout le prix.
> La peur d'un vain remords trouble cette grande âme:
> Elle flotte, elle hésite; en un mot, elle est femme.

The hard indomitable qualities implied in *superbe*, *implacable*, *intrépide* dissolve into the *sombre chagrin*, the *vain remords*: instead of action there is hesitation and indecision. Athalie herself completes the evidence. In the middle of one of her furious outbursts she is suddenly overcome by a sense of her own loneliness:

> Et moi, reine sans cœur, fille sans amitié.

When confronted with the child who she does not know is Joas she says:

Quel prodige nouveau me trouble et m'embarrasse?
La douceur de sa voix, son enfance, sa grâce,
Fait insensiblement à mon inimitié
Succéder ... Je serais sensible à la pitié?

It is of the essence of despotism that the ruler builds up a system
which is based on the suppression of the natural human virtues,
a system which rapidly develops into an unending process of
repression and destruction. In *Athalie* the personal tragedy of the
despot lies in the fact that it is the return of natural human weaknesses which actually leads to the collapse of the system. The despot
is a human being, and the remains of her humanity prove to be her
undoing.

It is important to realize that *Athalie* is not the study of an isolated
individual in the same sense as Racine's other plays. He sets Athalie
in her proper milieu, and one of the most impressive things in the
play is the study of the progressive moral deterioration of her
entourage and its influence on her policy. The bearing which this
point has on our present perplexities is obvious and it is worth
examining Racine's handling of it in detail. To do so, we must compare Mathan's speech in Act III. Sc. iii, with the High Priest's attack
on absolute monarchy in Act IV. Sc. iii.

Ami, peux-tu penser que d'un zèle frivole
Je me laisse aveugler par une vaine idole,
Pour un fragile bois que malgré mon secours
Les vers sur son autel consument tous les jours?
Né ministre du Dieu qu'en ce temple on adore,
Peut-être que Mathan le servirait encore,
Si l'amour des grandeurs, la soif de commander,
Avec son joug étroit pouvait s'accommoder.
Qu'est-il besoin, Nabal, qu'à tes yeux je rappelle
De Joad et de moi la fameuse querelle,
Quand j'osai contre lui disputer l'encensoir,
Mes brigues, mes combats, mes pleurs, mon désespoir?
Vaincu par lui, j'entrai dans une autre carrière,
Et mon âme à la cour s'attacha toute entière.
J'approchai par degré de l'oreille des rois,
Et bientôt en oracle on érigea ma voix.
J'étudiai leur cœur, je flattai leurs caprices,
Je leur semai de fleurs le bord des précipices.

Près de leurs passions rien ne me fut sacré;
De mesure et de poids je changeais à leur gré.
Autant que de Joad l'inflexible rudesse
De leur superbe oreille offensait la mollesse,
Autant je les charmais par ma dextérité,
Dérobant à leurs yeux la triste vérité,
Prêtant à leurs fureurs des couleurs favorables,
Et prodigue surtout du sang des misérables . . .

Mathan is a brilliantly ironical creation. He stands alone among Racine's characters, and to find anything comparable in French tragedy we have to turn to Félix in *Polyeucte* and Prusias in *Nicomède*. For by using his observation of the political scene, Racine created something which was a perfect vehicle for his criticism of the French Court. Mathan is the measure of the corruption of the life of the time; the weaknesses of human nature are set in their true perspective, enabling Racine to lay bare the roots of the evil.

The passage depends for its effect on the contrast between the hard, virile qualities suggested by *joug étroit*, *inflexible rudesse*, and the sinister, subterranean suggestions of *flattais*, *étudiais*, *mollesse*, *dextérité*. The worms "consuming" the idol indicate the moral softness of the sovereign and look forward to *offensait la mollesse*. Mathan alludes, with cynical humour, to his own softness when he declares that he was unable to submit to the discipline of the *joug étroit*. The image of the worms eating the wood of the idol is reinforced by *étudiais leur cœur*, for Mathan's method of insinuating himself into the confidence of the sovereign is identical with that of the worms and, by implication, the sovereign becomes a *vaine idole* —at any rate in the eyes of the "enlightened." The rhyme links *caprices* and *précipices*. For it is the unbridled passion that cannot submit to the *joug étroit* which contains the germ of dissolution. The fact that Mathan's defection to Baal was caused by some trivial dispute with Joad over the censer is the final damaging admission which sets his peculiar career and his unpleasant personality in their proper light.

From this we turn to the High Priest's warning to Joas:

Loin du trône nourri, de ce fatal honneur,
Hélas! vous ignorez le charme empoisonneur.
De l'absolu pouvoir vous ignorez l'ivresse,
Et des lâches flatteurs la voix enchanteresse.

Bientôt ils vous diront que les plus saintes lois,
Maîtresses du vil peuple, obéissent aux rois;
Qu'un roi n'a d'autre frein que sa volonté même;
Qu'il doit immoler tout à sa grandeur suprême;
Qu'aux larmes, au travail, le peuple est condamné,
Et d'un sceptre de fer veut être gouverné;
Que s'il n'est opprimé, tôt ou tard il opprime.
Ainsi de piège en piège, et d'abîme en abîme,
Corrompant de vos mœurs l'aimable pureté,
Ils vous feront enfin haïr la vérité,
Vous peindront la vertu sous une affreuse image.
Hélas! ils ont des rois égaré le plus sage.

I have already suggested that the theme of *Athalie* is not the study of the destructive forces at work in an otherwise stable order, but a conflict between two separate orders. One of them is wholly corrupt and must be destroyed as a preliminary step towards the restoration of "law." The other contains the possibility of a stable order, but stability can only be achieved provided that certain conditions are fulfilled. Joad's admirably "democratic" speech is a courageous criticism of the Court of Louis XIV. It is a description of the manner in which sovereignty degenerates into dictatorship and is of exceptional interest at the present time; but it only becomes fully intelligible when read in the light of Mathan's pronouncement. It is a statement of the problem from a different angle. Its intention is wholly constructive; it is a serious warning against dangers which may lead to a repetition of the disasters that overtook the *peuple saint* under the rule of Athalie. There is the same contrast between the *plus saintes lois* and the subterranean associations of *charme empoisonneur*, *voix enchanteresse*, *piège* and *abîme*. The effect, however, is to correct Mathan by restoring the values that he deliberately undermined. The *amour des grandeurs* is stigmatized as *ce fatal honneur*; the "passions" and the "caprices" are seen to possess a *charme empoisonneur* which inevitably corrodes what is best in civilization, which leads to an *ivresse* that is incompatible with *pureté* or *vérité*. Mathan's is the *voix enchanteresse*; he is one of the *lâches flatteurs* concealing the dangers, removing the *frein* from the supreme will of the sovereign. This time the situation is looked at objectively and the words are given a different value. The substitution of *frein* for *joug étroit* is an example. In other words, the elaborate subterfuge, the flowers strewn on the edge of the precipice, the *couleurs favorables* which hide truth, are cleared away and the full rottenness of the situation is exposed and judged.

It is interesting to notice that Athalie and her minions (like some of the most notorious of their modern exemplars) are *apostates*. They have abandoned one set of beliefs and set up an alien system in its place. It is characteristic of these substitute-religions, as we know to our cost, that they bear a close resemblance to the thing that they replace. At bottom, Athalie is a woman in whom the habits of mind of a Jansenist have survived the repudiation of the faith, and this is true of her entourage. They have a dogmatic system; they have above all the same uneasy consciences as the Jansenists,[1] and they are painfully aware of human weaknesses; but in their system the normal values are turned upside down and it is this that leads to disaster. It is true that there is no "love interest" in *Athalie*, but Athalie's infidelity is not less corrosive than Roxane's passion for her "brother-in-law" or Phèdre's for her stepson. Her collapse is an interior collapse, and though she is actually killed by the Levites, her physical death is simply the consummation of the process.

3

Athalie's great speech in Act II. Sc. v, is the centre of the play and must be examined in detail. For convenience sake it can be divided into three movements. The first is from l. 6 to l. 26; the second from l. 27 to l. 48; and the third from l. 50 to l. 88.

> Prêtez-moi l'un et l'autre une oreille attentive.
> Je ne veux point ici rappeler le passé,
> Ni vous rendre raison du sang que j'ai versé.
> Ce que j'ai fait, Abner, j'ai cru le devoir faire.
> Je ne prends point pour juge un peuple téméraire.

---

[1] In the speech from which I have already quoted, Mathan says:
> Toutefois, je l'avoue, en ce comble de gloire,
> Du Dieu que j'ai quitté l'importune mémoire
> Jette encore en mon âme un reste de terreur;
> Et c'est ce qui redouble et nourrit ma fureur.
> Heureux si, sur son temple achevant ma vengeance,
> Je puis convaincre enfin sa haine d'impuissance,
> Et parmi les débris, le ravage et les morts,
> A force d'attentats perdre tous mes remords!

I*

Quoi que son insolence ait osé publier,
Le ciel même a pris soin de me justifier.
Sur d'éclatants succès ma puissance établie
A fait jusqu'aux deux mers respecter Athalie.
Par moi Jérusalem goûte un calme profond.
Le Jourdain ne voit plus l'Arabe vagabond,
Ni l'altier Philistin, par d'éternels ravages,
Comme au temps de vos rois, désoler ses rivages;
Le Syrien me traite et de reine et de sœur;
Enfin de ma maison le perfide oppresseur,
Qui devait jusqu'à moi pousser sa barbarie,
Jéhu, le fier Jéhu, tremble dans Samarie.
De toutes parts pressé par un puissant voisin
Que j'ai su soulever contre cet assassin,
Il me laisse en ces lieux souveraine maîtresse.
Je jouissais en paix du fruit de ma sagesse.

This speech is Athalie's apologia and is addressed to Mathan and to Abner. It is important to distinguish in the first movement between the speaker's *intention* and the actual *effect* of her oration on her hearers, for the two are distinct. She opens on a note of proud disdain and when she declares:

Je ne veux point ici rappeler le passé,
Ni vous rendre raison du sang que j'ai versé,

she evidently intends to brush aside the past as unimportant; the consonants give the line an air of brisk determination and the short, precise words remind us of a person driving home her point by a series of taps on a table. The next lines appear to be a flat contradiction of this assertion, and the contradiction is caused by the pressure of the events forcing themselves into Athalie's mind and refusing to be lightly set aside. L. 9 is a concession to Abner and the moral associations of *devoir* are used to excuse Athalie's deeds in his eyes. The reference to *un peuple téméraire* is, perhaps, an unconscious inversion which reveals Athalie's uneasiness. She cannot admit that she is afraid, but instead the Jews are described as *téméraire(s)*. The associations of *devoir* are strengthened by

Le ciel même a pris soin de me justifier

which has the appearance of clinching the argument. "Heaven itself approves my course."

Athalie is trying to show that her position is at once "right" and "secure." She is trying to convince her hearers in order to convince herself. She dwells at some length on her material successes because they are a sign of divine approbation and also because they give her a sense of security. In the lines:

> Sur d'éclatants succès ma puissance établie
> A fait jusqu'aux deux mers respecter Athalie,

the *établie* is intended to have a solid, reassuring ring, but it is felt at once to be hollow and insecure. At the same time there is a shifting of the angle of vision. Athalie adopts an impersonal standpoint and looks at herself (inviting her hearers to do the same) from without. We are to stand back and gaze upon the great Queen whose power is firmly established as far as the two seas.

The position is consolidated by the catalogue of "successes" in which the supernatural and the natural are judiciously mingled. "It is thanks to me that Jerusalem—the Holy City—enjoys a deep calm," and the *profond* lends its support to *établie*. The peace extends over the whole country. She does not describe her victories over the Arab and the Philistine: she presents us with a *fait accompli*—

> Le Jourdain *ne voit plus* . . .

Only the careful manipulation of consonants suggests a faint disturbance which preceded the calm and perhaps indicates the mild exertion that was needed to repress the marauders.

There is a further change in l. 19. "The Syrian treats me as Queen and sister." Athalie—the "reine sans cœur, fille sans amitié"—inspires affection as well as respect. For the next six lines the rugged r's and v's give way to the hiss of the s's in *pousser, oppresseur, Samarie, puissant, assassin, maîtresse* as Athalie swoops down upon a different and far more formidable enemy. The vague triumphs over the anonymous hordes of Arabs and Philistines are suddenly exchanged for the uncomfortably precise

> Jéhu, le fier Jéhu, tremble dans Samarie.

The reasons for this are interesting. One has the impression that the victories over the Philistines and the Arabs were victories over phantom armies, but Jehu is a different proposition. Jehu was the person who killed Jezabel, and the death of Jezabel haunts Athalie from one end of the play to the other. Jehu was an object of hatred and fear, a physical as well as a psychological danger. Athalie tries desperately to convince herself that she has reduced him to impotence so that he cannot repeat his treatment of her mother in her own case.

Then the final picture of Athalie herself:

> Il me laisse en ces lieux souveraine maîtresse.
> Je jouissais du fruit de ma sagesse.

The material triumph is consolidated by *souveraine* and *sagesse*, a word with profoundly religious associations.

I have spoken of the difference between the intention and the effect of the passage. When it is studied closely, it is seen to be an elaborate pantomime in which Athalie recounts her triumphs over phantom armies. These phantoms have a deep psychological significance because they are an attempt to exteriorize fears to which Athalie cannot give a name. She tries to reassure herself by describing a victory over imaginary enemies in place of her own collapse in the face of real enemies whom she cannot overcome. The *effect* of the passage is, therefore, to create in the spectator's mind an impression of a precarious peace.

> Mais un trouble importun vient, depuis quelques jours,
> De mes prospérités interrompre le cours.
> Un songe (me devrais-je inquiéter d'un songe?)
> Entretient dans mon cœur un chagrin qui le ronge.
> Je l'évite partout, partout il me poursuit.
> C'était pendant l'horreur d'une profonde nuit.
> Ma mère Jézabel devant moi s'est montrée,
> Comme au jour de sa mort pompeusement parée.
> Ses malheurs n'avaient point abattu sa fierté;
> Même elle avait encor cet éclat emprunté
> Dont elle eut soin de peindre et d'orner son visage,
> Pour réparer des ans l'irréparable outrage.
> *Tremble*, m'a-t-elle dit, *fille digne de moi.*
> *Le cruel Dieu des Juifs l'emporte aussi sur toi.*
> *Je te plains de tomber dans ses mains redoutables,*
> *Ma fille.* En achevant ces mots épouvantables,
> Son ombre vers mon lit a paru se baisser.
> Et moi, je lui tendais les mains pour l'embrasser.

Mais je n'ai plus trouvé qu'un horrible mélange
D'os et de chairs meurtris, et traînés dans la fange,
Des lambeaux pleins de sang et des membres affreux,
Que des chiens dévorants se disputaient entre eux.

The opening lines of the second movement betray the insecurity of Athalie's "peace." The material success begins at once to crumble. The punctuation gives the impression of a series of strangled gasps. There is a conflict between Athalie's desire to conceal her dream and a desperate desire to confide in someone, to be reassured.

The crux of the passage, and perhaps of the play, is the word *songe*, and Athalie's voice sinks to a terrified whisper:

Un songe (me devrais-je inquiéter d'un songe?)

Her fear is powerfully augmented by the word *ronge*. Subterranean influences undermining normal life are one of the principal *motifs* of the play. The worms "consume" the wooden idols; the trickery of Mathan undermines sovereignty; and the dream undermines Athalie's peace of mind.

The celebrated line:

C'était pendant l'horreur d'une profonde nuit

focuses our whole attention on the dream, gathers up the emotion of the previous twenty lines and concentrates it on a single point. It is a wonderful example of Racine's power of condensation and of his dramatic sense. This line robs the material triumphs, sedulously catalogued in the first movement, of all their reality. For the rest of the play it is the dream world which is the reality, the shadow world of the supernatural which breaks through Athalie's psychological armour and destroys her. The terror and darkness suggested by the long, slow syllables of the *profonde nuit* extend over everything. The *calme profond*, for which Athalie had been fighting desperately, changes into another sort of *calme*—a silence in which terror reigns.

In place of the image of the proud and successful Athalie that was built up in the first movement, there arises a different figure. Jezabel is not merely Jezabel; she is Athalie herself. The description of Jezabel has a profoundly ironic significance—ironic because the subterfuge of Athalie's self-portrait is deliberately stripped away. The *pompeusement parée* refers to the insignia of royalty—the external symbols—on which Athalie herself has insisted. The décor is seen to be a disguise for her true feelings:

> Même elle avait encor cet éclat emprunté
> Dont elle eut soin de peindre et d'orner son visage,
> Pour réparer des ans l'irréparable outrage.

The unreal, painted figure is Athalie in her precarious and unreal security. The *sagesse* of l. 26 is not wisdom at all, but trickery. The hopeless despair behind the *irréparable outrage* gives the passage its tragic note.

The grim story of Jezabel's violent death is evoked more than once in this play. Joad dwells on it with a savage glee because he feels that it is the weak spot in Athalie's defences. Athalie herself refers to it because it has never ceased to prey on her mind until it has finally become a presage of her own death, and this explains the reference to Jehu in the first part of the speech.

Racine certainly intended the dream to be accepted as a supernatural warning, but its working is subjective. We must remember that Racine's Catholicism was a religion of intense subjective manifestations. The figure of Jezabel has much the same significance in this play as Venus in *Phèdre*. Once the fearful warning:

> Le cruel Dieu des Juifs l'emporte aussi sur toi

—which looks forward to Athalie's last despairing cry

> Dieu des Juifs, tu l'emportes!

—has been uttered, Athalie is a beaten woman. Her character disintegrates in precisely the same way as that of the other Racinian heroines.

The process of disintegration is described with consummate power in seven lines. One of the things that makes the passage effective is the *speed* of the process of disintegration. The painted Jezabel is presented in six lines; in six lines a sickening feeling of collapse is suggested by the poet. Then there is a pause; the painted figure hangs suspended in the darkness illuminated by a harsh, crude light which reveals its battered appearance. The warning is uttered; the *fille digne de moi* links the fate of mother and daughter, and the *digne* heightens the macabre comedy of the scene. Then the figure leans dramatically towards Athalie; Athalie raises her arms to embrace it or to assure herself of its reality or perhaps even to obtain some sort of support from it. Suddenly the figure crumples up leaving only a mass of torn and bloody flesh over which the mongrels fight. It is the outward and visible sign of the interior psychological collapse of Racine's heroine which is presented with a *hardiesse* that is without parallel in the whole of his work. It can now be seen how little truth there is in the theory that Racine's great monologues are frigid recitals of past events. His greatness does not lie least in the fact that the change which takes place in the personality of his characters actually happens before our eyes.

The third movement is no less important than the others, but it does not call for the same detailed analysis and is too long to set out in full here. It begins with a continuation of the dream:

> Dans ce désordre à mes yeux se présente
> Un jeune enfant couvert d'une robe éclatante . . .
> Mais, lorsque revenant de mon trouble funeste
> J'admirais sa douceur, son air noble et modeste,
> J'ai senti tout à coup un homicide acier
> Que le traître en mon sein a plongé tout entier . . .

The word *désordre* is of the utmost importance because of its many implications. The physical disorder to which it refers is the symbol of psychological disorder, but it is also out of this disorder that the new order will emerge. The child in his white robe is set against the bloody confusion of mangled flesh to emphasize the contrast between "innocence" and "corruption," "order" and "disorder." He may also be intended to suggest the Christ-Child because there is evidently a contrast between the disorder of the old world and the order of the new world of Christianity. Nor should we overlook the implication that the new world, for all its gentle beginnings, was a revolution that destroyed what was corrupt in the old. The dagger, for example, is probably a foreboding of Athalie's own death, but it is also symbolical of the stealthy way in which her destruction was brought about, and of the secret beginnings of Christianity.

The most important lines in the third movement are those describing Athalie's meeting in the Temple with the High Priest and Joas whom she recognizes as the child of the dream:

> Le grand prêtre vers moi s'avance avec fureur.
> Pendant qu'il me parlait, ô surprise! ô terreur!
> J'ai vu ce même enfant dont je suis menacée,
> Tel qu'un songe effrayant l'a peint en ma pensée . . .
> Il marchait à côté du grand prêtre.

At this point the two worlds—the dream world and the real world
—merge and consolidate against Athalie. The spectacle of the
High Priest and Joas making common cause against her suggests
better than anything the experience that we get from the last three
acts of the play. We have a sense, which at times becomes almost
oppressive, of the hostile forces closing in and paralysing Athalie;
but we also have a sense of liberation, a sense of the new order
symbolized by Joas taking shape and growing until it transcends
the narrow religion of the High Priest.

4

Although the play closes with the triumph of religion and the
reconstruction of the *tremblant État*, Racine was at some pains in
his Preface to remind us that this triumph was only a temporary one.
For many years Joas was a model king, but he ended his reign by
killing the High Priest of the time in the Temple in a fit of anger.[1]
In spite of its satisfactory ending, *Athalie* is shot through and
through with an unmistakable note of pessimism. Its nature becomes
clear from Joad's vision of the ultimate downfall of Joas, the
Babylonian captivity and the foundation of the Catholic Church:

> Comment en un plomb vil l'or pur s'est-il changé?
> Quel est dans le lieu saint ce pontife égorgé?
> Pleure, Jérusalem, pleure, cité perfide,
> Des prophètes divins malheureuse homicide!
> De son amour pour toi ton Dieu s'est dépouillé.
> Ton encens à ses yeux est un encens souillé . . .
>
>   Quelle Jérusalem nouvelle
> Sort du fond du désert brillante de clartés,
> Et porte sur le front une marque immortelle?
>   Peuples de la terre, chantez.
> Jérusalem renaît plus charmante et plus belle.

[1] This may have been a personal allusion to Racine's own excesses which
followed his model childhood at Port-Royal.

There is a striking contrast between the language used to describe the disasters and the language used to describe the foundation of the Church. The images of destruction are precise and concrete; the images of reconstruction vague and abstract. The dull lead smothers the glittering gold; the priest is killed in the sanctuary; the incense is "soiled." From these ruins there emerges a strange "repository" Church. The homely "lead" and the "soiled" incense emphasize the curious prettiness of the "Jérusalem nouvelle brillante de *clartés*" and of the "plus *charmante* et plus *belle*," which makes the Church seem beautiful at the expense of strength. It is probable that the imagery was suggested by church decorations, but this merely underlines the fact that the poet was obliged to rely on second-hand images to describe the triumph of religion. For the "new order" is somehow unreal, and its very unreality seems to reflect the poet's own disillusionment and the defeat of his hopes.

I think that we must conclude that Racine had come to feel that his great hope—the creation of a Christian society on the ruins of the society analysed in the secular plays—was not destined to be realized. The history of the past hundred and fifty years has abundantly justified his pessimism. It is true that France rid herself of the evils against which Joad solemnly warned Joas in the attack on absolute monarchy; but the cost to Europe as well as to France herself was appalling. For the remedy was to a large extent destroyed with the evil, and the suffering that this involved has not yet finished. Nor can we overlook the immense responsibility of the Roi Soleil for the fact that the same evil later took root in a neighbouring country.

Comment en un plomb vil l'or pur s'est-il changé?

It is a question on which we should all do well to meditate in a spirit of profound humility.

EPILOGUE

In an earlier chapter I suggested, with reservations, that the seventeenth century can be divided broadly into three ages and those ages named after France's three greatest dramatists. When I stand back and survey the three portraits from a distance, I am more conscious of the difficulties of this division and more aware of the continuity of the French tradition. Their work seems at first to be a study of three different people—the Man of Honour, the Natural Man and the Man of Passion—but the impression is perhaps misleading. The real theme of the seventeenth century is the fortunes of the struggle between Reason and Passion seen at three different moments, and the Man of Honour, the Natural Man and the Man of Passion are really three facets of the same person. It is, indeed, the story of the rise and fall of Reason in France; and we discover with surprise that at the end of the century the three dramatists, starting from three different places, converge on a single point, share the same disbelief in Reason.

Corneille set out in his earlier plays to establish the dominion of Reason; in the period of comparative calm which followed, Molière shows us the dominion of Reason as an accomplished fact and proceeds to satirize any deviations from it which threaten the balance of society. *Le Misanthrope*, however, does more than look forward to Racine. When Alceste declares impatiently

> Mais la raison n'est pas ce qui règle l'amour

he is not merely looking forward to Hermione's

> Tant de raisonnements offensent ma colère.

The *authors* of both plays are saying the same thing, are proclaiming their growing scepticism about the ability of Reason to solve the human problems that face it. What is really startling, however, is the discovery that, in his declining years, Corneille seems to have become a convert to the same way of thinking. We have seen that in *Pulchérie* "honour" wins too easily; but it is not a complaint that can be made against *Suréna*, the last play of all, which was produced in 1674. When Suréna remarks

> ... l'amour, jaloux de son autorité
> Ne reconnaît ni roi, ni souveraineté

is he not echoing words used only two years earlier by Roxane—

> Mais l'amour ne suit point ces lois imaginaires?

And Eurydice's injunction to her lover to marry some other princess for political reasons, but not to love her—

> Il faut qu'un autre hymen me mette en assurance.
> N'y portez, s'il se peut, que de l'indifférence

—recalls Atalide's boast

> Je vous ai vers Roxane envoyé plein de moi . . .
> Ce n'est point un amant en vous que je lui laisse.

In this last play Corneille's characters proclaim their love with a shamelessness which is worthy of the most abandoned of Racine's heroines. Reason is scarcely mentioned. "Duty" has become a political subterfuge which enables members of the ruling party to impose their will and break up the *mariages d'amour* of their rivals. Suréna and Eurydice only mention it to brush it rudely aside as an intolerable obstacle to their desires. The ideal of service and the acceptance of the political *mariage de raison* have gone by the board. Instead, they prefer to settle down to a leisurely enjoyment of the pleasures of *chagrin d'amour*:

> Je veux qu'un noir chagrin à pas lents me consume,
> Qu'il me fasse à longs traits goûter son amertume.

Thus Eurydice; and when she tries, not very convincingly, to persuade Suréna that it is his duty to marry another princess and give the State children who will emulate his own exploits on the field of battle, he disposes very briefly of her argument:

> Quand nous avons perdu le jour qui nous éclaire,
> Cette sorte de vie est bien imaginaire,
> Et le moindre moment d'un bonheur souhaité
> Vaut mieux qu'une si froide et vaine éternité.

Racine, one feels, can hardly have missed the point of that. He must have perceived the connection between Suréna's *imaginaire* and Roxane's *lois imaginaires*, must secretly have applauded Suréna's sentiments and reflected that his former "rival" had made splendid progress since his condemnation of *Britannicus* for dwelling too much on the *faiblesses* of human nature.

If *Suréna* falls a long way below Corneille's finest work it is not because "honour" wins too easily; it is because the characters, after ridding themselves of their troublesome scruples, no longer have the courage to seize the *bonheur souhaité*, to ensure the triumph of their passions. The only one of them who displays the true Cornelian fire is Suréna's sister, Palmis, who, when she sees the wilting Eurydice collapse and die very suddenly on the stage, brings the play to a close by declaring, in lines worthy of Corneille at his best:

> Suspendez ces douleurs qui pressent de mourir,
> Grands dieux! et dans les maux où vous m'avez plongée,
> Ne souffrez point ma mort que je ne sois vengée!

The death of Racine brings the *grand siècle* to a close. It is more than the end of an age; it is the end of a whole phase of human experience. With Racine the French classical theatre reached the summit of perfection; no further development along the same lines was possible. This did not prevent the eighteenth century from trying to continue the work of its predecessors; but in spite of the undoubted achievement of Marivaux and Beaumarchais, the attempt was a failure. The immense vitality of the seventeenth century depended, as I have tried to show, on its ambivalent attitude towards authority, on its attitude of acceptance-and-resistance. In the seventeenth century "the rules" were a constant subject of lively debate; it was not until the next century that the doctrines of classicism ceased to be controversial and were universally and passively accepted. This acceptance, and the divorce between reason and passion, explain the lifelessness of the eighteenth-century theatre. The work of the dramatists, as we can see from Voltaire's tragedies, became a boring imitation of "the Ancients." *Gloire*, which had had an immense glamour for the seventeenth century, degenerated into a counter; *passion* was no more than a frigid pose. The *philosophes*, using the methods which they had learnt from their distinguished predecessors, proceeded to apply them to the dissection of a dying society. They divided Man neatly into two, into a being who possessed the intelligence of a highly civilized person and the body of a highly trained animal. There was no longer any conflict between reason and emotion. For emotion was largely eliminated and replaced by sensation. The mind was simply an instrument for providing the body with agreeable sensations. The result was a drastic impoverishment of life which is amply reflected in eighteenth-century literature until the Revolution upset the balance and provided poetry with fresh and exciting material.

Racine's work was an end, but it was also a beginning, though what it began only becomes apparent a hundred and fifty years after his death. Professor Willey has shown that the materialism implicit in the Cartesian philosophy created a "climate of opinion" which was fundamentally hostile to poetry, but this is not the whole of the story.[1] The Cartesian philosophy did more than ruin traditional metaphysics. It marked the transition from a classical metaphysic to the idealist systems which have dominated modern literature.[2] I am not suggesting that Descartes had a direct influence on Racine, but it seems to me that a philosophy which makes the mind reflecting on its own processes—the *Cogito ergo sum*—its starting-point, and the preoccupation of the imaginative writer with what happens inside the individual mind, are manifestations of the same tendency and of a change which took place in the human mind during the seventeenth century. The work of Corneille and Molière was pre-eminently a study of man in society, of the Social Man. Now one of Racine's most startling innovations was not merely to shift the drama from the outer to the inner world, to transform the Social Man into the Individual Man; it was to make the inner drama his *exclusive* preoccupation, so that all his greatest characters might echo the words he used in one of his occasional poems: "Il y a deux hommes en moi." In his plays there is not, as there was in Corneille's and Molière's, a conflict between the claims of the individual and the claims of society; they reflect the disintegration of society within the consciousness of the individual. When Alceste turns his back on society and throws over the *bienséances* to set out in search of the *endroit écarté*, he performs a symbolical act. There are grounds for thinking that his creator felt tempted, at any rate for a moment, to follow his example; but he thought better of it and returned in his later work to his normal manner. It was

[1] *The Seventeenth-Century Background*, London, 1934, chapters V, VI and X.

[2] See Remy de Gourmont's interesting discussion of the connection between idealism in philosophy and the Symbolist Poets in *l'Idéalisme* (Paris, 1893), where he remarks (p. 27): "Le symbolisme est l'expression esthétique de l'idéalisme."

left to Racine to make the gesture a reality; the *endroit écarté* was both psychological and physical, and it can be argued that in Racine psychological and physical exile is an accomplished fact. In his greatest work he pushes the exploration of the human mind far beyond anything which had previously been attempted in France, and it was no doubt this tendency which prompted M. Pierre Brisson to say of Phèdre that "no other figure of the universal theatre gives away such dangerous secrets as hers."

In the eighteenth century, Racine's work was continued up to a point in the comedies of Marivaux. The strength and weakness of Marivaux would make an absorbing study, but this is not the place to undertake it. All that I can do is to point out that in Marivaux's comedies feelings become more and more rarefied and elusive until they seem to evaporate altogether like a delicate perfume. His work is a strange mixture of acute psychological insight and a special kind of verbiage for which the French coined the word *marivaudage*. It is the verbiage which chiefly interests us here. *Le Jeu de l'amour et du hasard* is a delightful comedy, but the very words of the title reveal its weakness and the poverty of the age which produced it. Its weakness is that the attitude behind it is altogether *trop voulu*. *L'amour* is not a powerful and dangerous emotion which continually threatens the balance of society, as it had done in the seventeenth century; it is an interesting state of mind, is no more than a "game." The characters are always asking themselves not simply "What do I feel?" but "How should I feel if I found myself in this or that situation?" In other words, the drama does not arise from a clash between powerful feelings or a conflict between a principle and a feeling, but from an absence of feeling, a *plein repos* which is very different from the state which Pascal analysed. Their dissatisfaction leads them to make use of *le hasard*, to invent artificial situations and then "see what it feels like." The two principal characters in *le Jeu de l'amour et du hasard* decide that it would be altogether too commonplace and uninteresting to meet, see whether they like one another and, if they do, marry. They hit independently on the same idea of disguising themselves as their servants and their servants as themselves. After a great deal of fun and misunderstanding, the couples find that they like each other very well, and marry. I think we must conclude from this that the seventeenth century had explored certain feelings so thoroughly that they were exhausted.

Now when a distinguished artist—and there is no doubt about Marivaux's distinction—is driven to manufacture artificial obstacles in order to create new feelings or to titillate old ones, there is clearly something wrong. His verbiage is not, as it sometimes appears to be, merely a playful *badinage* which is deliberately written to entertain the audience. It is a sign of sterility and it also marks the limit to which psychological investigation can be pushed *on the stage* without degenerating into a mere *jeu de mots*.

Marivaux, therefore, marks the transition from dramatic poetry to the short poem and the novel of our own times. The true heirs of Racine are not Marivaux and Voltaire, but the authors of the *Fleurs du mal* and the incomparable *Adolphe*. For Racine carried the dialogue of the mind with itself to the point where the debate could only be continued in private and in exile. No dramatist could push the exploration of the split personality further than Racine did in *Phèdre* or improve on the supreme technical accomplishment that he displayed in the role of Œnone; but it is the same voice that we hear when we listen to the cloistered Adolphe bitterly upbraiding himself for his treatment of Ellénore and to the dialogue between the anonymous travellers as they gaze in horror at the corpse dangling on the end of the gibbet on the shores of Cythère:

Ridicule pendu, tes douleurs sont les miennes!

It was probably only his immense respect for *les bienséances* which prevented Racine from saying precisely the same thing when he contemplated the dead Phèdre and brooded darkly over the *nuit infernale* which had swallowed her up.

TABLE OF DATES

BIBLIOGRAPHICAL NOTE

In addition to the works referred to in the text, the following may be consulted:

BOURGET, P., *Œuvres complètes, II, Critique*, Paris, 1900 ("Réflexions sur le Théâtre").

BRISSON, P., *Molière, sa vie dans ses œuvres*, Paris, 1942.

BROWN, A. M., M.D., *Molière and his Medical Associations*, London, 1897.

DESJARDINS, P., *La Méthode des classiques français*, Paris, 1904.

DUCLAUX, MARY, *The Life of Racine*, London, 1925.

FERNANDEZ, R., *Itinéraire français*, Paris, 1943.

GHÉON, H., *L'Art du théâtre*, Montreal, 1944.

GUIZOT, M., *Corneille et son temps*, Paris, 1852.

LANSON, G., *Corneille* (Les Grands Écrivains Français), Paris, 1898.

MAULNIER, T., *Racine*, Paris, 1936.

MICHAUT, G., *La* Bérénice *de Racine*, Paris, 1907; *La Jeunesse de Molière*, Paris, 1922; *Les Débuts de Molière à Paris*, Paris, 1923.

MORNET, D., *Histoire de la littérature française classique* (1660–1700), Paris, 1940.

SAINTE-BEUVE, C.-A., *Portraits littéraires* I (Corneille, Racine, "La Reprise de *Bérénice*"); *Portraits littéraires* II (Molière); *Nouveaux lundis*, VII ("Corneille: *le Cid*"); *Histoire de Port-Royal* II (Corneille); *Histoire de Port-Royal* III (Molière); *Histoire de Port-Royal* VI (Racine). (It is instructive to compare the studies of Corneille and Racine in the *Portraits littéraires* with the much more sympathetic approach in *Port-Royal*.)

SAINT-ÉVREMOND, C. DE, *Œuvres complètes*, I (ed. Planhol), Paris, 1927. ("Défense de Quelques Pièces de M. Corneille")

STRACHEY, LYTTON, *Landmarks in French Literature*, London, 1912; *Books and Characters*, London, 1922.

VALÉRY P., *Variété V, Sur Phèdre Femme*, Paris, 1944.

VAUVENARGUES, MARQUIS DE, *Œuvres complètes*, I, Paris, 1821 ("Réflexions sur Quelques Poètes").

VEDEL, V., *Deux classiques français vus par un critique étranger: Corneille et son temps—Molière*, Paris, 1935.

INDEX